Peace Accords and Ethnic Conflict

ICES ETHNIC STUDIES SERIES

Published in the same series:

Robert B. Goldmann and A. Jeyaratnam Wilson (eds), *From Independence to Statehood: Managing Ethnic Conflict in Five African and Asian States*, 1984

Dietmar Rothermund and John Simon (eds), *Education and the Integration of Ethnic Minorities*, 1986

R. Siriwardena (ed), *Equality and the Religious Traditions of Asia*, 1987

Neelan Tiruchelvam and Radhika Coomaraswamy (eds), *The Role of the Judiciary in Plural Societies*, 1987

K.M. de Silva, Pensri Duke, Ellen S. Goldberg and Nathan Katz (eds), *Ethnic Conflict in Buddhist Societies*, 1988

Ralph R. Premdas, S.W.R. de A. Samarasinghe and Alan B. Anderson (eds), *Secessionist Movements in Comparative Perspective*, 1990

K.M. de Silva and R.J. May (eds), *Internationalization of Ethnic Conflict*, 1991

S.W.R. de A. Samarasinghe and Reed Coughlan (eds), *Economic Dimensions of Ethnic Conflict*, 1991

Peace Accords and Ethnic Conflict

Edited by

K.M. de Silva and S.W.R. de A. Samarasinghe

INTERNATIONAL CENTRE FOR ETHNIC STUDIES,
SRI LANKA
in association with
The Canadian International Development Agency
The Friedrich Ebert Stiftung
The United States Institute of Peace

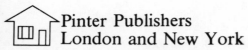

Pinter Publishers
London and New York

Distributed exclusively in the USA and Canada by St. Martin's Press

Pinter Publishers
25 Floral Street, Covent Garden, London WC2E 9DS, United Kingdom

First published in 1993

© International Centre for Ethnic Studies, 1993

Distributed exclusively in the USA and Canada by
St. Martin's Press, Inc., Room 400, 175 Fifth Avenue,
New York, NY10010, USA

British Library Cataloguing in Publication Data
A CIP catalogue record for this book is available from the
British Library

ISBN 1 85567 079 8

Library of Congress Cataloging-in-Publication Data
A CIP catalog record for this book is available from the
Library of Congress

Typeset by GCS, Leighton Buzzard, Bedfordshire
Printed and bound in Great Britain by Biddles Ltd., Guildford and King's Lynn

This volume is dedicated to the memory of
the late Edward E. Azar,
scholar, educator, humanist and friend

CONTENTS

NOTES ON CONTRIBUTORS

Reed Coughlan is Mentor/Unit Coordinator, North Central Regional Centre, SUNY Empire State College, State University of New York, Suite 606, State Office Bldg 207, Genesee Street, Utica, New York, USA.

Francis Mading Deng is Senior Fellow, Foreign Policy Studies Program, The Brookings Institution, Washington, DC, USA. Previously he was Jennings Randolph Distinguished Fellow, US Institute of Peace; Sudan's Ambassador to Canada, Scandinavia and the USA and Minister of State for Foreign Affairs.

K.M. de Silva is Foundation Professor of Sri Lanka History at the University of Peradeniya, Sri Lanka, and Executive Director, International Centre for Ethnic Studies, Sri Lanka. He is currently a Visiting Fellow of the Woodrow Wilson Center for Scholars, Washington, DC, USA.

Sucha Singh Gill is Lecturer and Reader in Economics at the Punjabi University in Patiala, India. He was also a professor of Economics at the Guru Nanak Dev University in Amritsar from 1987 to 88.

Kamala Liyanage is Lecturer in Political Science at the University of Peradeniya, Sri Lanka.

K.K. Panda is Director, Institute of Constitutional and Parliamentary Studies, Parliament House in New Delhi, India.

John M. Richardson Jr is Professor of International Affairs and Applied Systems Analysis and Director of Doctoral Studies at the School of International Service, The American University, Washington, DC, USA.

S.W.R. de A. Samarasinghe is Director, International Centre for Ethnic Studies, Kandy, Sri Lanka and Senior Economist and Faculty Member of the Development Studies Program affiliated to the American University, Washington, DC, USA.

Dale Thomson is Professor of Political Science, McGill University, Montreal, Canada. Previously he was Professor of International Relations at the Johns Hopkins University, Washington, DC, USA.

Jianxin Wang is a doctoral candidate in International Relations at the School of International Service, The American University, Washington, DC, USA.

ACKNOWLEDGEMENTS

All the chapters of this volume except the sixth and eighth are revised versions of papers presented at an international conference held in Colombo in July 1991. The discussions at the conference and the critical comments of many participants helped greatly in the revision of the papers. The editors of this volume would like to thank all the authors of these chapters. We are particularly grateful to Professor John M. Richardson Jr, Mr Jianxin Wang and Dr Kamala Liyanage for so readily accepting our invitation to contribute to this volume.

The conference of July 1991 was the fifth of a series on the comparative study of various aspects of ethnic conflict initiated by the ICES. The series of conferences was made possible through the financial support of the Friedrich Ebert Stiftung (FES). A grant from the Canadian International Development Agency (CIDA) helped us to organize this fifth conference. In addition we had the support of the United States Institute of Peace (USIP) in Washington, DC. The ICES would like to acknowledge our thanks to Her Excellency Nancy Stiles, the Canadian High Commissioner in Sri Lanka, and Mr Andre Vinette, Counsellor (Development) at the Canadian High Commission in Colombo and to Dr Reinhold Plate, the Resident Representative of FES in Sri Lanka for their encouragement and generous support. The research involved in the preparation and revision of the Sri Lankan papers was funded in part by a grant from USIP.

The organization of the conference was in the capable hands of Ms Ernaganie Karunaratne ably assisted by Ms Nalini Weragama, Mr T.M. Jayatilake and Mr Samarakoon Bandara. The preparation of the papers presented at the conference and the final text was done with customary efficiency and good cheer by Ms Sepali Liyanamana and Ms Bernadine Perera. Ms Kanthi Gamage, Librarian of ICES, handled the proof-reading of the papers, the revisions of the papers and their transformation into chapters of this book. Our Accountant, Ms Chalani Lokugamage helped in numerous ways in the organization of the conference and in the preparation of this volume, as she did on all previous such occasions.

The final stages in the preparation of this volume was done in Washington, DC. We would like to thank the Woodrow Wilson International Center for Scholars – where one of us (K.M. de Silva) is at

present a Visiting Fellow – for providing a congenial atmosphere, and
the library and other academic resources for this task.

K.M. de Silva
S.W.R. de A. Samarasinghe

ICES
554/1 Peradeniya Road
Kandy
Sri Lanka

7 June 1992

1 INTRODUCTION

K.M. de Silva and S.W.R. de A. Samarasinghe

I

Peace accords

The ethnic peace accords and peace negotiations reviewed in this volume were attempts to manage – if not resolve – some of the most protracted, more durable and, with the exception of Canada's, among the most violent ethnic conflicts in recent times, the conflicts in Canada, Cyprus, Punjab (India), Sri Lanka and Sudan. All these countries have been parts of the British Empire and Commonwealth in one form or another. The duration of that link was longest in Canada where it goes back to the 18th century, followed by Sri Lanka where it began in the last years of that century, and Punjab where the association with the British raj was at least a hundred years old at the time of Indian independence. The links were of much shorter duration in both Cyprus and Sudan. With the exception of the disputes in Canada, all the others, at least in their present form, emerged from the dissolution of the British Empire. They are, in short, post-independence conflicts.

Canada's tensions, in so far as they concern the English- and French-speaking groups in that country, have their roots in the earliest phase of the British conquest of the French possessions in Canada in the 18th century. The conflicts in Cyprus and Sri Lanka are no more than the latest phase in antagonisms and hostilities that go back several centuries in the case of Cyprus, and indeed a thousand years or more in the case of Sri Lanka. In both instances, as well as in Sudan and Punjab, responses and reactions to colonial rule affected the thinking and behavior of ethnic and religious groups in their rivalries and, after independence, in their tensions, as some sought a redress of historic grievances and others to protect hard won advantages from erosion by new policies.

The extent, duration and levels of violence, and the impact of these on the country's political structures and institutions in the course of these conflicts, have varied greatly. At one end of the scale is Canada where the violence has been minimal; in fact, the violence there could be regarded as practically non-existent in comparison with all the other conflicts reviewed in this book – Cyprus, Punjab, Sudan and Sri Lanka. All these countries have endured very high levels of violence ranging from sporadic but deadly terrorist attacks to virtual civil war, and sustained guerrilla warfare in parts of each country. Cyprus, where violent clashes, and the breakdown of the constitution and power-sharing arrangements eventually precipitated the intervention of a regional power which proceeded to use its army to partition the island and establish a separate political entity for the security of the Turkish minority there, would be at the other end of the scale. Cyprus is selected for this doubtful distinction not because the duration or level of violence were longer or higher than in the others but on account of the combination of very high levels of violence with the drastic changes in political structures that followed the Turkish invasion.

All these conflicts, save Canada's, have been internationalized to a greater or lesser degree either by affected minority groups within the country, or by diaspora elements living in voluntary or involuntary exile and working in association with representatives of the minority at home, or by interested external agencies ranging from neighboring states to prestigious international non-governmental organizations. The peace accords reviewed in this book, save those in Canada and Punjab, illustrate the processes of internationalization of ethnic conflict at work. Those processes have been most conspicuous and more complex in Cyprus than in all the others.

Specialists in international relations have generally tended in their writings to underestimate the significance of ethnic conflict if not to ignore it altogether.[1] The frequency with which ethnic conflicts have erupted in recent years and the speed with which they have been internationalized has led to a change in this situation, and the international dimensions of ethnic conflict have begun to engage the attention of scholars in international relations. The lead has been taken by specialists in conflict resolution studies: J.W. Burton, Francis Deng, I.W. Zartman, and the late E.E. Azar for example.[2] In the final chapter of this present volume Richardson and Wang provide a critical look at conflict resolution and conflict management theories, as well as a summary of conclusions on the efficacy of peace accords in dealing with protracted ethnic conflict.

The authors dealing with Cyprus, Sudan and Sri Lanka in this present volume examine the international dimension of ethnic conflict in each of these cases in considerable detail. Francis Deng, who writes on the Sudan, is uniquely qualified to review the negotiations involved in the effort to bring peace to that country through accords and treaties. He is not only a distinguished scholar who has made important contributions to the study of conflict resolution in Africa and on the Sudan's political crisis, but also an accomplished diplomat and an active participant in recent peacemaking efforts in his country.

The chapter on Cyprus written by Reed Coughlan is based on extensive interviews conducted with some of the principals in the dispute in that troubled island. These interviews provide fresh insights into the complexities of the peacemaking process in Cyprus. They show the difficulties that confront international efforts to reconstruct the pre-partition Cypriot polity to meet the aspirations of the two contending parties within the island; as well as the fears of the two regional states, Greece and Turkey, whose own history of conflict and suspicion of each other mean peacemaking on Cyprus is a most arduous undertaking.

K.M. de Silva's study of the making of the Indo-Sri Lanka Peace Accord of 1987 relies on a mixture of interviews with key figures involved in its making both in Sri Lanka and India, as well as on a study of the official minutes of discussions and documents in the various stages of the negotiating process. Above all, he has had access to the papers of President J.R. Jayewardene of Sri Lanka including the vitally important telegrams exchanged between him and the late Rajiv Gandhi immediately preceding the signing of the Accord, and thereafter.

The involvement of regional powers in the ethnic conflicts of Cyprus (Greece and Turkey) and Sri Lanka (India) are case studies that demonstrate an important theme in the impact of ethnic conflict on interstate politics, namely

> States that have close affective links with ethnic groups in another state will often not remain indifferent to the fate of these groups. Connor[3] ... is surely right to state that many governments hold transborder causes in more esteem than the traditions of international law. Such governments will often regard it their right and their duty to involve themselves in the ethnic problems of other states.[4]

Apart from a French attempt to internationalize Canada's ethnic conflict in the 1960s the Canadian dispute has remained free of international ramifications and is treated here as an internal problem of that country. India insists that the Punjab dispute is an internal problem and has resisted all efforts on the part of the Sikh minority to internationalize it. Even so, the Indian government has conceded – for instance in its well-known *White Paper* on the Punjab crisis published in 1984 – that 'external forces, with deep-rooted interest in the disintegration of India . . .' had a role in exacerbating the tensions within Punjab. Although the 'external forces' officially identified are the Sikh diaspora groups in North America and Western Europe and especially the separatist groups among them, Pakistan is often seen, and criticized, as the principal source of external support for Sikh separatist groups operating in Punjab.

II

The Canadian dispute

The Canadian dispute, as we have seen, has the longest history among the conflicts reviewed in this volume. The origins of the Canadian dispute go back to 1763 when New France, the French possessions in present-day Canada, were ceded by France to Britain. From that, as Kenneth D. McRae points out:

> . . . three future lines of cleavage in Canadian politics were born simultaneously. A colony of France founded on the Roman Catholic religion, the French language, and the civil law of Paris was annexed to a British Empire founded on a Protestant establishment of religion, the English language, and the English common law. In the aftermath of the conquest, the most noteworthy concerns were religious and legal. After a decade of uncertainty, the Roman Catholic religion and the French civil law received guarantees in the Quebec Act of 1774. . . . American independence . . . had consequences for the old province of Quebec, for it introduced a new problem of refugees from the United States that was mainly English-speaking and Protestant . . .[5]

Dale Thomson's chapter on Canada argues that:

> Canada has known so little ethnic-derived violence since it assumed responsibility for its internal affairs that it is often cited as an example of peaceful ethnic co-existence. Yet today there is the very real possibility of its breaking up along ethnic lines. So perhaps the Canadian case is instructive, not as representing the success or failure of a specific accord, but of a series of accords or arrangements that have enabled the country to remain intact without however resolving the ethnic tensions once and for all.[6]

The fact is, that the tensions within Canada – religious and linguistic – have exercised the minds of Canadian and British politicians at various times for the better part of two centuries since the Quebec Act of 1774. The history of Canada provides an excellent case study in the durability of ethnic discord and tensions, and their capacity to survive the best efforts of politicians and statesmen to devise solutions. A number of legislative enactments beginning with Pitt's Canada Act of 1791 two hundred years ago, and a succession of policies, were adopted in efforts to defuse or moderate these tensions. Sometimes, as in the early 19th century, the two Canadas would be united in an ill-concealed effort to erode the distinctive French identity and when these efforts failed to achieve the desired results, the diametrically opposite policy of protecting the autonomy of French Canada was adopted in the hope that this would help reduce tensions. Neither policy succeeded in its objectives. Lord Durham's masterly report on the problems of Canada and his pathbreaking recommendations on constitutional and other reforms in Canada is a major landmark in the history of efforts at a resolution of Canada's ethnic conflict. Although he was far from generous to the French, the eventual adoption of the constitutional reforms he recommended brought together Canadian politicians, both English and French, in taking responsibility for managing their country's affairs. This included searching for policies of accommodation and compromise that would help preserve its unity in the face of the sharp divisions that persisted between the English and French. The introduction of these constitutional reforms in the mid-19th century gave Canada the lead in the evolution of responsible government in the colonies of the British Empire. In less than 20 years after the introduction of this bold constitutional experiment, Canada followed with yet another – the establishment of a Canadian federation in 1867 at a time when the outbreak of the American civil war had sapped confidence in the staying power of federal structures.

The long-term success of the Canadian experiment in federalism, however, was also the source of many of the country's difficulties in the 20th century. It undoubtedly strengthened Canada's persistent efforts to push the limits of responsible government to the point where it assumed the status of a self-governing dominion of the British Empire. Canada was always the pioneer in this, well ahead of Australia, New Zealand and South Africa and the great contribution made by the French element in Canadian politics to this assertion of Canada's rights in its relations with the metropolitan country needs to be emphasized. In the long run, however, the success of Canadian federalism in preserving and fostering French Canadian autonomy in Quebec, came at a price – the protection given to the distinctive French identity in that province became the foundation on which a resurgence of separatist movement was built in the 1960s. Religion is much less significant as a factor in that resurgence, in its present form, than language but some scholars argue that the current language dispute in Quebec is no more than a continuation, in a disguised form, of the religious disputes of the past.[7]

Dale Thomson reviews these issues against their historical background in his chapter of this book. More important, in the second paragraph of his introduction he draws our attention to the enormously significant new development in Canada's experiments with ethnic autonomy:

> The Canadian case is also interesting at the moment in that two principal ethnic conflicts are manifest, one between French and English speaking Canadians, and the other between the aboriginal populations (themselves originally from Asia) and the more recent immigrants and their descendants. The two conflicts impact on one another: in 1990 the Meech Lake Accord between French- and English-speaking Canadians was blocked at the last moment by an aboriginal member of a provincial legislature because it did not address his people's problems. As a result it is now acknowledged that both conflicts have to be addressed simultaneously, thus greatly complicating the situation.

For the first time in Canadian history what Thomson calls the 'aboriginal challenge to the status quo' will receive as much attention as the two centuries old conflict between the English- and French-speaking Canadians.

III

Negotiating identity

Problems of identity, national and or ethnic, appear in high relief in all the disputes reviewed in this book. We concern ourselves, at this point, with the problems of Sudan and Cyprus. In his chapter on Sudan, Francis Deng argues that:

> In virtually all the agenda items that have been suggested for negotiations, or constitutional talks, the issue of national identity has figured prominently. Sometimes, it is phrased as a problem of competing nationalities or as a conflict of identity factors, such as race, culture, language or religion. The question often posed is whether the country is Arab, African, Afro-Arab or Arab-African. From a religious perspective, the cultural question is whether the country is to be considered Islamic, governed by Sharia law, or secular with constitutional guarantees for religious freedom and equality.

With some modifications appropriate to a different setting, the central theme of the argument, the issue of conflicting identities is equally valid for Cyprus, and explains why and how that strategically located island was polarized between Greek and Turk. It also explains how this polarization led to civil war, the Turkish intervention, the partition of the island and the present statement in negotiating a settlement.

Reed Coughlan's chapter provides succinct summary of the history of Cyprus, and the historic conflicts that have bedeviled efforts at maintaining a stable system of government after the colony gained independence from Britain.

> The Greeks first settled on the island during the second millennium BC. The Turkish population was introduced during the period of Ottoman rule between 1571 and 1878. The island was ceded to Britain in 1878 and it was annexed by the British at the beginning of World War I; it was given crown colony status in 1925. By mid-century anti-colonial nationalism began to take hold in Cyprus under the auspices of the guerrilla movement EOKA, which combined its determination to oust the British with an aspiration to bring about union with Greece. Enosis, as it is known, was not a new idea; it has first surfaced following the Greek war of independence in the 1820s. In 1955 the violent campaign to oust the British and unite Cyprus with Greece galvanized the Greek Cypriots and simultaneously antagonized the Turkish Cypriot minority on the island. The Turkish Cypriots quickly established the Turkish Resistance organization and formulated an oppositional ideology that espoused the notion of Taksim, or partition, with a view to the alignment of each of the ethnically distinct territories with the respective motherlands . . .

While Francis Deng has emphasized identity as a factor in the Sudanese conflicts, he has very little to say on the Sudanese experience under the British connection, or on the latter's influence on the development of the current conflict. Other African scholars are inclined to attach a great deal of the blame for the Sudanese crisis to the British connection, as the following extract from a chapter in a recent book co-edited by Francis Deng shows:

> The origins of the present conflict in Sudan must be traced to its colonial past, when Great Britain employed 'divide and rule' tactics effectively. Apart from using Egypt under the Condominium Agreement as an intermediate power to rule Sudan, the British fostered real division between the North (Arab and Moslem) and the South (African and non-Moslem). In 1919, the Southern provinces were formally cut off from the north and were declared closed to all northerners except government officials. Southerners were taught English and Arabic, and they were isolated from Arab and Islamic traditions. . . . Therefore, when Sudan became independent in 1956, it was a country with

south and north deeply different from one another. Great Britain's southern policy had bequeathed a perpetual source of division within the new multinational republic.

Within the Arab Muslim communities of the north, the British further entrenched clan and religious division...[8]

This forceful criticism of the 'divide and rule' policies of the British has its parallels in the evaluation of the impact of British rule in other parts of the Third World. But the distance between the period of colonial rule and the current realities of indigenous rule or misrule grows longer. As this happens, one tends to view these attempts to transfer the blame for all the problems that elude solution by the legatees of the British to the former colonial rulers' Machiavellian 'divide and rule' policies, with greater scepticism and as emotional reactions rather than dispassionate assessments of a former metropolitan nation's responsibility for a colony's post-independence problems. Divisions in colonial societies were sharp and deep enough on their own and colonial administrations and officials were often drawn into disputes through the machinations of local elites. We also need to consider the post-colonial ruling elites' own contribution to the breakdown of political systems and the atrophy of democratic institutions – through short-sighted policies in the pursuit of sectional interests, whether these be the interests of an ethnic group or a political party.

Francis Deng's strictures on the British are more perceptive because he sets these, realistically, in the context of what went on before the British and what happened after independence.

Arab migration and settlement in the South was discouraged by natural barriers, climatic conditions and the hostilities of slavery. The Turko-Egyptian and Mahdist raids of the nineteenth century further aggravated the Southern apprehension of waves of invasions from the North. With the British came peace, but the gulf between the South and the North was re-enforced and extended into the modern context by the infamous 'Southern Policy' reversed only nine years before independence.

Post-colonial governments aimed at unifying the country through a centralized system, supplemented with assimilationist policies. The South, on the other hand, wanted a federal system initially pursued through constitutional channels. When that was rejected and repressed, Southern demands escalated to a separatist armed rebellion. But increasingly, the Northern view of national identity as Arab and Islamic became challenged not only by scholars, but also by nationalist leaders from the South.

IV

Rajiv Gandhi's Peace Accords

The Peace Accords in Punjab and Sri Lanka reviewed over four chapters – two each on the two accords – are linked together by being part of a series of three such accords negotiated by the late Rajiv Gandhi between July 1985 and July 1987, beginning with the accord in Punjab discussed here in the two chapters by K.K. Panda and Sucha Singh Gill. There are subtle but none the less significant differences in the approaches of the two authors to the very controversial issue of the Punjab crisis. Panda's chapter could easily carry a subtitle 'A View from New Delhi' where he lives and works, just as Gill's chapter is 'A View from Punjab' where he lives and works.

Taking over as Prime Minister, as his mother's successor after her assassination by her Sikh bodyguards, Rajiv Gandhi immediately sought a mandate from the people. In the event he secured an endorsement that was quite as overwhelming as, if not even more so than, the one his mother had won in the immediate aftermath of the liberation of Bangladesh. Treating it as a mandate for fresh initiatives and dramatic changes he picked on two of the thorniest issues he had inherited from his mother for early resolution – Punjab and Assam. The Punjab crisis, quite naturally, took priority, and he began negotiations within a few weeks of his massive electoral victory. The man he chose to negotiate with, Harchand Singh Longowal, is seen by Panda as a moderate among the Akali Dal leaders, while in Gill's view he was 'the virtual dictator' of the Akali Dal's agitation of the early 1980s, and by implication something other than a moderate.

In Punjab as in Assam Indira Gandhi had pursued a dual policy. One feature of this policy was a shrewd and calculated exploitation of existing divisions in the ranks of the Akali Dal in Punjab as well as among the other radicals and activists in Punjab and Assam. This helped her to establish and maintain a governing coalition in the two states, in which the Congress I formed the indispensable core. The chapters by Panda and Gill, and especially the latter, will show that this policy did not work in the way she hoped it would, but its failure was more pronounced in Punjab than in Assam. The second prong of the policy was the commencement of discussions, if not formal negotiations, with some of the opposition groups especially with those who were seen to command the loyalties of significant groups in those states.

The policy of negotiations went further in Assam than in Punjab.

Between 1980, when she returned to power after her defeat in 1977, and the end of 1982 she had conducted a series of talks with the activist leadership in Assam.[9] They were resumed in 1984, after an appalling outbreak of ethnic violence and a successful boycott of the polls had rendered the Assam general election of 1983 a meaningless exercise and had deprived those elected on that ridiculously low poll of any semblance of a credible claim to represent the views of the people.[10] Thus, in regard to Assam, Rajiv Gandhi could use the negotiations conducted by his mother as a useful base for the fresh initiative he had in mind. In Punjab he did not have this advantage, but even with regard to that state he could turn to the Akali demands embodied in the Anandpur Sahib resolution of 1973 and the demands made in 1981–82. Panda's chapter contains an analysis of the former, while Gill shows how important the latter were in the negotiations that culminated in the signing of the Punjab Accord.

One is struck by the speed with which Rajiv Gandhi acted once he had made up his mind to reach a settlement with the man whom he regarded as the most credible of the Akali Dal leaders and one with whom he could do business. By 25 July he had signed an accord aimed at healing Punjab's suppurating political crisis. In less than three weeks of this he signed an accord on Assam, and chose the occasion of the celebration of India's independence on 15 April 1985 to announce this. Rajiv Gandhi was on the crest of a wave of popularity. The euphoria of those early weeks of his honeymoon with the electorate did not last long. The assassination of Longowal his co-signatory on the Punjab Accord coming as it did less than a month from its signing should have shattered any illusions he may have had on bringing peace to strife-torn Punjab. He refused to be deflected by this grim reminder of how pervasive Punjab's political violence was, to any early return to the policies his mother had followed. A general election was held in Punjab, where despite attempts by extremist groups to disrupt the polls as had happened in Assam two years earlier, two-thirds of the registered voters went to the polls and gave the Longowal group of the Akali Dal a resounding victory. Congress I suffered a setback. Although early signs were propitious, Gill's chapter will show how the promises made in the Accord were not fulfilled, and how the situation drifted to a state of political paralysis accompanied by a reversion to the pre-accord cycle of violence and repression which destroyed thousands of lives. In Assam, however, Rajiv Gandhi's Peace Accord achieved some success in giving that isolated state a measure of political stability it had not enjoyed for some time, and the people at large more peace than at any time in the early 1980s. The opposition groups which won power at the general election of 1985 succeeded in holding on although they had only a plurality at the polls.[11] More important, unlike in Punjab, no attempt was made to undermine its position in order to build a coalition around Congress I.

As for Sri Lanka, there was a qualitative difference in the fact that the Peace Accord Rajiv Gandhi was negotiating between the two sovereign states concerned an ethnic conflict in one of them (Sri Lanka) involving a minority (the Tamils) which has affective links with the people of a state of the Indian union, Tamil Nadu. The negotiations between the two countries had commenced under Mrs Gandhi as early as August 1983 and had gone on for over a year before coming to an abrupt end in December 1984, shortly after Mrs Gandhi's assassination, with very little achieved.

Rajiv Gandhi began the talks anew. Unlike in the Assam case there was no attempt to use the pre-1985 negotiations as the basis for the resumption of talks between the two countries although the issues remained the same. In making this decision Rajiv Gandhi was hoping to ensure a more cordial atmosphere for the negotiations with the Sri Lankan government than his mother had been able to achieve.

From the resumption of talks with the Sri Lanka government in the second quarter of 1985 his objective, very clearly, was the drafting and signing of yet another Peace Accord. As K.M. de Silva's chapter would show, he very nearly succeeded in this objective less than two months from the signing of the Punjab Accord. By 30 August 1985 his principal negotiator had succeeded in gaining the agreement of representatives of the Sri Lanka government to a framework of proposals for a resolution of the ethnic conflict in the island. A draft accord which came to be known in official circles as the Delhi Accord was initialled on 30 August by representatives of the two governments. This draft formed the basis of all future negotiations between them on Sri Lanka's ethnic problems in so far as these concerned the Tamil minority. The signing of the Accord were not fulfilled, and how the situation drifted to a state of political paralysis accompanied by a reversion to the pre-accord cycle were reluctant. The Liberation Tigers of Tamil Eelam (LTTE) the most violent of these groups, who had considerable and rapidly growing public support among the Tamils, refused to endorse it. The Tamil United Liberation Front (TULF) who had been consulted in the framing of the Delhi Accord and had given its concurrence to it, were unwilling to take the risks involved in ignoring the wishes of the LTTE on this matter. The kidnapping and assassination of two TULF stalwarts, both former MPs resident in Jaffna, the principal town in the Tamil dominated Jaffna peninsula of Sri Lanka's Northern province, between 1 and 3 September 1985 by the LTTE, was a clear reminder of the perils involved in disregarding their views. Coming as it did so soon after the assassination of Longowal in Punjab it ensured that Tamil representatives would not sign the Delhi Accord.

The Peace Accord that Rajiv Gandhi had in mind for Sri Lanka in 1985 came two years later after tortuous negotiations between the two governments, and with representatives of Tamil interests in Sri Lanka. The two year gap between the signing of the first of the accords, the Punjab Accord, and the third, the Indo-Sri Lanka Accord, should have provided time for reflection on the strengths and weaknesses of this mode of peacemaking. There is very little evidence to suggest anything of the sort was done either in New Delhi, or for that matter in Sri Lanka.

In Sri Lanka as in Punjab the Indian army was used in a calculated demonstration of military power to impose the will of the Indian government in support of what were seen to be India's national and strategic interests. The difference was that in Sri Lanka the use of the Indian army followed the signing of the Accord and flowed from its clauses, while in Punjab the Accord itself had to deal with the consequences that flowed from the army's intervention. In both instances the use of the army did little to resolve the conflict; on the contrary, the consequences were well-nigh disastrous for India's own national interests, and not least for the two leaders who ordered the resort to force. Mrs Gandhi was assassinated by her Sikh bodyguards within a few months of Operation Blue Star, as the army assault on Amritsar's Golden Temple was called; Rajiv Gandhi was assassinated nearly four years after he sent the Indian army to the north and east of the island, an assassination which is widely believed to have been carried out by the LTTE on the orders of the LTTE leader to avenge the deaths caused by the Indian army in Jaffna and elsewhere in the north and east of the island.

The use of the Indian army in Punjab on that fateful occasion was a purely internal matter for the Indian state, and one for which there were precedents in India's recent history. There were very few precedents in international politics for the decision to use an army in an attempt to resolve an ethnic conflict in a neighboring state. One such precedent was the Indian intervention in East Pakistan which led to the creation of Bangladesh, and the other was the Turkish intervention in Cyprus. These were unilateral decisions of the two governments, India and Turkey. In contrast, the use of the Indian army, in the north and east of

Sri Lanka had the support of the Sri Lanka government and of its president at that time, J.R. Jayewardene.

The chapter in this book by Samarasinghe and Liyanage on the responses to the Indo-Sri Lanka Accord deals with the nature, extent and sources of support, and on the opposition to it. That Accord had provoked the most widespread anti-government riots in the post-independence history of Sri Lanka and, while these lasted, gravely imperilled the stability of the government. Two features of the Accord, above all others, explain the violent upsurge of opposition to it: the decision to use the Indian army in a peace-keeping role in Sri Lanka, and the decision to amalgamate the Northern and Eastern provinces into a single administrative unit. The first decision, as we have seen, was not a unilateral one. The responsibility for it has to be shared by the two signatories of the Accord, Rajiv Gandhi and J.R. Jayewardene. The second was the result of Indian pressure on a reluctant Sri Lankan government to accept an unpalatable decision for which there was no public support in the country. Indeed, neither of Rajiv Gandhi's other accords committed his co-signatory and his party or group to a line of action that was so clearly unpopular with the electorate.

The opprobrium attached to the Indo-Sri Lanka Accord was concentrated on its architects within the government, and especially President Jayewardene. The Janatha Vimukthi Peramuna (JVP), the most virulent and violent critics of the Accord, called for his assassination through posters and inflammatory speeches. The slogan 'Kill JR' was scrawled on walls in all parts of the country and painted in white across public highways. On 18 August 1987 the JVP almost succeeded in assassinating him, in a daring attempt on his life within the parliamentary complex. As for Rajiv Gandhi an infuriated Sri Lankan sailor assaulted him with the butt of his rifle at a guard of honor ceremony in Colombo on 30 July 1987. Gandhi deftly evaded the full force of his assailant's blow.

V

Conclusion

A review of the ethnic Peace Accords peace negotiations studied in this book leaves us in little doubt about the formidable difficulties that confront mediators seeking to resolve ethnic conflicts, especially where these have persisted over long periods of time measured generally in

14   *K.M. de Silva and S.W.R. de A. Samarasinghe*

decades, or sometimes over generations (as in the case of Canada). As Richardson and Wang show in the concluding chapter of this book ethnic conflict is less favorable to mediation than other conflicts, including conflicts between states. In many cases – Punjab and Sri Lanka are good examples – there is a multiplicity of interested and conflicting parties, as well as divided authority on one or more sides, all of which makes it difficult to reach agreement or to make an agreement stick once it has been reached. Besides, leaders of extremist groups including some of the factions of the Akali Dal in Punjab or the LTTE and many of its rivals in Sri Lanka see few gains in a peaceful outcome, and have little or no interest in the give and take of mediation. External forces with a stake in the outcome, India in the case of Sri Lanka or Greece and Turkey in the case of Cyprus are complicating factors. Sometimes such a regional power – Turkey for instance – may see its interests best served by the prolonging of a stalemate until the situation forces a settlement it can accept, rather than commit itself wholeheartedly to the course of conflict resolution. Generally, however, the principal sources of intractability in the ethnic conflicts reviewed in this book, have been indigenous forces rather than external allies and mentors.

Notes

1. Ryan, Stephen (1990) *Ethnic Conflict and International Relations*, Aldershot: Dartmouth. See particularly the discussion on pp. 1–50.
2. Among the more important works of these authors are: Azar, E.E. (1990) *The Management of Protracted Social Conflict: Theory and Cases*, Hampshire, England: Dartmouth; Burton, J.W. (1987) *Resolving Deep Rooted Conflict*, Lanham, Md.: University Press of America; Azar, E.E. and Burton, J.W. (eds.) (1987) *International Conflict Resolution*, Brighton: Wheatsheaf; Deng, F. and Zartman, I.W. (eds.) (1991) *Conflict Resolution in Africa*, Washington, DC: The Brookings Institute; and Zartman, I.W. (1989) *Ripe for Resolution: Conflict and Intervention in Africa*, 2nd edn, New York: Oxford University Press.
3. The reference is to Connor, W. (1980) Ethnic political change and government responses, in Sugar, P.E. (ed.) *Ethnic Diversity and Conflict in Eastern Europe*, Santa Barbara.
4. Ryan, Stephen, *op. cit.*, p. 35.
5. McRae, K.D. (1990) Canada: reflections on two conflicts, in Montville, J.V. (ed.) (1991) *Conflict and Peacemaking in Multiethnic Societies*, Lexington, Mass.: Lexington Books, pp. 197–217. The extract quoted is in pp. 197–98.
6. *Ibid.*, p. 200.
7. On this issue see Asch, M. (1984) *Home and Native Land, Aboriginal Rights*

and the Canadian Constitution, Toronto; Barsh, R.L. (1991) Aboriginal rights and Canadian credibility, in *Human Rights Forum* Canadian Human Rights Commission, 2(1) 5–7; Salisbury, R.F. (1986) *A Homeland for the Cree: Regional Development in James Bay*, Kingston.

8. Nyong'O, P.O. (1991) The implications of crisis and conflict in the Upper Nile Valley, in Deng, F. and Zartman, I.W. (eds) *Conflict Resolution in Africa*, pp. 95–114. The quotation is from pp. 104–5.

9. On the problems of Assam see Weiner, J. (1978) *Sons of the Soil: Migration and Ethnic Conflict in India*, Princeton: Princeton University Press; Baruah, S. (1986) Immigration, ethnic conflict and political turmoil in Assam, 1979–1985, in *Asian Survey* 26 (XI), November; and Singh, Jaswani (1984) Assam's crisis of leadership, *Asian Survey*, 24 (X), October.

10. The Assam election of 1983 is discussed in Shourie, A. (1983) Assam's elections: can democracy survive them? *India Today*, 31 May.

11. The Assam elections of December 1985 are reviewed in Baruah, S. (1986) Lessons of Assam, *Economic and Political Weekly*, (hereafter *EPW*), 15 February; see also *India Today*, 15 January, pp. 22–35.

2 THE QUEST FOR DURABLE FRENCH-ENGLISH AND IMMIGRANT-ABORIGINAL ACCORDS IN CANADA

Dale Thomson

Introduction

At first glance, Canada might seem to be an unlikely case study for a conference on peace accords. A 'peace accord' is usually understood to be a formally negotiated settlement analogous to a treaty following a period of violence. Canada has known so little ethnic-derived violence since it assumed responsibility for its internal affairs that it is often cited as an example of peaceful ethnic co-existence. Yet today, there is a real possibility of its breaking up along ethnic lines. So perhaps the Canadian case is instructive, not as representing the success or failure of a specific accord, but of a series of accords or arrangements that have enabled the country to remain intact without, however, resolving the ethnic tensions once and for all.

The Canadian case is also interesting at the moment in that two principal ethnic conflicts are manifest, one between French- and English-speaking Canadians, and the other between the aboriginal populations (themselves originally from Asia) and the more recent immigrants and their descendants. The two conflicts impact on one another: in 1990 the Meech Lake Accord between French- and English-speaking Canadians was blocked at the last moment by an aboriginal member of a provincial legislature because it did not address his people's problems. As a result it is now acknowledged that both conflicts have to be addressed simultaneously, and this greatly complicates the situation.

This chapter reviews briefly the various French-English accords or constitutional arrangements over the years as a backdrop to the current, and most critical, quest for a new one. I will deal with the aboriginal challenge to the *status quo* only in the current context. I will approach the subject from the perspective that, in both instances, the challenge to the *status quo* is closely related to the modernization process. This process has not only made members of the two ethnic groups acutely conscious of their situation of inferiority, but has provided them with the means to do something about it.

Analytical framework

In developing my analysis, I will be guided by the *Integrative Theory of Inter-group Conflict* elaborated by the late Henri Tajfel, social psychologist at the University of Bristol, and his associates.[1] Tajfel posits that ethnic groups evolve through various stages in their search for a positive social identity, and that an understanding of where a particular group is situated on that continuum is useful for the analysis of its current dynamism. In traditional societies, he argues, ethnic groups accept their 'social categorization' or customary place in the larger society. As modernization brings out changes within the group, its members pass through a phase of 'self-evaluation' or clarification and questioning of that social identity. This process leads in turn to a phase of 'intergroup comparisons', that is, comparisons on the level of both values and material assets with other groups about which they have information. Finally, groups move into a phase of 'competition' with proximate out-groups whose lives touch on theirs. With regard to Tajfel's competition phase, I have distinguished between individual and group competition. In the case of individual competition, the goals pursued are more likely to be equal opportunity in the workplace, freedom from discrimination in social relations and individual rights. If competition is group-based, then the objective becomes more to eliminate all unfavourable comparisons between groups as a whole, and attempts are made to mobilize the entire membership for that purpose. Minor conflicts are more likely to escalate into serious crises and calls for radical solutions, including, in the case of ethnic conflict within a single country, demands for independence.

I have chosen to emphasize this distinction between forms of competition since both are evident in the Canadian public debate, and are indeed in competition with one another for popular support. For purposes of simplification, the model of individual competition is usually associated with the thinking of former Prime Minister Pierre Trudeau, and the model of group competition with that of his long-time adversary, the late Premier of Quebec Rene Levesque. Trudeau's solution to French-English tensions in Canada was to guarantee as much as possible the individual rights and opportunities of French-speaking Canadians within Canada as a whole. Levesque, for his part, saw the solution in the creation of a sovereign state of Quebec for the French-speaking collectivity which would negotiate future relationships with what remained of Canada.

Looking back

History usually casts its long shadow over inter-ethnic relations. In the Canadian case, certain past events maintain their salience. First among these is the fact that the French initially colonized the territory and exercised their dominion over it for more than two centuries. Most French Canadians can trace their ancestry to those original 8,000 settlers. Today they number some seven million, of whom 80 per cent live in the Province of Quebec where their forefathers first settled. They make up about a quarter of the Canadian population. Deeply ingrained in their collective psyche are two bitter memories: the British conquest, and France's abandonment of them without a struggle more than two centuries ago. With slogans such as '*Je me souriens*' and '*la survivance*', they maintained the principal traits of their ethnic identity – their French language, Roman Catholic religion, local laws and customs. The feeling of being an oppressed group stimulated their feeling of solidarity.

The British, for their part, soon abandoned any thought of forced assimilation, and devised a colonial policy that was subsequently to mark the whole Empire, indirect rule through local elites. By the Quebec Act of 1774, the distinctive qualities of the French-speaking settlers, including their language and religion, were confirmed. This historical document might be considered the first accord between the English and French of Canada. The dual ethnicity of the population was recognized.

In 1791 the first parliamentary institutions were introduced, with an Executive Council, a Legislative Council, and a Legislative Assembly. While the powers of the popularly elected Assembly were limited, French Canadians soon recognized its usefulness in defending their interests. Moreover, since the colony was divided at the same time into two parts each with its own Assembly, they were assured of a majority in the Lower Canadian one. Indeed, the first outbreak of violence between French and British occurred when the French Canadian Speaker of the Assembly became involved in a power struggle with a particularly undemocratic British Governor, and eventually led an uprising against him. The French population, sympathetic but cautious, did not respond to the call to arms as expected, and the uprising was quashed. The lesson: democracy, not force, was the most effective means of survival.

The British reacted by re-uniting the two parts of Canada with a single Parliament where the English settlers would have a majority of seats. They also proscribed the French language in debates, but in vain. The language restriction was ignored; and stable government was soon proven impossible without French participation. The principle of double majorities, or equal Cabinet representation from the two groups (not unlike the present theoretical framework of consociational democracy) evolved. In an age when political party discipline was still rare, this system soon fell prey to the switching of alliances, and consequently to political instability.

Out of this chaos arose the British North America Act, 1967, which we can consider the second Canadian accord. Negotiated in large part by the two principal ethnic leaders, John A. Macdonald and George-Etienne Cartier, the BNA Act established a federal system in which French Canadians would have a majority in one province (member-state) Quebec, and proportionate representation within the institutions of the central government. Quebec, and the other provinces, were given jurisdiction over all matters of local concern, including education and civil rights. The French and English languages were both given official status in the Quebec legislature and courts, and separate school systems were continued for the two groups. At the federal level too, both French and English were made official languages of Parliament and the courts. In the other provinces, there was no specific provision for the use of the French language, but there too the existing system of separate schools was maintained. (The school systems were religious, not language based, but each was free to choose its language of instruction).

While the BNA Act was designed to provide the French Canadians with a safe haven from English Canadian influence, all the more important since the immigration pattern was tipping the balance more and more in favour of the latter, it had the effect of condemning them to permanent minority status. In Tajfel's words, in accepting the new constitution, French Canadians through their leadership categorized themselves as French-speaking Roman Catholics, and committed themselves to maintaining that social categorization. For most of the next century, the two ethnic groups co-existed with relatively little contact and consequently little serious friction. The major exceptions occurred during the two World Wars, when the English Canadian majority imposed military conscription to force the French Canadians to support the allied (for French Canadians, the British) cause.

Modernization and its effects

Inevitably, outside influences did penetrate Quebec society through foreign investments, industrial development, telecommunications and population movements; a trend that accelerated after World War II. It was reflected in 1960 in the election of a reform government in Quebec committed to modernizing the state infrastructure, developing the economy, and meeting the rising aspirations of the population for greater services. French-speaking Quebecers had clearly entered Tajfel's second phase of self-evaluation, and even the third phase of social comparison.

This 'Quiet Revolution', as it came to be called, was also marked by a resurgence of ethnic consciousness, or nationalism, but in a less defensive mode. The Algerian and Cuban liberation movements were frequently referred to by a new generation of Quebecers as models. Writers such as Franz Fanon and Regis Debray were sources of inspiration. The remark was frequently heard: if such-and-such a colonial people can become independent and run its own affairs, why not we? In marked contrast to the old cautious conservatism, Quebec was caught up in a new atmosphere of hope, progress and liberation from old constraints.

Fortunately for Canada as a whole, a new government took power in 1963 under the leadership of Lester B. Pearson and the new modernizing elite of Quebec was strongly represented. It was thus able to throw its support behind the Quiet Revolution, except of course in its more overtly nationalistic manifestations. For instance, a Royal Commission on Bilingualism and Biculturalism was established to find ways of ensuring the equality of 'the two founding peoples' throughout Canada. Without waiting for the Commission to report, the government undertook to increase the proportion of French-speaking Canadians in the public service to correspond to their proportion of the total population, and to give them the opportunity to work in their own language. A larger share of joint tax fields was ceded to the provinces – at Quebec's insistence – to enable them to develop their own programmes. A long-standing constitutional irritant was tackled anew: when Canada became independent in 1931, Ottawa and the provinces had been unable to agree on a formula for amending the constitution in areas of shared jurisdiction, or of vital importance to both levels of government. Accordingly, the amending authority in that regard had remained in the hands of the British authorities. The matter was taken up again at the request of the Quebec government, and in 1965 agreement was reached in principle. By that time, however, the new Quebec nationalists were calling into question the Province's place within Canada, and were concerned that any resolution of the amending formula problem would consolidate the *status quo*. The Quebec government retreated and no action was taken. The new nationalism had become a force to be reckoned with.

Modernization led to an increasingly pluralistic society in Quebec, but out of the process emerged two broad political options identified for convenience with two leaders, Rene Levesque and Pierre Trudeau. Levesque had been a member of the Liberal government that had initiated the Quiet Revolution but, always a strong nationalist, he had left the party after its defeat in 1966 to form the Parti Quebecois (PQ). The PQ's principal plank was sovereignty-association, or independence combined with a common market relationship with the rest of Canada. This objective was based on the concept of Quebec society as essentially an integrated ethnic community with a common history, language and values and, as practical assets, a state infrastructure and a clearly defined territory. The fact that some 20 per cent of the population was not French-speaking was dealt with by declaring that in a democracy the majority decides, and that at any rate minority rights can be protected. In striking contrast, Trudeau saw society in terms of individuals and sought to ensure fair opportunities and freedom from discrimination through guarantees of civil rights and other forms of legislation. In that sense, he saw the role of government with regard to French Canadians as helping or even goading them to be able to compete with English Canadians. In that framework, he conceived of language legislation, for instance, as maximizing opportunities for them to live their own lives and make their living in French, and therefore to communicate with their government, whether federal or provincial, in that language.

Thus, if we assume that by the late 1960s Francophone Quebecers had entered Tajfel's final stage – that of social competition – in their quest for a positive social identity, we see Levesque and Trudeau representing its two manifestations, group and individual competition. When Trudeau became Prime Minister of Canada in 1968, and Levesque Premier of Quebec in 1976, Canadians witnessed a classic conflict in the political arena between those two approaches to their principal national problem.

Achieving office first, Trudeau made a major effort to resolve the problem of the amending formula, and came very close to doing so in 1971. However, the then Quebec government, led by Robert Bourassa, again backed off at the last moment because of fears of the nationalist reaction. Its concerns were at least understandable; the Parti Quebecois was by then the Official Opposition in the legislature, and political violence had merged on the Quebec scene for the first time in more than a century. In the early 1960s, a few bombs had been exploded in the predominantly English quarter of Greater Montreal, and two innocent lives had been lost, but the perpetrators had been arrested in short order, and the terrorist activity was nipped in the bud. Then in 1970, members of the Front de Liberation du Quebec kidnapped a British diplomat and a Quebec Cabinet Minister, killing the latter before being apprehended. Traumatized by the events, the Bourassa government had requested the federal government to send troops into the Province to maintain order and to declare martial law so that the provincial police could more effectively seek out the terrorists. The population was deeply shaken, many being sympathetic to the terrorists at the outset but then revolted by the murder of a leading French-speaking Quebecer. The Parti Quebecois tried desperately to dissociate itself from these acts of violence.

The election of the Parti Quebecois in 1976 can be explained in part by the shortcomings of the Bourassa government, and also by the fact that its commitment to sovereignty-association was softened by a further commitment not to proceed with the project unless the public gave its approval in a referendum. Formed by history to be cautious of uncertain ventures, Quebecers were reassured that they were still able to control their leaders through the democratic process. When the referendum was held in 1980, French-speaking Quebecers split almost evenly, but the others voted massively against the proposal, and it was defeated by 60 per cent to 40 per cent.

A few points have to be made about this democratic process. First, the Canadian government and Canadians as a whole accepted that, while they were strongly opposed to the separation of Quebec, they must respect the wishes of Quebecers whatever the latter decided. Second, Levesque and his colleagues accepted the popular verdict in the referendum and agreed to continue to govern the Province within the federal system. Third, Prime Minister Trudeau made a firm commitment during the referendum campaign to bring about constitutional changes to meet the concerns of Quebecers. That appeal appears to have been effective in the outcome. In effect, Quebecers were given a good reason – and by a French Canadian – to at least postpone their final word on their relations with the rest of the country.

In 1982 Trudeau did make good on his promise of constitutional changes, but not in the way that most Quebecers expected. He succeeded in resolving the problem of amending the constitution and also incorporated it in a charter of Rights and Freedoms. To meet the demands of some premiers, he also strengthened the provinces veto on future constitutional changes, and added a provision to permit any province to override the provisions of the charter when its vital interests were at stake. But he did all this over the objections of the Levesque government. The move was legal in the sense that, under the previously existing constitutional arrangements, no single province could block it, but it was more questionable in political terms. Trudeau argued that he had the support of all but one of the Members of Parliament from Quebec and that they represented the population of the Province just as much as did the Parti Quebecois. Indeed, public opinion polls indicated that Quebecers supported the changes in a proportion of three to one.

None the less, the question must be asked: can the 1982 arrangements be considered a further French-English accord? Probably not, in the light of the fact that it was not accepted by the Quebec government, and that it became a subject of further negotiations with that Province.

The Meech Lake Accord

Trudeau retired before the 1984 elections and his party was defeated in those elections by the Conservatives, led by another Quebecer, Brian Mulroney. Half French and half Irish in origin, Mulroney was bilingual; he also had close contacts with the Quebec nationalists. In fact, since his party had practically no organization in the Province, he made a deal with the Parti Quebecois to help his party's candidates campaign and a number of those candidates had close ties with the PQ. With that combination, the Conservatives won a majority of Quebec seats in the federal Parliament. On the provincial level, the following year the Parti Quebecois was defeated, and Robert Bourassa became Premier again.

Both Mulroney and Bourassa took office with firm commitments to renegotiate the 1982 constitutional arrangements to make them acceptable to Quebec. They were soon able to agree on a set of changes, and in 1987 they succeeded in persuading the other premiers to accept them almost unaltered. Thus was born the Meech Lake Accord, named for the conference site near Ottawa where the heads of government meeting took place. Under its terms, Quebec enlarged its veto power over future constitutional amendments relating to Parliament and the Supreme Court. Future appointments to the Senate and Supreme Court from Quebec were also to be made by Ottawa from lists submitted by the provincial government. In the field of immigration, a joint federal-provincial responsibility under the constitution, Quebec would have greater powers to select and integrate immigrants to the province. With regard to shared-cost federal-provincial programmes, Quebec could opt out of any of them and receive the same amount of money from Ottawa, providing it created its own programme 'compatible with the national objectives'. Finally, Quebec was to be recognized in the constitution as a 'distinct society' and the constitution was to be interpreted in the sense that the Quebec government had a specific role to 'preserve and promote' it.

The Meech Lake Accord was put together by the heads of government in two short series of intensive discussions lasting almost around the clock. The terms were also agreed to without the other premiers' advisers being present. Why the haste? It was part of Mulroney and Bourassa's strategy, and the other premiers grasped the opportunity to bring Quebec, in Mulroney's words, 'back into the Canadian family'. They even agreed to submit the document to their respective legislatures without allowing any changes to be made. In short, the Accord was accepted in a wave of goodwill towards Quebec and a sense of euphoria that a solution to the constitutional disagreements had been found.

The constitutional provisions of 1982 had provided for a three-year delay in approving future amendments. That proved to be the Achilles' heel of the Meech Lake process. Bourassa had the Accord approved promptly by the Quebec legislature. Mulroney followed suit in Parliament and was supported by the official Opposition. Most of the other premiers did likewise. But before three years passed, three provincial governments changed hands through general elections, and in every case the new government took office with commitments to secure changes in the Accord. Most of the proposed changes stemmed from complaints from important sections of Canadian society that *their* concerns should have been dealt with as well as Quebec's. These included aboriginal rights, women's rights, Senate reforms to enhance Western Canada's influence in Ottawa, recognition of other cultural communities, and the situation of certain major economic groups such as the farmers and fishermen. Serious reservations were also expressed in English Canada about the long-term implications of the 'concessions' made to Quebec, and particularly the distinct society clause. Could it not be used by Quebec, some asked, to acquire a different status from that of the other provinces, and even to bring about a form of *de facto* separation? Such fears were fuelled by indiscreet statements by Bourassa and other politicians to their fellow Quebecers that the clause was an open door for such changes as Quebec would need in the future.

With the three-year time limit for constitutional changes only weeks away, Prime Minister Mulroney convened the premiers again for a final marathon negotiating session. His strategy of threatening them with the consequences of failure proved misguided; opinions had hardened in both Quebec and English Canada. The three new premiers demanded that their concerns be addressed in the Accord; Bourassa for his part could not afford to make any concessions. While the secret bargaining sessions went on late into each night, the media portrayed the denouement in cataclysmic tones. In the end, one of the three hold-outs, Premier McKenna of New Brunswick, acquiesced for the sake of national unity. Another, Premier Filmon of Manitoba, agreed to submit the Accord to his legislature with slight modifications. The third, Premier Wells of Newfoundland, agreed to consult either his legislature or the population of the province.

Premier Filmon did attempt to introduce the document in the Assembly, but because of time constraints, he had to ask for special permission to do so. It was refused by the sole aboriginal member of the Assembly, Elijah Harper. Harper, who was acting on instructions from the assembly of native chiefs, became an instant hero among his own people, and also among a great many other Canadians. Premier Wells did succeed in introducing the measure in his legislature, but realizing that it was going down to defeat in Manitoba, he adjourned the debate and allowed Harper to take the credit, or opprobrium, for its demise.

Post-Meech trauma

The failure to approve the Meech Lake Accord before the deadline of 23 June 1990 drew attention to, and even greatly exacerbated, the division between the two linguistic groups in Canada. For most French-speaking Quebecers (French Canadians in other Provinces see their interest in maintaining the integrity of Canada) it was seen as a denial of their distinctive language and society, and of their demand for equality within the whole country. Their pride was deeply wounded. The English Canadian reaction was more complex. Some people, who had accepted the Accord as imperfect but preferable to the probable consequences of failure, were deeply disturbed. Others who felt that their own grievances should also have been addressed, or who saw the concept of Quebec as a distinct society as incompatible with their vision of a united Canada, were relieved. Ethnic prejudice, always latent, was also stirred up by the vigorous debate in the last days of the Accord. Another feeling resurfaced in English Canada: a deeply-rooted lack of confidence in the viability of the country. In periods of adversity, Canadians are prone to question whether their national enterprise is not an impossible dream. In the summer and fall of 1990, discussions turned more around the likelihood of the break-up of the country, and the material consequences for Canadians of such an occurrence, than around ways of saving it.

In view of the strong feelings aroused on both sides of the linguistic barrier, the level of overt animosity was surprisingly low. Asked in a public opinion survey conducted two weeks after the collapse of the Accord if they disliked members of the other group, not more than eight per cent of English- and French-speaking Canadians answered in the affirmative. On the other hand, most thought that the members of the other group disliked them. The survey also revealed that a strong majority of both groups desired to keep the country together in some form.

His constitutional strategy in tatters, and with the Parti Quebecois buoyed up by the recent events, Premier Bourassa declared that Quebec must henceforth decide its own future. He established and enlarged a legislative committee (that is, a committee composed of members of the legislature plus representatives of labour, business and other large sectors of society) to hold hearings and consider the constitutional future of the province. The only option that was precluded was the *status quo*. Bourassa also charged a committee of his own party with proposing a new policy to replace the one that had come to a dead end. In the meantime, he announced, he would have no discussions with the other provinces, and any future negotiations would be restricted to one-on-one communications with the federal government.

The two Quebec committees reported in early 1991. The legislative committee, whose deliberations were marked by intense bargaining between the political parties, called for a referendum on independence by October 1992 unless a binding and acceptable offer of a highly decentralized federal regime was received from the rest of Canada before that date. The Liberal Party committee staked out a tough bargaining position: it proposed the transfer of 22 fields of jurisdiction from the federal to the Quebec government. If effected, it would have not only created a very distinctive Quebec society, but would have rendered the federal government incapable of keeping the country together.

General de Gaulle once declared that no nationalist movement could be stopped short of full independence if the population supported it. Two questions face Canadians in that regard. First, whether his conclusion, drawn from his experience with the decolonization of Africa, is a firm socio-political law, and whether it applies to the Canadian case, and secondly what light Tajfel's competition phase of ethnic progression throws on the current situation. Let us recall that he identified four stages in the quest of an ethnic group for a positive social identity, the last being competition with one or more out-groups. I have distinguished between group vs. group competition and competition between individuals, and have postulated that the former is more likely to lead to separation. The evidence derived from an analysis of the Meech Lake crisis seems to indicate that group consciousness was heightened dramatically in Quebec, and that therefore the group competition model became more significant. To the degree that it became more salient, de Gaulle's statement is more plausible, and policy planners would do well to think in terms of negotiating the dissolution of Canada under the most mutually advantageous terms. Since there is already broad agreement that economic hardships should be minimized logic would call for a new accord in the form of a confederation of two or more sovereign states or a regime analogous to the European Community. This second option was what de Gaulle had in mind for Canada, and it is the goal of the Parti Quebecois.

Yet another last chance for Canada?

But is de Gaulle's scenario the only feasible one? Is another still conceivable which would both build on the common experience and accomplishment of the past, including the lessons of the Meech Lake episode, and also ensure a greater measure of equity and benefits for French Canadians within the Canadian system? Such a prospect would imply an individual model of competition. Is it still a credible alternative? One positive indication is that the modernization of Quebec has led to an increasing appreciation of individual rights. There is even evidence that modernization, together with a long common experience in a similar geographical environment, have greatly increased the shared values and interests of all Canadians. A high proportion of Quebecers now accept the challenge of individual competition, both among themselves and with other Canadians. This is particularly true of the most prestigious group of Quebecers at the present time, the business elite. For the first time, a cadre of entrepreneurs, some managing firms of international scope and inspired more by market than nationalist considerations, are serving as role models for the younger generation. The province's business schools are thriving as never before.

After spending the summer of 1990 in a seeming state of shock and confusion, Canadian leaders outside of Quebec began to react to the

Bourassa government's challenge to put forward a set of precise proposals. Sensitive to the widespread criticism that the Meech Lake process was too secretive and even undemocratic, the federal government established a Citizen's Forum on Canada's future. It was, in fact, a travelling committee of well-known personalities, mostly professional communicators, whose task was to engage in a dialogue with ordinary Canadians, and encourage them to express their views on the state of the nation and possible ways of improving it. The federal government also established a parliamentary committee to investigate alternative methods of amending the constitution to replace the unanimity provision that had led to the failure of the Meech Lake Accord. It also authorized a Royal Commission to examine the situation of the aboriginal population. And finally, it announced plans to create yet another parliamentary committee, with additional representation from the provinces and perhaps other groups, to bring all the strands of the puzzle together and to make specific recommendations to Parliament on how to meet the challenge thrown out by Quebec. At the provincial level, most of the other governments also set up consultative bodies to draw up policy positions. Add to all that the countless public debates, intellectual panels, journalistic analyses, almost weekly opinion polls and other forms of political communication, and one has a picture of a dialectical marathon of truly impressive proportions.

The federal Citizens' Forum delivered its report in late June of this year. Based on consultations with some 350,000 persons, its impressions of the state of public thinking were necessarily heterogeneous, but a few broad strains were evident. English Canadians were far more attached to their country than was evident from the debate over Meech Lake, and, indeed, they had quite strong feelings about the national identity. For that reason, they resented deeply both Quebec's threats to it, and the actions of politicians such as Prime Minister Mulroney whom, it was felt, placed it in jeopardy by their actions. They were prepared to make considerable concessions to Quebec to keep the country together, but none that would change it fundamentally. There was more understanding for the situation of the aboriginal population. The Forum spent far less time in Quebec, and it was less forthcoming regarding public reaction there. Throughout the report was an implication that strong and clear leadership acceptable to all parts of Canada could still rally the diverse elements of the population around an imaginative set of proposals for reform, but that no such leadership seemed to be available at the moment.

The parliamentary committee on amending the constitution was understandably more precise in its recommendations, which it also submitted in late June. Essentially, it sought to provide greater input from the regions and the population as a whole in the amending process. Since Quebec has about a quarter of the Canadian population, it is considered a region for this purpose, and would thus have a veto on the most important proposals for amendments. In addition, a majority of Senators from Quebec, who it is anticipated would be appointed in future in consultation with the Quebec government or even elected, would have to approve any federal legislation affecting the French language and culture. And finally, provision would be made in the constitution for the first time for referenda on vital national issues. All in all, this set of recommendations constitutes a positive contribution to the constitutional debate, but they were premised on the assumption that Quebec would remain within the Federal system.

Two years after the failure of the Meech Lake Accord, what do all these consultations indicate about the possibilities of negotiating a new agreement, whether a modified form of federalism or a treaty sanctioning the independence of Quebec? In the interval, there has been some moderation in public attitudes in both English and French Canada. Opinion polls indicate that Quebecers, while still feeling aggrieved at what they consider to have been a humiliating rejection by English Canada no longer feel strongly on that score. Reflecting the increasingly pluralist nature of their society their views are far from unanimous. Less than a quarter can be classified as hard core independentists at any price. A larger number are what might be termed 'soft' separatists, that is, they are favourable in principle to independence but uneasy about its possible consequences, and would accept an offer from English Canada that would justify giving Canada still another 'last chance'. The rest of the population of Quebec is either in favour of remaining in Canada with some unspecified changes in the federal system, or satisfied with the *status quo*, or simply uninvolved in the whole question. Perhaps it would be fair to say that some two-thirds of Quebecers prefer to stay within Canada, in part because of the uncertainties and possible economic costs of separation. For most of them that would be a rational, not an emotional choice, and would have to be based on credible reasons.

English Canadian opinion has also evolved in the past two years. A genuine attachment to Canada has dampened the satisfaction over the defeat of the Meech Lake Accord, and there is a greater disposition to accept a constitutional reform package, providing it deals with the concerns of English Canadians as well as Quebecers. One of the unknown factors is the future of the Reform Party of Canada, a new party originating in Western Canada which takes a hard line against Quebec. In a sense, it is the English Canadian counterpart of the Parti Quebecois. So far it has attracted mainly those Canadians who are upset over the political 'concessions' to Quebec but, in the absence of strong federal leadership, it could extend its clientele to other groups.

The aboriginal factor

Of all the non-Quebec issues in the equation, none is as important as the demands of the aboriginal population for a fairer share of the benefits of Canadian society. Following Elijah Harper's coup in derailing the Meech Lake Accord, they have taken fresh hope that a comprehensive new accord can be wrenched from the Canadian authorities for them as well. They are determined to block any further accord with Quebec until that goal is achieved. Historically, many native chiefs did sign 'treaties' with the Canadian authorities, ceding the title to huge parcels of land for smaller 'reserves' and some additional benefits. In more remote areas, no such documents were signed, and land rights remained undefined. As the country was developed by the European and other immigrants, the natives were pressed back into their reserves or the hinterland, and eventually their way of life was endangered. Even in the Arctic region, they became more and more wards of the state, living near and off the white settlements. At the present time, the native youth are passing through a particularly difficult transitional phase, having largely abandoned their traditional way of life but not having been integrated into the mainstream of Canadian society.

What are the demands of the aboriginals or 'first nations' as they now designate themselves? By and large, self-government in their own territories; but those territories still have to be defined. As a starting point, they lay claim to what they consider to be their traditional homelands, which sometimes include large urban centres, and in the case of Quebec, 80 per cent of the province. Because of their lack of economic opportunities, particularly in the northern regions, they also need the massive support of the Canadian authorities for the foreseeable future. That implies that they are in favour of a strong federal government, a position that puts them at odds not only with Quebec but with some other provinces.

The conflict between the aboriginal and Quebec agendas is illustrated with regard to the development of the hydro-electric resources of northern Quebec. The provincial government sees in that project an opportunity to strengthen the economy; some nationalists even argue that it would nullify the economic argument for remaining within Canada. At the same time, the project would ruin vast stretches of land for hunting and fishing. The aboriginal leaders in the area, supported now by others in the rest of the country, are determined to block the hydro-electric project until their interests are protected. And they are calling on the federal government, with its primary responsibility for native rights and also for environmental protection, to stand by them. They have threatened to use violence if necessary in defense of their cause, and there is good reason to think that it is no idle threat.

The leaders of the first nations have also made impressive progress in co-ordinating their efforts and in developing common strategies and goals. The new head of the association of chiefs, elected in June 1991, is a lawyer with evident leadership and negotiating talent. They will have to be an integral part of the next round of constitutional negotiations.

Conclusion

What insights does the Canadian case offer to the study of inter-ethnic conflict and to the negotiation of peace accords? It has been, on the whole, non-violent except on the verbal level, so 'peace' in the usual sense has not had to be negotiated. And the current quest for a new accord between Quebec and the rest of Canada continues to be fruitless. Perhaps the case does offer some insights, however, into the rise of ethnic tensions in a developed liberal democratic society, and into the particular problems of dealing with them. The respective roles of political leaders and the general public are also of possible interest. During the Meech Lake process, the two seemed often to be out of synchrony and to be functioning at different levels. The politicians appeared to be pursuing their own agendas, competing with one another, and uttering dire warnings of impending doom if their positions were not accepted. The public, on the other hand, remained relatively uninvolved, uninformed about the various options, more moderate than the general tenor of the political debate, and more interested in the pecuniary than the legalistic facets of the issues. For instance with regard to the distinct society clause, around which the public debate revolved, less than 10 per cent of both English- and French-speaking Canadians were aware of the actual text and its legal ramifications. Indeed, over the years the public has been wearied and exasperated by what it has perceived as political wrangling. Even at the height of the Meech Lake crisis, opinion polls indicated that a majority of both French and English Canadians gave higher priority to economic than to constitutional issues. In the light of these findings, it is fair to speculate that the more the public is involved in the next spate of deliberations, whether through referenda, public fora, a constituent assembly or national convention, the less radical the outcome is likely to be.

Another conclusion that can perhaps be drawn from the Canadian case is that inter-ethnic conflicts are seldom resolved; they are at best 'managed' with a minimum of eruptions. The most productive efforts made in the past three decades to reduce tensions between French- and English-speaking Canadians have been piece-meal steps towards a new set of norms and rules to govern the relationship. The attempts to reach a single, comprehensive 'final' solution have all failed, but in the meantime, French-English relations, and French Canadians' place within Canada, have evolved in a very positive manner. Perhaps the most vivid example is the evolution of bilingualism since the establishment of the Royal Commission on Bilingualism and Biculturalism in 1963.

Finally, I return to Tajfel's model and specifically to the distinction between group and individual competition. As we have seen, French Quebec society has evolved rapidly in what is, historically speaking, a short period of time from a predominantly conservative, group oriented and defensive attitudinal mode to a much more outgoing, self-confident and enterprising one. While group solidarity is still part of the common psyche, the pursuit of individual self-interest is much more manifest in daily life. Indeed that pursuit of individual self-interest frequently underlies current ethnic attitudes in Quebec. In other words, group mobilization, or group competition, is used as a means to enhance individual competitivity. Accordingly, I would hypothesize that to the degree that French-speaking Quebecers feel that they have a fair opportunity to live and work within Canada, in their own language and with a standard of living comparable to that of other Canadians, they will be disposed to accept a new accord to consolidate that situation. If they do not, they will opt sooner or later for a group-based solution, that is, a form of separation. That is the bottom line in the quest for a new accord.

Notes

1. See H.D. Tajfel (1978) *Differentiation Between Social Groups*, New York: Academic Press.

APPENDIX
Strengthening the Canadian Federation: The Constitution Amendment, 1987*

Canada stands on the threshold of a stronger partnership based on a renewed respect for the regional and linguistic diversity that gives our country its unique identity.

The door was opened on June 3, 1987, when the Prime Minister and all 10 Premiers followed up their April meeting at Meech Lake by agreeing to place the *Constitution Amendment, 1987* before Parliament and the provincial legislatures for adoption.

This booklet sets out and explains the text of an amendment that strengthens Canadian unity.

Unfinished business – Wrapping up unfinished business, the *Constitution Amendment, 1987* complements guarantees already written into the Constitution for our multicultural heritage, for aboriginal rights and for official-language minorities in every part of Canada.

Quebec was left out of the agreement that led to the *Constitution Act, 1982*, and adoption of the *Amendment* will bring it back into the Canadian constitutional family as a full and willing partner in future progress.

Spirit of federalism – The *Constitution Amendment, 1987* meets Quebec's concerns, affirms the equality of all provinces and promotes the national interest.

It offers every province a chance to cooperate with the federal government through national institutions and to share in setting common goals for the future.

While existing social programs like medicare and policies like family reunification in immigration remain unchanged, the *Amendment* sets out means for sharing the cost of new national programs and pursuing national objectives in areas of provincial jurisdiction, while respecting special concerns and needs in each province.

It will also ensure better federal-provincial coordination through annual meetings of the Prime Minister and the Premiers to discuss constitutional and economic issues of interest to all Canadians.

In this way, it realistically reflects the essence of federalism – a central government and provincial governments, all strong in their own spheres but working together on behalf of the public.

*Government of Canada, August 1987.

Step by step – The *Constitution Amendment, 1987* is the latest step in a continuing process of nation-building.

Canada has one of the oldest written constitutions in the world, and the federal and provincial governments have been at work for two decades to bring it up to date as a living document that meets the evolving needs of Canadians.

A major step was taken in 1982 when the *Canadian Charter of Rights and Freedoms* became part of our Constitution and an amending formula for future constitutional change was put in place.

But that reform remained incomplete: Without Quebec, it was more difficult to secure further constitutional amendments requiring the consent of two-thirds of the provinces with half the nation's population and impossible to secure those calling for unanimous agreement.

The problem of Quebec's constitutional isolation – a legacy of 1981–82 and a potential source of conflict and disunity – is not one we will be leaving to our children.

Built on past achievements and on continuing consultations over the years, the *Amendment* squarely faces this problem and takes another careful step forward.

Looking ahead – Adoption of the *Constitution Amendment, 1987* will not be the end of constitutional reform in Canada.

The Constitution reflects what Canadians are – equals who take pride in the way they have made their diversity a building block of unity, not a stumbling block.

It is also a tool for achieving their hopes for the future, and this *Amendment* creates a framework within which the nation's elected leaders, federal and provincial, will meet the challenges that Canada faces.

An agenda for future constitutional discussion is already taking shape.

Linguistic duality and Quebec's distinct society

The presence of two major language groups is one of the most enduring and obvious facts about Canada.

About a quarter of our people are French-speaking while almost all the rest speak English, sometimes in addition to another language.

Historically, it is this linguistic duality that has made diversity, not 'the melting pot,' a Canadian ideal.

There are English-speaking and French-speaking Canadians in all parts of Canada. But most French-speaking Canadians live in Quebec, while most English-speaking Canadians live in the other provinces and the territories – and this is an important part of what makes Quebec a distinct society within Canada.

Basic facts – The *Constitution Amendment, 1987* gives constitutional standing for the first time to these basic facts.

Clause 1 recognizes Canada's linguistic duality and the role of Parliament and all provincial legislatures in preserving this feature of our national life.

It also recognizes the key role of the legislature and government of Quebec in preserving and promoting the identity of that province as a distinct society within Canada.

Minority rights

Recognition of linguistic duality and Quebec's distinct society in the *Constitution Amendment, 1987* complements the recognition of rights already enshrined in the Constitution.

Official languages – The presence of Anglophones in Quebec and Francophones in the other provinces is part of the linguistic duality that clause 1 of the *Amendment* recognizes.

Existing constitutional rights to use either English or French in Parliament and federal courts as well as in certain provincial legislatures or provincial courts, and minority-language education rights spelled out in the *Canadian Charter of Rights and Freedoms* remain unchanged.

Aboriginal rights – The historic and treaty rights of Indians, Inuit and Métis – Canada's aboriginal peoples – were protected in the Constitution in 1982, and clause 16 of the *Constitution Amendment, 1987* reaffirms these rights.

Attempts to further define aboriginal rights in the Constitution have not yet been successful, although four Conferences of First Ministers have been convened in the past five years.

But the federal government is still committed to this goal, maintaining contact with aboriginal associations and the provinces in a search for a consensus that would make formal constitutional talks on this issue practical.

Multiculturalism – Canada's multicultural heritage was also previously protected by the Constitution, and clause 16 of the *Constitution Amendment, 1987* confirms this guarantee.

The federal government will, of course, continue its support for multiculturalism programs that help make the heritage of millions of Canadians a living reality.

The spending power

When Canada's Constitution was first written in 1867, the future importance and cost of such programs as education, health and social services could not be foreseen.

While the provincial governments were made responsible for these programs, not all provinces could afford to provide adequate levels of services, so the federal government makes equalization payments to them.

In addition, the federal government has assisted in establishing such national programs as hospital insurance and medicare by sharing the costs with the provinces.

But the federal government's power to establish such national programs has often been a source of controversy because these programs were in areas of provincial jurisdiction.

The *Constitution Amendment, 1987* is designed to make sure that the diversity of our country is fully reflected when new national programs are created to meet the needs of Canadians.

Clause 7 will ensure that no province is penalized for setting up programs of its own instead of participating in national programs in areas of exclusive provincial jurisdiction.

If the provincial program or initiative is compatible with the national objectives, the province will get 'reasonable compensation' – in effect, the money that the federal government would have contributed to the shared-cost program in that province.

Flexibility – What is new in the *Amendment* is a guarantee that provinces can pursue national objectives in their own way, if that is what their electors want, without losing their share of federal funds.

Every province has always had the right not to take part in shared-cost programs; Parliament has never had the power to make them do so.

As public needs are defined, new shared-cost programs will be established, as they have been in the past. But provinces will have a say in how these programs will be designed.

And the elected representatives of the people, at both the federal and provincial levels, will be able to focus on meeting the needs of Canadians without squabbling about how to divide the bill.

Economic conferences – Federal-provincial conferences on social and economic issues have long been an important forum for meshing the policies of the two orders of government.

The *Constitution Amendment, 1987* breaks new ground in making sure that First Ministers meet at least once a year to discuss economic and other matters and to foster increased understanding and cooperation.

Regular exchanges of views will help First Ministers keep abreast of needs in all parts of the country and work together in designing their policies to avoid duplication.

Immigration

The federal and provincial governments, under the existing Constitution, share responsibility for immigration, though federal law overrides provincial law if there is a conflict.

Because of their social and economic priorities, provinces sometimes want to receive immigrants with particular aptitudes, and six provinces now have agreements with the federal government about immigrants coming to live within their borders.

Clause 3 of the *Constitution Amendment, 1987* will require the federal government to negotiate such an agreement with any province that wants to have a say in immigration.

However, the federal government will keep supreme authority over national standards and objectives like family reunification, which is a major feature of the Canadian approach to immigration, and over total numbers of immigrants admitted each year.

In addition, the federal government remains solely responsible for granting citizenship.

Freedom of choice – Immigrants will not be forced to settle in a particular part of the country, any more than they can be now.

And once in Canada, they will continue to have the same freedom as everyone else under the *Canadian Charter of Rights and Freedoms* to move from one part of the country to another.

Because of its concern for promoting its distinct society with a Francophone majority and an Anglophone minority, Quebec has always had a special interest in immigration.

With the support of all 10 Premiers, the federal government is committed to negotiating an agreement ensuring that Quebec has the right to select a number of immigrants, including refugees, that will allow it to maintain its relative weight within Canada.

Procedures for selecting immigrants to Quebec will remain largely the same as they have been since 1978, except that Quebec will get an expanded role in the selection of immigrants who apply from within Canada.

Nothing will force immigrants to choose Quebec as their destination; it will be up to Quebec to attract them.

The agreement with Quebec will also let the province assume responsibility for services to immigrants that would otherwise be provided by the federal government, so the province can assist the integration of new immigrants into Quebec's distinct society.

National institutions

Partnership between the federal and provincial governments is the core of federalism.

In federalism, each order of government is responsible for certain matters – education in the case of the provinces and defence in the case of the federal government, for example – and they share the task of making the country work as a whole.

The *Constitution Amendment, 1987* will strengthen the federal nature of two key institutions – the Supreme Court of Canada and the Senate – by giving provincial governments a say alongside the federal government in choosing members.

The Supreme Court – One of the central roles of the Supreme Court of Canada is to settle disputes about the meaning of the Constitution, including disputes between the federal and provincial governments.

Yet, until now, all appointments to this Court have been made by the federal government alone.

Clause 6 of the *Constitution Amendment, 1987* will enhance the federal character of the Supreme Court as the referee of constitutional disputes by giving the provinces a voice in the selection of judges.

The appointment will be made by, and will have to be acceptable to, the federal government as the voice of all Canadians, but it will have to choose from names submitted by the provinces.

Ever since the Supreme Court was created, a third of the judges have come from Quebec, to ensure that the Court can deal with cases based on Quebec's system of civil law, as well as those based on the common law system of the rest of the country.

This will continue, and Quebec can submit names when any of the three 'civil law' judges is appointed, while the nine other provinces can submit names when the other six judges are appointed.

The Senate – At the time of Confederation, the Senate was intended to provide a forum for regional voices in the national Parliament, and each province has a constitutional right to be represented in the Senate.

Clause 2 of the *Constitution Amendment, 1987* takes this principle a step further.

A new Senator will have to be acceptable to both the federal government and the government of the province the Senator represents.

Appointments to the Senate will continue to be made by the federal government, but provinces will have a say in who is appointed.

Thus Canada ceases to be the only major federation in the Western world where members of the second chamber are chosen solely by the central government.

As evidence of its commitment to address fundamental Senate reform, the federal government has agreed to start applying this rule immediately.

Further reform of the Senate is one of the items on the agenda for future constitutional talks.

The amending formula

One of the most important parts of any constitution is the formula for amending it; usually the more fundamental the provision concerned, the higher the degree of agreement needed to make changes.

Under Canada's Constitution, the general rule is that amendments require the consent of Parliament and the legislatures of two-thirds of the provinces accounting for half the population. This will not change with the current amendments.

But the consent of Parliament and all legislatures is required for some of the most important amendments – the composition of the Supreme Court, for example, and the amending formula itself.

Unanimity protects the vital interests of all provinces when amendments to key national institutions are planned.

Clause 9 of the *Constitution Amendment, 1987* will give *all* provinces a say over additional areas of fundamental importance.

Unanimous agreement has been achieved repeatedly in Canadian history – on the establishment of unemployment insurance and old age pensions, for example, and on the *Constitution Amendment, 1987* itself. So unanimity need not be a straitjacket.

Compensation – Clause 9 also provides that when a provincial power is transferred to Parliament, a province that is not affected will get reasonable compensation to ensure that its residents are not taxed for services they do not receive.

The future of constitutional reform

The intent of the current round of constitutional reform was to address a limited number of issues designed to convince Quebec to rejoin the Canadian constitutional family and, thereby, to unblock the process of further constitutional change.

Now, many other issues can be addressed in the coming years, as Canadians chart the path into the future.

Although there have been several proposals for further Senate reform over the years, for example, agreement has been elusive.

The federal and provincial governments, together with representatives of territorial governments and the Indian, Inuit and Métis peoples, also still face the challenge of providing a more precise constitutional definition of aboriginal rights.

Canada still has unfinished business on the constitutional agenda and, as a modern and growing society, it will confront new problems in the years ahead.

Instead of ignoring unresolved constitutional issues, the *Constitution Amendment, 1987* will establish a forum for dealing with them.

Clause 13 provides for a conference at least once a year, starting in 1988, where First Ministers can tackle other constitutional issues. As with the current amendments, the outcome of such conferences would be debated fully in Parliament and the provincial legislatures.

Public participation

Canadians have a chance to take part in the constitution-making process.

Joint Senate-House of Commons hearings will explore the implications of the *Constitution Amendment, 1987* so it is well understood by everyone.

Perhaps more important, evidence before the hearings by experts and interested members of the public and the report of the Joint Committee will help set the agenda for First Ministers when they start their series of regular constitutional conferences under the *Amendment*.

A stronger partnership

Canada is a land where respecting each other's differences has made it possible to work together in building a strong nation.

This is the spirit of the *Constitution Amendment, 1987.*

It gives both federal and provincial governments a say in key national institutions, the federal spending power, immigration and certain constitutional amendments.

It puts in place machinery for federal-provincial cooperation in pursuing constitutional reform and in meeting the economic needs of Canadians.

It adds the dimension of linguistic duality and Quebec's distinct society to the constitutional recognition of other community values like multiculturalism and aboriginal rights.

In doing these things, it cements Canadian unity.

* * *

Constitution Amendment, 1987

Following is the text of the Constitutional Accord approved by the Prime Minister and all provincial Premiers on June 3, 1987, which provided the basis for submitting a resolution to Parliament and the provincial legislatures, seeking approval of the *Constitution Amendment, 1987.**

1987 CONSTITUTIONAL ACCORD

WHEREAS first ministers, assembled in Ottawa, have arrived at a unanimous accord on constitutional amendments that would bring about the full and active participation of Quebec in Canada's constitutional evolution, would recognize the principle of equality of all the provinces, would provide new arrangements to foster greater harmony and co-operation between the Government of Canada and the governments of the provinces and would require that annual first ministers' conferences on the state of the Canadian economy and such other matters as may be appropriate be convened and that annual constitutional conferences composed of first ministers be convened commencing not later than December 31, 1988;

AND WHEREAS first ministers have also reached unanimous agreement on certain additional commitments in relation to some of those amendments;

NOW THEREFORE the Prime Minister of Canada and the first ministers of the provinces commit themselves and the governments they represent to the following:

1. The Prime Minister of Canada will lay or cause to be laid before the Senate and House of Commons, and the first ministers of the provinces will lay or cause to be laid before their legislative assemblies, as soon as possible, a resolution, in the form appended hereto, to authorize a proclamation to be issued by the Governor General under the Great Seal of Canada to amend the Constitution of Canada.

2. The Government of Canada will, as soon as possible, conclude an agreement with the Government of Quebec that would

   (*a*) incorporate the principles of the Cullen-Couture agreement on the selection abroad and in Canada of independent immigrants, visitors for medical treatment, students and temporary workers, and on the selection

---

*While the general principles described in the introductory pages of this booklet are clear from a reading of the text, the proposed amendments include a number of technical provisions and there are frequent references to the *Constitution Acts 1867 to 1982*. For a detailed understanding, it is therefore necessary to consult the *Constitution Acts, 1867 to 1982*, which can be found in libraries or ordered (Catalogue No YX1-1/1986E) at a price of $4.25 each ($5.10 outside Canada) from the *Canadian Government Publishing Centre, Supply and Services Canada, Ottawa, Ontario, K1A 0S9*. Cheques and money orders are payable to the Receiver General for Canada.

of refugees abroad and economic criteria for family reunification and assisted relatives,

(*b*) guarantee that Quebec will receive a number of immigrants, including refugees, within the annual total established by the federal government for all of Canada proportionate to its share of the population of Canada, with the right to exceed that figure by five per cent for demographic reasons, and

(*c*) provide an undertaking by Canada to withdraw services (except citizenship services) for the reception and integration (including linguistic and cultural) of all foreign nationals wishing to settle in Quebec where services are to be provided by Quebec, with such withdrawal to be accompanied by reasonable compensation,

and the Government of Canada and the Government of Quebec will take the necessary steps to give the agreement the force of law under the proposed amendment relating to such agreements.

3. Nothing in this Accord should be construed as preventing the negotiation of similar agreements with other provinces relating to immigration and the temporary admission of aliens.

4. Until the proposed amendment relating to appointments to the Senate comes into force, any person summoned to fill a vacancy in the Senate shall be chosen from among persons whose names have been submitted by the government of the province to which the vacancy relates and must be acceptable to the Queen's Privy Council for Canada.

3 STALEMATE IN CYPRUS: NEGOTIATIONS BETWEEN THE GREEK AND TURKISH CYPRIOT LEADERSHIP

Reed Coughlan

This chapter seeks to provide an explanation for the political stalemate in the intercommunal negotiations in Cyprus in the period 1989 to the present – 1992. The explicit intent of the research on which it is based was to discover why the process had broken down and attempt to provide a set of tentative answers through an analysis of the interests and negotiating positions of the two sides in the conflict. A necessarily truncated review of the historical background prefaces a discussion of the perspectives held by the leaders of the two communities, with whom interviews were conducted in the late spring of 1991. The author interviewed both Rauf Denktash, a leader in the Turkish community since 1955, when the troubles originated, and currently President of the Turkish Republic of Northern Cyprus, and the Greek Cypriot President, George Vasiliou who was elected to lead the Republic of Cyprus in 1988. The latter had come to office with little political experience, having established himself as a successful businessman. He did have, however, the unofficial support of the Communist party, AKEL. Two other interviews were also completed: the first with Glavkos Clerides, who has been an active participant in the political arena for thirty years. He served as acting President of the Republic for a brief period in 1974, has been the leader of one of the major political parties and negotiator for the Greek Cypriot community at the UN-sponsored intercommunal talks for a number of years. He opposed Vasiliou in the most recent presidential race, losing by a narrow margin in run off elections. Finally, Oscar Camillion, special envoy of the UN Secretary General shared his views regarding the status of negotiations and the prospects for settlement.[1]

The viewpoints expressed in these interviews are taken to reflect the contrasting interests of the two communities. It should not be assumed however, that there are no differences of opinion within each of the communities. The diversity of perspective among both Greek and Turkish Cypriots is quite substantial. None the less, for heuristic purposes, we will treat the perspectives articulated in these interviews as if they fairly represent the constituencies from which they have been drawn.

Cyprus has a population of 690,000; approximately 18 per cent is Turkish and 78 per cent is Greek. Since 1974, when Turkey invaded Cyprus, the island has been partitioned along an east–west line. The Northern territory, approximately 37 per cent of the island, is controlled by the Turkish Cypriots, and is occupied by 35,000 troops from mainland Turkey. It is separated from the Greek Cypriot Republic in the South by a buffer zone manned by a UN peace-keeping force. Movement across the 'green line' by Greek and Turkish Cypriots is prohibited.

The Greek Cypriots want the Turkish army to leave and they want the island reunified. They insist that the refugees who were displaced as a result of the Turkish invasion of 1974 be allowed to return to their ancestral homes and they want the settlers who have come to the North in the last 17 years to return to Turkey. They look forward to the time when Cypriots can own property, and travel and settle anywhere on the island, regardless of ethnic origin. The Greek Cypriots claim that their's is the legitimate and sovereign government of Cyprus and they refuse to acknowledge the existence of any other government in Cyprus.

The Turkish Cypriots, for their part, assert their own right to self determination, have set up their own republic in the North, and seek international recognition of their sovereignty and independence. They cherish the protection afforded by the presence of the Turkish army, and they are determined to maintain two separate territorial zones in the event of a federal reunification. They want to be treated as equals at the bargaining table and in any political arrangements with the Greek Cypriots.

Since 1974 the Greek Cypriots have enjoyed considerable success in securing support from the UN and other international fora. They have focused world attention on the invasion by Turkey in 1974 and the continuing presence of an occupying army in the North. In their view this is a matter of foreign intervention. The Turkish Cypriots, on the other hand, are inclined to a longer view of history which draws attention to the relations and interaction between Turks and Greeks within Cyprus. They claim that their constitutional rights were abrogated in 1963 and their participation in the Federal government was prevented by the constitutional amendments proposed by the Greek Cypriots. The failed attempt by the majority to impose union of Cyprus with Greece helps to explain why the invasion occurred and why the presence of Turkish troops is necessary to protect the rights of the minority.

Following a brief account of the background to the struggle, we will review efforts to bring about a settlement. We will then discuss these competing interpretations of history and assess the different views on the contemporary situation.[2]

While the bi-communal nature of the population has a fairly long history, the territorial bizonality of the island is a more recent development. The Greeks first settled on the island during the second millennium BC. The Turkish population was introduced during the period of Ottoman rule between 1571 and 1878. The island was ceded to Britain in 1878, was annexed by the British at the beginning of World War I and was given crown colony status in 1925. By mid-century anti-colonial nationalism began to take hold in Cyprus under the auspices of the guerilla movement EOKA, which combined its determination to oust the British with an aspiration to bring about union with Greece. Such a union, 'Enosis', as it is known, was not a new idea; it had first surfaced following the Greek war of independence in the 1820s. In 1955 the violent campaign to oust the British and unite Cyprus with Greece galvanized the Greek Cypriots and simultaneously antagonized the Turkish Cypriot minority on the island. The Turkish Cypriots quickly established the Turkish Resistance organization and formulated an oppositional ideology that espoused the notion of Taksim, or partition, with a view to the alignment of each of the ethnically distinct territories with their respective motherlands. The competing ideologies of Enosis and Taksim polarized the two communities within Cyprus between 1955 and 1959 and brought the island to the brink of civil war.

Prior to the outbreak of violence in 1955, relations between the two ethnic groups were relatively calm. Greeks and Turks lived together in mixed villages throughout Cyprus. However, in the decade following the start of the campaign to oust the British and unite the Island with Greece, the Turkish Cypriots increasingly withdrew into the safety of their own territorial enclaves.

Trilateral talks between Britain, Greece and Turkey were convened in order to find a solution that would accommodate these competing aspirations. Tentative agreements were hammered out in Zurich and were finalized in London in 1959. While representatives of the two Cypriot communities signed the relevant documents they did not participate in the negotiations and had no say in the political arrangements imposed on the island in 1960 when Cyprus was granted independence. The London-Zurich agreements established the essential elements of the constitution and laid out what became known as the Treaty of Guarantee, the Treaty of Establishment and the Treaty of Alliance. The Treaty of Guarantee was designed to ensure the territorial integrity and independence of the new republic by assigning the three guarantor powers – Britain, Turkey and Greece – the right to intervene in the event that the arrangements secured by these agreements were breached. The explicit intent was to prevent the partition of the island or the unification of Cyprus with either Turkey or Greece. The Treaty of Establishment allowed the British to retain ownership of two large military bases. The Treaty of Alliance specified that Greece would be permitted to station a military contingent of 950 men and Turkey 650 men on the island. The three powers further pledged to co-operate in their common defence. The constitutional arrangements provided for proportional representation from the two communities in all spheres of government. Seats in the legislature and cabinet posts were to be distributed in a ratio of seven to three, among Greeks and Turks respectively.

The uneasy truce established in 1959 broke down in December 1963 when the President, Archbishop Makarios, proposed changes in the constitution which the Turkish Cypriots deemed unacceptable. There had been numerous difficulties encountered in the implementation of the 1960 agreements. Disagreements between the two communities centered on constitutional issues and on the proportional allocation of civil service jobs. Turkish Cypriots comprised 18 per cent of the population but had been guaranteed 30 per cent of the security and civil service jobs. The strength of the safeguards written into the agreements and the relatively favorable terms that accrued to the Turkish Cypriots reflected the unequal distribution of power between Greece and Turkey at the bargaining table in Zurich and London. The proximity and military superiority of Turkey, combined with its importance to NATO and western security provided leverage in the negotiations that Greece was unable to match.[3] While the Turkish Cypriots argued that the disproportionate allocation of public sector jobs would redress imbalances evident during the period of British rule, Greek Cypriots resented the concessions that had been made and refused to comply.

Intercommunal fighting broke out in December, 1963. Peace was restored in March 1964 when the United Nations introduced a peace-keeping force to quell the violence. The effective exclusion of the Turkish Cypriots from political power led to the establishment of separate judicial, administrative and legislative structures within the Turkish enclaves scattered across Cyprus.

The period 1964–1971 witnessed a number of unsuccessful efforts to bring about a reconciliation. In 1971 EOKA was resurrected to force a union of Cyprus with Greece; a terrorist campaign was directed at the regime of President Makarios and received military and financial assistance from Greece over the next three years. On 15 July 1974 the EOKA, supported by the military Junta in Athens staged a *coup d'etat* which succeeded in overthrowing Makarios. Having escaped the violence, Makarios went to New York where he described the coup to the UN security council as an invasion. The Turkish Community, through its leader Rauf Denktash, sent up a cry for help from Turkey to stop Greece from taking over the island. In the event, Turkey invaded Cyprus from the North, quickly taking control of the northern third of the Island, and thereby creating a safe haven for the embattled Turkish Cypriots. The Greek military regime which had supported the coup in Cyprus collapsed on 23 July. Glavkos Clerides served as President until Makarios' return in December. By now the Turkish army had wrested control of the northern third of the country and the Turkish Cypriots proceeded to construct their own administrative organizations. Over the course of the next year arrangements were worked out whereby approximately 160,000 Greek Cypriots moved to the South and 45,000 Turkish Cypriots joined their compatriots in the North. Roughly one third of the population of each of the two communities was displaced.

In 1975 Rauf Denktash was declared President of the Turkish Federated State of Cyprus. Sporadic and basically unsuccessful intercommunal talks were held under UN sponsorship between 1974 and 1976. Then, in January 1977, Denktash and Archbishop Makarios reached an historic compromise agreement in which the basic parameters of a settlement were laid out.[4]

While this outline Agreement serves as a contemporary point of reference, it was never ratified. Talks seemed to flounder over the degree to which the new central government would assume a Federal or a confederal form. The death of Archbishop Makarios in August of that year temporarily put a halt to further initiatives.

Progress was uneven over the next two years. In 1979, however, a new set of agreements was worked out. The essential aspects of the second round of so called 'high level' talks, this time between President Kyprianou and Denktash serve as a second point of reference for current discussions about the possibilities for a settlement.[5]

In the course of these talks the notion of a bizonal state was introduced. Various proposals also specified adjustments to the boundary demarcations by which portions of the Turkish held territory would be ceded to the Greek Cypriot side. In the late 1970s and early 1980s such territorial proposals were put forward by the two sides though no agreement was ever achieved. The intercommunal talks stalled for another year, then in August 1980 the UN Secretary General outlined the areas of agreement that had been reached to date:

(a) Both parties have reaffirmed the validity of the high level agreements of 12 February 1977 and 19 May 1979;
(b) Both parties have reaffirmed their support for a federal solution of the constitutional aspect and a bizonal solution of the territorial aspect of the Cyprus problem;
(c) Both parties have indicated that the matter of security can be raised and discussed in the intercommunal talks. It is understood that this matter will be discussed, having regard to certain practical difficulties which may arise for the Turkish Cypriot community, as well as to the security of Cyprus as a whole;
(d) Both parties have appealed to the Secretary General for the continuation of the intercommunal talks.[6]

At various points in the negotiation process the Greek Cypriots have attempted to internationalize the Cyprus problem in an effort to mobilize support for their goals in the global arena. The Turkish Cypriots resent these initiatives because, from their viewpoint, the Greek Cypriots thereby consolidate the impression that theirs is the legitimate government of Cyprus struggling to deal with a secessionist minority. This is a fairly accurate assessment of the outcome of these efforts. The UN has consistently sided against the Turkish position. It is perhaps ironic that these efforts by the Greek Cypriots to bring about reunification of the island through international diplomatic pressure has had quite the opposite effect. Every time a new initiative is launched in the UN or other international fora, the Turkish Cypriots have responded with moves that effectively consolidate partition and the *de facto* reality of two separate states on the island. In May 1983, for example, when the UN General Assembly passed resolution 37/253 reiterating its call for the withdrawal of foreign troops, and deploring the importation of settlers in the North, Denktash threatened to boycott the intercommunal talks. Several months later the Turkish Cypriots made a Unilateral Declaration of Independence through the creation of the Turkish Republic of Northern Cyprus (TRNC). Predictably, the UN Security Council responded with a resolution which deplored the Declaration of Independence and dubbed it illegal and invalid. Further, it called upon all states not to recognize it. Other international bodies such as the Commonwealth Heads of Government Conference and The Council of Europe concurred with the UN judgment.[7]

Having defied international pressure, the TRNC continued to present themselves at the negotiating table but did so now with the insistence that any new settlement talks be aimed at a bizonal federation based on the partnership of two politically equal communities. A new round of UN sponsored discussions, known as the Proximity Talks, was begun in September 1984. Over the next several months Kyprianou, President of the republic in the South and Denktash, President of the TRNC, communicated through Secretary General De Cuellar who served as intermediary. This arrangement by which the Secretary General played a sort of shuttle diplomacy made some form of communication possible in spite of Kyprianou's refusal to negotiate unless the Declaration of Independence was withdrawn. The optimism engendered by the proximity talks subsequently led to direct 'high level' talks conducted in New York in January 1985. Despite the impression that differences between the two sides had dissipated, no agreement was ultimately reached. The failure of the summit was met with disappointment on both sides. The Draft Agreement presented by the Secretary General had stipulated a recommitment to the high level agreements of 1977 and 1979, the establishment of a bi-communal federal constitution and a bizonal territorial arrangement. The legislature was to be composed of a lower chamber with a 70–30 composition and an upper chamber with a 50–50 representation. The President and Vice President were to symbolize the equality of the two communities and the unity of the country. The issues surrounding the three freedoms, that is, the freedom of movement for all Cypriots, the freedom of settlement and the right to own property anywhere on the island, were to be addressed by a special working group. Territorial adjustments were to be specified, as would a timetable for the withdrawal of non-Cypriot troops and the provision of security guarantees for the two communities.

The impasse that led to the breakdown of the summit arose over the degree to which the details of the agreement were to be determined before the signatories put pen to paper. While Denktash wanted to conclude the agreement as it stood, Kyprianou felt the need for closure on particulars before he would sign the document. The following year a new draft agreement was forwarded by De Cuellar with no more movement or success. The most recent round of initiatives (1988–89) was launched on the heels of a meeting between the Greek Prime Minister, Papandreou, and the Turkish President, Ozal, at Davos, Switzerland. This effort at rapprochement between the two motherlands combined with the optimism arising from the electoral success of Vasiliou in the Greek Cypriot Presidential race led to an atmosphere of high expectation. In interviews with the journal *World Marxist Review* in 1988 both leaders expressed cautious optimism and referred to the positive environment created by the Davos initiative, the improved international relations associated with the easing of cold war tensions, and the commitment of their respective communities to seek a negotiated settlement.[8] Denktash and Vasiliou met in Geneva and then New York. Their efforts quickly foundered, however. Following the meeting in New York between the two leaders, the Greek Cypriots claimed that Denktash had dug in his heels over the right to self determination for the Turkish Cypriots. Denktash, for his part, claimed that Vasiliou broke off the talks and now refuses to speak with him about the Cyprus problem at all.

There were three points of disagreement. The first had to do with Denktash's objection to the Secretary General taking an active role in preparing a draft agreement. The UN Security Council overruled Denktash on this point. The second issue, which Vasiliou apparently refused to concede, was Denktash's insistence on the right of the Turkish Cypriots to self-determination. The third question hinged on whether the talks could proceed before the second point was resolved. Denktash suggested that they could, Vasiliou that they could not. Yet Vasiliou claimed that Denktash had put forward the issue of self-determination as a prerequisite to a consideration of the draft agreement.

The motivation to achieve a negotiated settlement provides another focus for discussion and debate. Both sides claim to want to proceed in good faith, and each side attributes to the other intransigence and a lack of interest in bringing about a change in the present situation. President Vasiliou, for example, maintained that:

> The main constraint in solving the Cyprus problem has nothing to do with ethnic conflict, but it is simply the desire of Denktash and some people around him and of President Ozal of Turkey to maintain the *status quo*.... When I met with Denktash in New York I went there with the intention of negotiating a settlement. You know what Denktash has said, 'let us consider,' he said, 'that a non solution is another option. That an option is a non-solution', by which he means continued partition of the island.

Clerides made a similar point when he said that:

> I believe that Denktash has lost interest in a solution to the Cyprus problem.

If he had to chose between being vice President of a slightly larger state, or the President of a smaller state, he would opt to be President of a smaller state, and I think that Denktash is much more concerned in perpetuating the situation in the hope of being recognized than in the hope that a solution will be found.

Denktash is also skeptical of the other side's goodwill. He attributes the lack of interest among the Greek Cypriots to the success with which they have convinced the world community that the Republic in the South constitutes the legitimate government of Cyprus. Denktash said:

We have every interest in reunification. It would benefit us economically and politically. But the Greek Cypriots look at it from the point of view of the Republic of Cyprus, and they say, since we are the Republic of Cyprus and its legitimate government *vis a vis* the world, what need have we got to take back a partner that we threw out in order to become the Government of Cyprus?

The assessment of the prospects for a settlement and the concrete steps that will be required to reopen the talks differ markedly. The Greek Cypriot view that Denktash has lost interest seems to have a counterpart in Denktash's claim that Vasiliou will not even talk with him. When asked what will be necessary to resume discussions, Vasiliou ignored Denktash, and focused on Ozal, the President of Turkey. This is consistent with the Greek Cypriot strategy of 'internationalizing' the problem, and conveying to the global community their definition of the situation: Turkey invaded Cyprus in 1974; since that time, it has garrisoned a 35,000 man army of occupation on the northern third of the island. The Greek Cypriots argue from this premise that the UN must enforce its resolutions and make Turkey withdraw both its army and the settlers that were brought over from the mainland. As Vasiliou put it:

It is all a question of President Ozal deciding that the solution is to his country's benefit. Unfortunately, judging by some of his latest remarks, I am not very encouraged.

President Vasiliou believes that progress must begin with the withdrawal of Turkish troops and he thinks that decision must be made by President Ozal of Turkey. He exhibits little interest in negotiating with Denktash both for this reason and because he refuses to acknowledge Denktash's claims for self-determination. Denktash for his part has no more regard for the legitimacy of the government in the south. He argues that the Turkish troops came in 1974 not as an invading force to occupy Cyprus but as an army of liberation whose presence guarantees the continued security of the Turkish Cypriots. Denktash explained that the Turkish Cypriots are determined to preserve the rights they had been guaranteed in the Zurich Agreements, and that the Greek Cypriots are equally determined to hold on to their claim to represent the Government of Cyprus. Denktash expressed frustration and anger at what he regards as the injustice of world opinion:

> People think that we are opposing the legitimate government of Cyprus. They don't realize that our fight is against a Greek Cypriot Republic which is trying to impose itself in place of the government of Cyprus which was bi-communal. They don't realize that this is what the fight is about. For 28 years august bodies have been deciding that in Cyprus the Greek Cypriots are our government. If Greek Cypriots are our government, then we are what the government says we are: a rebellious nuisance of a minority helping an enemy to divide Cyprus and keeping Cyprus occupied. How can we be treated like this?

Denktash's perspective is that the problem is a domestic one, internal to the island of Cyprus. It arose as a consequence of the attempt by the majority to impose a political arrangement on the minority which was unacceptable. The minority–majority relationship was a quintessential case of ethnic conflict. Referring to the Turkish Cypriot insistence on a bizonal territorial solution, Denktash says:

> Bizonality arose because of our need for security. Integrated we could not live. They made it impossible. So our people moved to the north, theirs moved south, and we agreed on this bizonality. When we agreed on bizonality the idea of security was ensured. Security is one of the underlining factors of any settlement.

In contrast, Vasiliou's definition of the situation not only focuses on the inernational arena and emphasizes the external dimensions, but also goes so far as to deny that the problem should be seen as a case of ethnic conflict:

> I don't believe that the term ethnic conflict is a proper way of describing the situation in Cyprus. There has been even very little overall conflict in history, especially among ordinary Greek Cypriots and Turkish Cypriots, who have coexisted peacefully on this island for four centuries. What we had was organized conflict, very artificial in its essence, and this hardly coincides with a sociologist's definition of ethnic conflict. What I want to say by this is that whatever conflict there has been in Cyprus, it has not essentially mobilized the emotions and the being of ordinary Cypriots who have mostly been the

innocent victims and quite often the mere spectators of a situation involving their own existence. If you have had the opportunity to witness meetings between Greek and Turkish Cypriots, you would easily understand what I mean. Unfortunately very few such meetings were and are permitted by the Turkish Cypriot leadership.

Clerides expressed a similar view in as much as he argued that Greek and Turkish Cypriots had little trouble living side by side, though he readily admits that the mutually exclusive ethno-nationalist aspirations of the two communities lie at the heart of the problem.

The Greek Cypriots deny that there is a problem in their interaction with Turkish Cypriots and they tend to recount the history of the troubles with reference to the invasion of 1974. Vasiliou refers to the lack of conflict in daily interaction; Clerides talks about the friendliness of the exchanges between attorneys in an office setting. There is no question that Greeks and Turks can live 'side by side' as they put it.

Denktash, however, is vehement in his assertion that this is not the case, and his temporal perspective is substantially deeper. He began his account of the Cyprus problem with stories his grandfather used to tell him about the persecution of Turkish Cypriots by Greek Cypriots. He talked about how his grandfather had to spend the night hiding in the lemon groves to escape the violence of Greek Cypriots. Denktash also recounted the fate of the well to do Turkish Cypriots who were imprisoned for the duration of World War I, their positions and wealth ruined as a consequence. For Turkish Cypriots village life held no sweet memories of harmonious communal relations; rather, the recollections of inter-ethnic conflict has led them to conclude that partition and separate territorial jurisdiction are crucial to any solution of the Cyprus problem.

Oscar Camillion serves as the special envoy of the UN Secretary General in Cyprus. His assessment of the obstacles to a settlement hinge on the historically accumulated mistrust that characterizes the relationship between the two communities. We have seen this in the attribution of motives elaborated by the leadership on both sides. It is also symptomatic of the intransigence of double minorities.[9] Denktash put it this way:

> At the center of the conflict here is the fear of one community which is smaller in size, but bigger and stronger in the area, trying to protect its identity and its political equality.

Within Cyprus the Turkish community is in the minority and, prior to

1974, the Greeks felt they had the upper hand. Within the larger Mediterranean region, the opposite is the case. The boldness of the Turkish Cypriot community derives not only from their perception of the strength of their position given the proximity and military superiority of Turkey in the region, but also from the historical memory of group superiority that lingers from the three centuries of Ottoman rule.[10]

Mistrust and the history of failed negotiations weigh against a settlement. On the other hand, the present international conjuncture suggests the possibility that new initiatives may enjoy some prospects for success. The outcome of the Gulf War points to the potential and strength of the UN in settling and/or mediating trouble spots in the global arena.

The Gulf War has been used as an analogy in several ways. Some have argued that the Turkish intervention in 1974 was similar to the American led counter-offensive against Iraq. The Greek Junta had supported the overthrow of a sovereign government. Turkey exercised its prerogative enshrined in the Treaty of Guarantee, and prevented the takeover of Cyprus by Greece. This scenario suggests that once the *coup d'etat* had been foiled and Makarios reinstated, Turkey should have withdrawn. The second analogy suggests a parallel between Iraq's invasion and occupation of Kuwait and Turkey's invasion and occupation of Northern Cyprus. This would lead one to conclude that the weight of world opinion and appropriate pressure from the US and others should be brought to bear to force Turkey to comply with the various UN resolutions calling for the withdrawal of foreign troops from Cyprus. Political realism seems to prevail among the Greek Cypriot leadership on this issue, however. While the Gulf War has helped to highlight the efficacy of the strategy of internationalization, as Clerides put it, it is unreasonable to think that the US could or would pressure Turkey into acquiescence, especially in light of the support Turkey provided during the Gulf War. He pointed out however, that if a settlement in the Middle East could be negotiated, it would likely undermine the geostrategic strength enjoyed by Turkey and thereby create an opening for the solution of the Cyprus conflict.

Denktash offers a different interpretation of the lessons of the Gulf War. He maintains that if the UN looked at the facts of the case,

> then they should say this to the Greek Cypriots: Saddam destroyed the sovereignty of a neighbor. He was pushed back. You did something worse. You destroyed the shared sovereignty of your partners, and then you

disowned your own signature, you destroyed the partnership, and you pretend to be the government of the whole island when you were not able to control these people and to impose your political will on them. When they declared their independence we did not recognize them. Now we see it was wrong. We should have recognized them so as to give you motivation for finding a solution on the basis of partnership again. This is how we see the Cyprus problem, and, therefore, when looked at coolly and objectively, the Gulf is an example in our favor.

Denktash does not recognize the Greek Cypriot government. It does not represent the Turkish Cypriots, according to Denktash, and has not done so since December 1963 when the late Archbishop Makarios attempted to curtail the Turks' constitutional rights; the Turkish Cypriots consequently refused to participate in the central government. Denktash points to the constitution of the Republic which stipulates that the Presidency is constituted by the bi-communal offices of President and Vice-President, the first occupied by a Greek Cypriot the second by a Turkish Cypriot. Vacancy in one of the offices, he claims, abrogates the authority of the other, and thereby undermines the legitimacy of the Presidency writ large. The Turkish Cypriots demand recognition as political equals and they require an arrangement by which the Presidency is rotated between the two communities. They want guarantees that they will not be relegated to a minority status and the best way to do this is to ensure that the two communities remain territorially separate, and for Turkey to be written into any agreement as a guarantor nation.

The issue of legitimacy and official recognition is one of the major stumbling blocks to negotiations past and present. The Greek Cypriots refuse to acknowledge the Turkish Cypriot administration in the north. They are determined to avoid even the appearance of recognition and therefore shun any official governmental interaction. Further, President Vasiliou takes the position that talks need to be undertaken with President Ozal of Turkey, both because Denktash has no official standing and because, in Vasiliou's view, the main source of the problem is the presence of Turkish troops on Cypriot soil. In those instances when Vasiliou and Denktash have met, the negotiations were mediated by the UN and Vasiliou was careful to make it clear that he spoke with Denktash only in his capacity as the leader of the Turkish Cypriot community. Denktash, for his part, insists upon formal recognition and goes further in his claim to political equality for the Turkish Cypriots in the negotiation arena and in any subsequent administrative arrangements on the island.

The two sides appear to have mutually exclusive aspirations, yet there have been several moments in the negotiation process when agreement was reached, concessions were made and a settlement was very nearly consummated (for example, in 1960, 1977, 1979 and 1985). It seems unreasonable to expect that the Greeks and Turks on Cyprus will live peaceably 'side by side' as they say. A loose confederation is, however, possible; it will take the form of a bi-communal constitution, bizonal in its territorial aspect and shorn up by guarantees that satisfy the perceived security needs of both communities.

Conclusion: prospects for change

The global environment of the 1990s may well presage real change in Cyprus. The rapprochement between East and West, the disintegration of the Warsaw Pact which had been so significant in shaping the alliances in the Middle East and in the entire Mediterranean, suggest that what might have been unthinkable five years ago may be thought of as commonplace tomorrow. Furthermore, as Camillion points out, the structural conditions of group conflict within Cyprus have been inalterably transformed. Changes brought about in Cypriot society as a consequence of the shift from a rural agricultural economy to an urban service economy have eliminated the conditions under which communal strife had been spawned. Villages have become cities and the parochialism of rural life has been supplanted by the cosmopolitanism of a modern economy dominated by tourism, insurance, banking and multinational commerce.

None the less, in a divided society such as Cyprus, change will be possible only if it is desired. The political leadership on both sides must want change, and they must believe that their counterparts on the other side of the Green Line are interested in helping to bring it about. The themes of mistrust and suspicion that run through the conversations reported in this chapter point to the difficulties faced by this divided society. The second problem highlighted by these interviews has to do with the definition of the problem and the proposed solutions that are consequent upon those definitions. Each side casts the problem as an exclusive matter; that is, the Greek Cypriots see it solely as a matter of foreign intervention, the Turkish Cypriots as a domestic/ethnic conflict. Any successful negotiation will need to address both dimensions of the problem, and it will be necessary for both sides to recognize the other's viewpoint.

These interviews were arranged in the anticipation that the political leadership on both sides might express a willingness to participate in a new dialogue and to move toward a resolution of this long-standing stalemate. The disintegration of the Warsaw Pact, the realignment of geopolitical realities, the presumed boost to the status and leverage of the United Nations as a consequence of the Gulf War might have been seen to have opened the door to change. The thrust of these interviews presents a much less optimistic forecast however. The views of history and of the origins and present nature of the conflict expressed by the leadership do not appear to have changed substantially. Their positions on various issues have hardened if they have changed at all. Denktash's persistent fears about the Greek Cypriot's aspirations for Enosis, Vasiliou's concerns over the lingering effects of the Ottoman influence and Clerides' reference to the Greek Cypriot fear of Turkish expansionism seem redolent of an earlier period in history.

Further, developments in the global arena tend to be interpreted by each side in such a fashion as to support their previously formulated world-view. The differing perspectives on the lessons drawn from the Gulf War, and from the upsurge of ethnic conflict in the Soviet bloc illustrate this selective perception.

Certainly the optimism that characterized the set of interviews published in *World Marxist Review* three years ago is no longer in evidence. At that time it appeared that relations between Greece and Turkey showed prospects for improvement and Vasiliou brought a new and presumably untainted perspective to the negotiating table. Since that time Mr Vasiliou has decided that discussions with Denktash are pointless and Denktash, in turn, has become discouraged by the unresponsiveness of the Greek Cypriot leader.

It may well be that the political constraints within which the Cypriot leadership operates suggest the wisdom of adopting a rather different and much less public set of strategies for reaching a settlement of the problem. Assuming that the will to change is there, and recognizing the difficulties inherent in that assumption, we might introduce the notion of 'Track Two Diplomacy'. It has been described by J.V. Montville as follows:

'Track Two Diplomacy' is unofficial, informal interaction between representatives of adversary groups or nations which aims to develop strategies and create an environment which could contribute to the resolution of their conflict. It must be understood that track two diplomacy is in no way a substitute for official, 'track one', government to government or leader to leader contact. Rather, track two activity is designed to assist official leaders by compensating for the constraints on them imposed by the psychologically understandable need for leaders to be, or at least be seen to be, strong, wary and indomitable in the face of the enemy.... Track two diplomacy, then, is conceived of as several levels of process designed to assist official leadership in the task of resolving, or in the first instance managing, conflicts by exploring possible solutions, out of public view, and without the requirement to formally negotiate or bargain for advantage. Track two diplomacy on its more focused level seeks political formulas or scenarios which might satisfy the basic security and esteem needs of all parties to a dispute. On its more general level, it seeks to promote an environment in a political community, through the education of public opinion, that would make it safer for public opinion to take risks for peace.[11]

The tenor and substance of these interviews provide an important barometer for assessing the mood and atmosphere for negotiation. It is equally true however, that the articulated viewpoints are developed in large part for public and political consumption. The mass media and the political culture in Nicosia, on both sides of the Green Line, as well as those in Athens and Ankara also intrude on the ideas expressed by political leaders in Cyprus.[12] To the extent that Vasiliou and Denktash feel the need to put forward the appearance of being 'indomitable in the face of the enemy' it may be that their public expressions are more inflexible than the more private postures that could be adopted through two track diplomacy. Again, such an initiative presumes a measure of goodwill which is not immediately evident. Reticence and intransigence, on the other hand, are perhaps the trademarks of conflicting parties in the Middle East and the Eastern Mediterranean. Such progress as has been made or anticipated in recent months and years has been facilitated by pressure from third parties. Clerides may have been correct in his assessment of the best prospects for a solution of the Cyprus problem. He argued that, once a settlement is imposed on the Middle East, the geostrategic strength of Turkey will shift and negotiation of the Cyprus issue will then be made possible.

Clearly, it would be preferable to settle this dispute without outside interference. However, the analysis presented here leads to the conclusion that the attitudes of the leaders on both sides of the Green Line are entrenched; developments outside of Cyprus that might have been expected to make progress possible or, indeed, likely, have little or no effect. The only plausible scenario out of which real change seems likely to occur involves the active intervention of third party actors. The role of the United States in bringing about agreement on the Middle East peace conference presents one such model. It seems likely that the Green Line and all that it represents will remain firmly in place until the world

turns its attention from the Middle East to a resolution of the difficulties
that beset Cyprus.

Notes

1. The author would like to express his appreciation for the courtesies
   extended to him by those who so graciously agreed to the interviews.
   Thanks are also due to Professors Otto Jones, Karen Pass, Ellen Rocco,
   Tom Rocco and Ken Abrams for their collegiality and to the Frederick
   Polytechnic Institute for their generous hospitality.
2. For a fuller discussion of the history of these negotiations, see Joseph
   Joseph (1990) The International Dimensions of the Cyprus problem,
   Cyprus Review 2 Autumn pp. 15–39; *The Cyprus Problem* (1989) Nicosia:
   Press and Information Office; Rauf Denktash (1982) *The Cyprus Triangle*
   Boston: Allen and Unwin; Ziam Necategil (1989) *The Cyprus Question and
   The Turkish Position in International Law*, Oxford: Oxford University Press.
3. Joseph Joseph (1985) *Cyprus: Ethnic Conflict and International Concern*,
   New York: Lang.
4. *The Cyprus Problem*, Nicosia: Press and Information Office, 1989.
5. Zaim Necategil (1989) *The Cyprus Question and The Turkish Position in
   International Law*, Oxford: Oxford University Press, p. 135.
6. *Ibid.* p. 135.
7. For a discussion of resolutions and measures drawn up by the EEC, see
   Charalambos Tsardanidis (1988) The European Community and the
   Cyprus problem since 1974 *Journal of Political and Military Sociology* 16,
   pp. 155–71; and by other regional security organizations, see Constantine
   Danopoulos (1988) Regional Security Organizations and National Interest:
   Analyzing the NATO – Greek Relationship, *Journal of Political and Military
   Sociology* 16, pp. 263–77.
8. Flashpoints (1988) *World Marxist Review* 31, pp. 39–43.
9. The notion of double minorities is discussed in Frederick Boal and Douglas
   Neville (eds) (1982) *Integration and Division: Geographical Perspectives on
   the Northern Ireland Problem*, London: Academic Press. The concept may
   be applied to Cyprus and suggests the parallels that may be drawn between
   Cyprus, Northern Ireland and Sri Lanka with regard to territorial and
   demographic relationships, and their common experiences of British
   colonialism. Some of these connections have been sketched out in Eamonn
   Breen (1990) *The Three Islands: International Agreements in Northern
   Ireland, Cyprus and Sri Lanka*, Belfast: Queens University Press, but see
   also, Dominick Coyle (1982) *Minorities in Revolt: Political Violence in
   Ireland, Italy and Cyprus*, Rutherford, NJ: Farleigh Dickenson University
   Press and Stephen Ryan (1990) *Ethnic Conflict and International Relations*,
   Aldershot: Dartmouth Publishing.
10. See Peter Worsley, Communalism and Nationalism in Small Countries: The
    case of Cyprus pp. 1–20 in Peter Worsley and Pascallis Kitromilides (eds)
    Small States in the Modern World. Worsley says, for example, that, while the
    Ottoman Empire contained and tolerated many different ethnic groups,

'All others, certainly, were inferior in status to Turks and Muslims, amongst whom the ruling class exercised a singularly ruthless repression to any challenge to its authority'. (p. 3) As Worsley suggests, the consolidation and institutionalization of religion and ethnic community under Ottoman rule may well account for the singular cohesion of ethnic identity in contemporary Cyprus.

11. J.V. Montville, quoted in Paul Arthur, *ibid*, p. 403.
12. Clearly the political culture is not intimidatory in the way that Belfast might be described, as in Paul Arthur (1990) Negotiating the Northern Ireland problem: One or two track diplomacy? *Government and Opposition* **25**, pp. 403-18. It is none the less, a deeply divided society in which the two ethnic communities are highly politicized, and to that extent, pronouncements by political leaders are closely scrutinized in the press and in politics.

4 NEGOTIATING IDENTITY: DISHONOURED AGREEMENTS IN THE SUDANESE CONFLICT

Francis Mading Deng

Introduction

During the discussions of a technical committee that was considering the application of regional autonomy throughout the Sudan – building on the experience of the South as a result of the 1972 Addis Ababa Agreement which granted the South regional self-government – President Jaafar Mohamed Nimeiri, speaking in 1979 with remarkable candor, made a startling but revealing confession. In response to fears that autonomy might lead to separatist tendencies and risk the eventual disintegration of the nation, he swore to tell the truth in front of God and said that when they had initially accepted the arrangement for the South, they had entertained similar fears and had planned the agreement only as a temporary means of persuading the rebels to surrender their arms. Their intention was to tear up the agreement within two or three years. To their surprise, regional autonomy had worked so well in the South that they now wanted to apply it to the whole country. Fears of separatism resulting from autonomy were therefore unjustified.

Nimeiri thus alluded to the principal problems with agreements that purport to end conflicts without addressing the root causes with sincerity. They tend to be clever ploys aimed more at undermining the cause of the adversary than they are genuine efforts to find lasting peace. Part of the problem is that causes of conflicts in such sharply divided countries as the Sudan deal with deeply felt issues of identity and their implications for participation in the shaping and sharing of power, wealth and other deference or material values. They are therefore very difficult to negotiate, far less to resolve.

The conflict of identities in the Sudan is often expressed in terms of the dichotomy between the Arab Islamic North and the African Christian and Animist South. But since the racial and cultural configuration of the country is a more complex fusion of the African and the Arab elements even within the North, these dichotomies do not adequately explain the diversities involved. Indeed, part of the problem is the crisis of national identity generated by the anomalies of racial and cultural make-up. But whether the division is racial or cultural, the critical question is what provides a common ground for a uniting national identity.

The identity issues which have torn the country apart have now been sharpened by the emerging Islamic agenda in the North and the counterforce of secularism by the Sudan People's Liberation Movement and Sudan People's Liberation Army (SPLM/SPLA) from the South. The issue of *sharia* or Islamic state should however be seen as symbolic of all the identity issues which have divided the country into the Arabs and Muslims on the one hand and Black Africans, Animists and more recently Christians on the other hand. This cleavage was more formalized into the North–South dichotomy under British rule.

Ever since 1974 when the British reversed their separatist policy toward these two parts of the country, the task of the leadership on both sides has been to negotiate a framework for mutual accommodation through various constitutional arrangements. But since the core issues involved tend to be difficult to resolve, the tendency has been either to evade them or to agree on arrangements that reflect partial resolutions or look good on paper but are intended to provide temporary relief from the conflict rather than to be honored in the long-term perspective.

With this as the pervading theme, this chapter will review the history of negotiations and agreements beginning with the Juba Conference of 1947, when the separatist policy was reversed. Following this we move to the Round Table Conference of 1965, when both sides agreed on an arrangement but implementation was blocked by a reversal of the conciliatory attitude of the central government; then to the Addis Ababa Agreement of 1972, which halted the war for ten years. To conclude, the more recent efforts to end the current war will also be considered.

The identity factor

In virtually all the agenda items that have been suggested for negotiations, or constitutional talks, the issue of national identity has figured prominently, though it has been approached in different ways. Sometimes, it is phrased as a problem of competing nationalities – or as a conflict of identity factors, such as race, culture, language or religion. The question often posed is whether the country is Arab, African, Afro-Arab of Arab-African. From a religious perspective, the critical question is whether the country is to be considered Islamic, governed by *sharia* law, or secular with constitutional guarantees for religious freedom and equality.

M.W. Daly has recently observed:

> The civil war . . . has as one of its principal causes fundamentally opposing views of what it means or should mean to be a Sudanese. These form bases for historical visions that are incompatible. . . . Resolution of the conflict may therefore involve a major change in the social and political structure of the Sudan, and may in turn influence national politics and nation-building elsewhere in the region.[1]

Southern reaction to the Northern identification of the country with Islam and 'Arabism' was to invoke an equal and even greater claim to the identity of the nation. This included endorsing secularism as the best means of ensuring religious freedom and equality – placing Christianity and traditional beliefs at par with Islam – and to advocating a foreign policy based on those domestic adjustments.

The evolution of North–South dichotomy

Sudan People's Liberation Movement and the 'Revolution for National Salvation' which seized power on 30 June 1989 are the culminations of contrasting historical processes in the North and the South. Arabization and Islamization in the North were brought about through stratifying and discriminating processes that favored the Arabs, their religion and their culture over the African race, religions and cultures. These assimilationist forces did not extend to the South which remained indigenously African in race, culture and religion until the advent of Christianity and Western influence.

Arab migration and settlement in the South was discouraged by natural barriers, climatic conditions and the hostilities of slavery. The Turko-Egyptian and Mahdist raids of the 19th century further aggravated the apprehension in the South, caused by waves of invasions from the North. With the British came peace, but the gulf between the South and the North was reinforced and extended into the modern context through the infamous separatist 'Southern Policy', reversed only nine years before independence.

Post-colonial governments aimed at unifying the country through a centralized system, supplemented with assimilationist policies. The South, on the other hand, wanted a federal system initially pursued through constitutional channels. When that was rejected and repressed, Southern demand escalated to a separatist armed rebellion. But increasingly, the Northern view of national identity as Arab and Islamic became challenged not only by scholars, but also by nationalist leaders from the South. This challenge has now been expanded and consolidated by the SPLM/SPLA under the leadership of Dr John Garang de Mabior.

Developments in both the North and the South have evolved through three parallel phases which could be characterized as traditional, transitional, and modern, even though they overlap or coexist. In the North, the tribal structures of indigenous Sudanese or Arab societies have been transcended, though not obliterated, by sectarian Islam and the broader concept of Arabism which, though objectively cultural, is subjectively perceived as also racial. As a result of this 'conservative' blend of tradition and sectarian Islam, several movements appeared as a modernizing reaction, among them the Communist Party, the wider 'Democratic Front', the Republican Brotherhood and the Muslim Brotherhood.

The Communist Party and their leftist sympathizers were destroyed by the Nimeiri regime after the 1971 abortive coup. The Republican Brotherhood was demoralized and rendered ineffective by the execution of their leader, Ustadh Mahmoud Mohamed Taha for apostasy in January 1985. The Muslim Brotherhood broadened its political net in the 1960s under the banner of the Islamic Charter Front and more recently reorganized politically into the National Islamic Front. The Front is now widely recognized as the brain trust behind the Revolution for National Salvation, the fundamentalist military regime which took over on 30 June 1989.

In the South, tribal structures have been transcended, though not obliterated, by the educated Christian, Westernized secular elite that has assumed political leadership in the modern context. The SPLM/SPLA represents the latest phase in the modernizing evolution of the symbols or models of identity in nationbuilding.

In both the North and the South, there are forces in the center with a range of conservative–liberal disposition, including professional associations, trade unions, farmers' associations, women's and youth organizations and student unions, who have periodically played key roles in instigating popular uprisings against military dictatorships, but have never offered a sustainable political agenda at the center.

Negotiating hidden agendas

Throughout the history of North-South relations, negotiations have centered on how to manage the politics of the dualistic identity of the country. The options within the unitary framework have ranged from a call for some form of recognition of the dualism to various forms of integration and assimilation. While the North has been in the driver's seat of integration and assimilation, more recently adjusted to accommodation of diversity in varying forms and degrees of decentralization, the South has shifted from a call for secession, which was unnegotiable to the North, to the postulation of a 'new Sudan' where the inequities of race, culture, language, religion or gender would be eliminated.

The stratifying equations of this power struggle have been pivotal in determining the critical margin beyond which the disadvantaged South explodes with violence or within which peaceful interaction, dialogue and reform have been possible. A significant factor in determining the critical margin has been the extent to which policies or actions of the central government have promoted or diminished a sense of belonging or identification with the country on more or less equitable footing with the North.

What these historical highlights indicate is that while there are moments when agreements promise a mutually acceptable framework and are accepted, there are also times when the agreements are dishonored, the North attempts to impose its Islamic Arab vision on the whole country and the South falls back on violent resistance. The challenge of breaking the cycle of promises and violations, and instead formulating and sustaining a viable framework for a just and lasting peace for the Sudan, becomes increasingly more difficult as the commitment gets more entrenched, extending into the demand for restructuring central power and related institutions.

As Donald Rothchild has recently observed, among the factors that are not easily amenable to negotiation are: 'a fear of restratification and the loss of political dominance; an assertion of group worth and place; the existence of negative remembrances and images; the determination to resist a controlling group's effort to spread its language, culture or religion; and evidences of a sense of superiority on the part of a politically or economically dominant minority'.[2] Accordingly, 'where ruling state elites and their constituents fear the consequences of a fundamental reordering of regime procedures, or where political minorities remain deeply anxious over their subordination or their cultural or physical survival, ethnic conflicts are likely to be intense and, in some cases, highly destructive of lives and property. Adopting an 'essentialist' perception regarding their ethnic adversaries ... allows little scope for negotiated, mutual gains and outcomes.'[3]

Several occasions in the history of North–South relations will illustrate the range of outcomes which have been envisaged in negotiating identity, and the manner in which positions have evolved toward even more difficult options. Among these are the Juba Conference of 1947, the Round Table Conference of 1965, and the Addis Ababa Accord of 1972.

Juba Conference

The first major forum in which Northerners and Southerners sat together to negotiate a common future was the Juba Conference of June 1947. The issue there was whether the South was prepared to join the process of political development in the North by sending representatives to the national Legislative Assembly about to be formed or would prefer first to have an Advisory Council of the kind that had preceded the establishment of the Assembly in the North. The British had already decided on unity and the only issue was to agree on transitional measures that would accelerate political and economic development in the South so that when independence came, Southerners would be able to hold their own in equal partnership with the Northerners.

The initial Southern reaction to the question of joining the national Legislative Assembly and in some cases even to the already decided issue of unity was to accept the principle, but allow time for learning the art and skill of government and for observing the attitude of the Northerners before making up their minds finally. However, on the second day of the conference a number of Southerners, mostly among the civil servants, reversed their position in favor of immediate participation in the national Assembly. Sorror Ramley, who was a participant in the 'very long struggle' to persuade the Southerners to change their minds later recalled that after receiving 'some sort of assurances or something like that [they were] very genuine for unity'. He confessed, however, that the task of winning the Southerners took 'a complete day's work'. One of the prominent spokesmen of the South, Clement Mboro, an administrator who later became a leading figure in the Southern movement, stated 'that since the conference of the day before he had fundamentally changed his mind and that the best way in which the Southerners could protect themselves would be to go to Khartoum now to legislate together with the Northerners ... in spite of their backwardness . . . Southerners must defend themselves and speak and think for themselves'.[4] James Tembura 'agreed emphatically with . . . Clement Mboro'.[5] When asked by the chairman why he had changed his mind, Tembura replied 'that Judge Shingeiti had said that if they did not do so they would have no say in the future government in the Sudan, and he had thought this over very carefully the previous night after considering what had been said during the day'.[6]

Many factors were of course involved in the perspectives of the Southerners and in particular the educated members. Among these could be cited the anti-colonial sentiment which they shared with the North, though in varying degrees, the promise of promotion to a level of equality with the North, both in positions and financial rewards, and paradoxically a sense of faith in the justice of the government which the British Administration had firmly established and which the Southerners thought would be sustained in an independent Sudan. But perhaps the critical factor was the inadequacy of Southern representation and comprehension of the real issues involved. It is clear that Southerners did not match their Northern counterparts and British superiors, whether by education, experience, sophistication or administrative status, and this unfair advantage explains why they were swayed to the joint Northern-British agenda. There could not have been a meeting of minds, as subsequent developments clearly demonstrated.

The Round Table Conference
The 1965 Round Table Conference on the Southern Problem convened by the Transitional Government of Sir El Khatim El Khalifa, which took power from the military rule of General Ibrahim Abboud, was the second occasion when representatives of the two regions met to discuss their mutual concerns. Again, the central issue was the negotiation of ways in which the diverse elements of national identity could be accommodated through unity in diversity.

Unlike the Juba conference, there was more symmetry in the representation of the two regions and the level of sophistication. After all, the Southern Problem and the military role of the Southern Sudanese Liberation Movement had been significant factors in the overthrow of the military government and Northerners were prepared to give the South its due. But what the South stood for, even in its widely varying range, proved to be unpalatable for the North. The South presented a long list of grievances due to Northern mistreatment and historic animosities with either federalism, self-determination or outright separation as the remedy.

The Northern parties suggested a measure of 'regional government' which the Southerners dismissed as equivalent to an 'unconditional unity', and made their own suggestions which were tantamount to a loose federation or confederation. Despite these disagreements, the conference adopted a resolution which stipulated measures for bettering the situation in the South and went on to say: 'The Conference considered some patterns of Government for the Sudan and could not reach a unanimous resolution as required by the rules of the Conference. We have, therefore, appointed a twelve-man committee to dwell on the issue of the constitutional and administrative set-up which will protect the special interest of the South, as well as the general interest of the Sudan'.[7]

The twelve-man committee deliberated and eventually reached agreement on a number of issues, among them the transfer of some central powers to the regions, the preservation and development of Southern languages, the establishment of a legislative body in the regions, the adoption of a parliamentary system of government, the establishment of a national development committee with branches in the regions, and the selection of a technical committee to recommend financial arrangements for the proposed system.[8]

There was considerable disagreement on a number of issues, which according to Abel Alier 'initially appeared innocuous. But in the course of debate and informal exchange of views, it became clear that there were fundamental differences, reflecting the conflicting values between North and South, on which a nation-state could stand or disintegrate.'[9]

With such sharp disagreements in the twelve-man committee and in the National Constitution Committee, 'Southern representatives said enough was enough. In December 1968 we packed our bags and left the committee.'[10]

The Addis Ababa Agreement
The hope for a more lasting reconciliation between the South and the North came on 25 May 1969, when young officers, under the leadership of Major Jaafar Mohamed Nimeiri, seized power and announced socialism for the whole country and autonomy for the South. They started in alliance with the Communist Party, and when there was opposition from the Ansar – the Mahdists – the Government clamped down on them. A Ministry for Southern Affairs was set up under a southern minister, Joseph Garang, an avowed Communist who believed 'The cause of the Southern problem is the inequality which exists between North and South by reason of an uneven economic, social and

cultural development. All the ills in South-North situations spring from this situation.'[11] Consequently, for Joseph Garang, the solution was development and the elimination of economic and social disparity.[12] Under him, a number of reforms were introduced, but the implementation of the autonomy was impeded, partly because of Garang's preference for practical developmental steps to a constitutional settlement and partly because of the ambivalence of the North about the proposed arrangement. While Southerners first welcomed the declaration of autonomy with enthusiasm and voiced their support of the Government the passage of time without any significant change brought back skepticism and suspicion.

In the meantime, the alliance between the Communists and the Government was weakening, and although some Communists, including Joseph Garang, remained in the Cabinet, the alliance rapidly disintegrated, finally ending in the abortive coup of 19 July 1971. Nimeiri returned to power after three days of apparent, though uncertain, Communist success. Those found responsible, including Joseph Garang, were convicted and executed.

Abel Alier, a young Southerner who had played a significant role in Southern politics and in whom the Southerners within the country, and, to a large extent, outside, had great confidence, replaced Joseph Garang as Minister for Southern Affairs.

Soon after the Communist coup was suppressed, Nimeiri presented himself to the Sudanese people in a plebiscite and was chosen by an overwhelming majority to be the President of the Democratic Republic. Abel Alier became one of the two Vice-Presidents while also continuing as the Minister for Southern Affairs.

Alier persuaded the President to hold talks with the rebels, a strategy which Joseph Garang had opposed. Once the talks were started, both sides worked diligently to make them a success. A long period of very delicate negotiations in which the World Council of Churches and the All African Council of Churches played a pivotal role with moral guidance and reinforcement from Emperor Haile Selassie, eventually ended in the Addis Ababa Agreement of February 1972. The President promptly enacted the agreement into law – the Southern Provinces Regional Self-Government Act 1972 – which came into force on 3 March 1972.[13]

Clearly, it was when Nimeiri's needs dictated reaching out for the South that he disregarded internal opposition and proceeded with negotiations. He had alienated both the right and the left and was building on the support of the center, which his key advisors suggested could include the South as the strongest alternative political and military power base. Nimeiri was persuaded against the opinion of his military advisors and senior officers, some of whom resigned from the Revolution Command Council in protest. These officers argued that it would be disgraceful for the military to negotiate with the rebels. President Nimeiri, who was well known for his decisiveness, argued that as the leader of the revolution, any disgrace or dishonor for the military would first and foremost fall on him, a risk he was prepared to take.[14]

The regional and international circumstances also favored Nimeiri's position. By his heroic victory against the communists, he had endeared himself to the West with whom the Sudan had broken relations since the six-day war of 1967 in the Middle East. With a Foreign Minister bent on normalizing relations with the West and an international, mostly Western, community desirous to assist the Sudan with the humanitarian task of relief, rehabilitation and reconstruction in a peaceful Sudan, especially in the South, where the new policy of the Government was attracting significant numbers of returnees, there was much to gain and little, if anything, to lose in ending the war. Alier himself had gone to Europe and Scandinavia and met with international governmental and private organizations, including the churches, to solicit assistance. The conference of the United Nations specialized and voluntary organizations on relief, resettlement and rehabilitation of returning refugees, which took place only a week before the Addis Ababa Agreement, resulted in pledges for assistance which created a favorable international climate for peace in the country.

But perhaps the most critical factor was the role of Abel Alier, a Southerner whose modesty, loyalty, and commitment to the peaceful resolution of the conflict had been tested. Unlike the ideologically committed marxist Joseph Garang, Alier appeared to be almost a pacifist, with considerable command of respect and trust across the political spectrum. After the abortive communist coup, which ended with the execution of Joseph Garang, he emerged as the obvious alternative and one in whom Nimeiri, and the North as a whole, placed their trust, enhanced by a compensational zest for not having heeded his wise counsel in the first place. But Alier was by no means a Northern stooge or puppet. He had been a prominent member of the Southern Front which advocated self-determination for the South, had resigned his position as a judge to participate in the Round Table Conference and had been the Southern spokesman in the constitution draft committee of 1968. That he was chosen by Nimeiri to mastermind the peace process and to lead the government delegation to the peace talks that resulted in the Addis Ababa Agreement is one of the anomalies of negotiation that requires a contextual understanding. In a way, it reflects both the effectiveness of an authoritarian leadership in the negotiation process and, in view of the eventual fate of the Addis Ababa Accord, the weakness and unsustainability of such narrow-based settlements. Alier's leadership of the Sudanese mediation team almost made the Addis Ababa negotiations a South-South dialogue. This was only balanced by his sensitivity and deep sense of evenhandedness. As he has written,

> I headed a delegation, essentially Northern Sudanese in both composition and disposition. I had not recommended any Southerner for the delegation, aware that even one or two more might make the talks appear one-sided, merely talks between Southerners. Indeed my leadership of the delegation was later criticized on these grounds. It was said that the Sudan Government delegation was a Northern delegation whose leadership should have been Northern Sudanese – a valid criticism, although the background leading to the talks was not known by many, including some members of the Sudan delegation.[15]

This is an important insight as it reflects the narrow base of the peace initiative and process. As Alier himself has intimated, 'the government had only gradually been reconciled to this initiative through a series of proposals and declarations'.[16] Alier testifies that the Sudan delegation worked as a team with the Northern Sudanese maintaining their freedom to meet and plan alone, without him and with his full appreciation. This was particularly the case when the serious issue of security arrangements was under discussion: 'The sensitivity of the subject was such that, though I was leader of the Government delegation, I was excluded from the talks which were secretly organized and concluded by the members of my delegation when the subject became the main preoccupation of both sides'.[17]

> I gave my colleagues the impression that I was not aware of their unease and what they were doing. For my part, what they did was quite legitimate and necessary. They represented the North and in that capacity were entitled to discuss the subject without me. It was acceptable to me that they took this secret initiative, although I was aware of their meeting since it took place in the room next door to mine.[18]

Alier's role represented an unusual blend of representation, negotiating positions and perspectives on issues. This may account both for the remarkable success of the talks and for the paradoxically feeble foundations of the agreement that later made it possible for Nimeiri to dismantle it unilaterally.

When the threat from the sectarian political parties and the Muslim fundamentalists proved sufficiently serious, especially after the 1976 armed attack by the opposition groups from bases in Libya, Nimeiri decided to reverse his Southern policy to pacify Northern opposition, believing that the Southern potential to rebel had been effectively and decisively neutralized.

His policies of Islamization, division of the South, manipulation of oil reserves and water resources, and the final stroke of the attempt to move Southern troops to the North to undercut the capability for a potential rebellion all combined to trigger the resumption of hostilities.

Perhaps the most significant lesson from the experience is the dilemma of whether to deal with dictators who are decisive and practical in doing what should be done to end a conflict, but are unlikely to secure a broad-based support that can sustain the settlement in the long run, or to embark on a democratic process that is more unlikely to bring about a workable consensus, but can sustain any solution reached through such a consensus. This dilemma remains a major puzzle for the cause of peace in the Sudan.

Dynamics and prospects

Since Nimeiri's overthrow by a popular uprising in April 1985, there have been efforts in the peace process which could be classified into three main strands: negotiations between the parties, third party mediation, and scholarly or intellectual dialogue involving participants representing or reflecting the positions of the parties and neutral resource persons.

The most relevant for our present purpose are the direct negotiations between the parties, of which only two occasions resulting in the Koka Dam Declaration and the Mirghani-Garang Agreement, were successful. Even this success was only partial in two respects. First, the agreements were merely procedural, aimed at facilitating progress toward a constitutional conference and did not provide a comprehensive settlement of the substantive issues. Secondly, they were not comprehensive in their representative capacity but, on the contrary, excluded some pivotal factions. As with the Addis Ababa Agreement, which eventually suffered from reliance on Nimeiri alone, these partial agreements met with the opposition of the excluded factions and died in one way or another.

It is now widely recognized that the war is stalemated in the sense that neither party can exact a decisive victory and impose its vision for the nation on the other. It is also obvious that the nation is suffering gravely from the war and its implications in human costs, famines and economic devastation. Yet, neither party seems to be feeling the pressure enough to indicate a willingness to make significant concessions on their fundamental objectives crystallized in the government Islamic agenda and the SPLM/SPLA commitment to secularism.

This raises the question of when a conflict becomes mutually hurting: Is it when a nation bleeds to a dangerous point or when the leaders themselves feel the threat to their political survival? Nimeiri's Sudan was not bleeding to death when he negotiated the Addis Ababa Agreement, but he was feeling himself and his regime severely threatened by the opposition forces. The Sudan of the post-Nimeiri regime is a nation at the brink of total collapse, but the leaders themselves have apparently not felt the personal threat of imminent demise. The SPLM/SPLA on the other hand, finding dignity in their commitment to self-liberation through a protracted armed struggle, are not about to make another Addis Ababa type compromise that would retain the conventional equations of the power structure in the country.

Meanwhile, the situation on the ground appears to be developing an impasse that avoids the critical issues which would have to be confronted in any serious negotiations. This means that lack of progress in negotiation may indicate a *de facto* separation which neither side would acknowledge since the rebels' stated objective is the liberation of the whole country while the government retains its claim to the sovereignty of the whole country. On the other hand, this may prove to be a postponement of an issue that will sooner or later have to be confronted.

What are the prospects of resolving that issue, if and when it is confronted? Speculations on this question are becoming increasingly pessimistic. This pessimism which is generated by the dismal record of North–South relations is implicit in the sub-title of Abel Alier's recent book: *Southern Sudan: Too Many Agreements Dishonored.* One of the most significant parts of the book is Alier's statement of options:

> Options which would be available within the unity frame of reference range from administrative decentralization which was tried in the Northern Sudan in 1980, regional autonomy which was tried in the Southern Sudan from 1972 to 1983 and federation which was partially tried in the form of regional autonomy, to confederation which has not been tried.

The second option is one which splits the nation-state into two or more sovereign entities. Separation, which was, by agreement, ruled out in the Addis Ababa Agreement of 1972, but which has been less remote since 1983 when the Agreement was abrogated ... could only be obtained either in the battlefield or by a violent and reactionary revolution in the Northern Sudan determined to adopt a theocratic system of government and an all-out Arab nationalism making no provision for African nationality. But if that stance were adopted in Khartoum, it could well spell the end of a Sudanese nation-state.[19]

To conclude, the manner in which agreements have been made that were either not seriously intended or were subsequently dishonored, and the on-going ambivalences of perpetrating the war while yearning for peace, or upholding the principle of national unity while contemplating separation, all emanate from hidden agendas. These in turn relate to the divisions that divide the country, the parties' perceptions of the cleavages, and the seeming conviction that they are unbridgeable and therefore undiscussable or if discussed, unresolvable. The issues involved are essentially those of competing identities and the alternative visions they offer the nation. But are the issues of Sudanese identity really unresolvable or are there alternative bases for reconceptualizing the country's self-perception to be more collectively and equitably accommodating? This is the question which the Sudanese and all those concerned with the welfare and future of the country must confront and address realistically, courageously and creatively.

Notes

1. M.W. Daly (1989) Islam, Secularism, and Ethnic Identity in the Sudan, in Gustavo Benavides and M.W. Daly (eds) *Religion and Political Power*, New York: State University of New York, p. 83.
2. Donald Rothchild (1991) Africa's interethnic conflicts: The linkages among demands require strategies and management of conflict, in Francis Mading Deng and I. William Zartman, *Conflict Resolution in Africa*, Washington, DC: The Brookings Institution, p. 194.
3. Ibid.
4. Proceedings of the Juba Conference on the Political Development of the Southern Sudan, June 1947, Appendix 9 in Mohamed Omer Beshir, *Southern Sudan Background to the Conflict* (London, C. Hurst and Company 1968; second and third impressions by Khartoum University Press, 1970 and 1979) pp. 136, 146–7.
5. Ibid.
6. Ibid.
7. Mohammed Omer Beshir (1968) *The Southern Sudan Background to the*

Conflict, London: C. Hurst and Company; second and third impressions by Khartoum University Press, 1970 and 1979, Appendix 19, p. 184. Mr. Beshir was secretary to the conference.

8. Some issues were left unresolved, among them whether the national parliament would be empowered to override regional legislatures or not, the effect of state of emergency on the regional powers and institutions, the nature of financial relations between the regions and the center, and the degree to which regional governments would assume charge of security.

9. *Id.*, p. 36.

10. Ibid.

11. *Revolution in Action*, Speeches by Joseph Garang, 1970, p. 8.

12. Joseph Garang's extreme commitment to development as the real solution is obvious in this passage from an address he made at the British House of Commons on 16 April 1970, to a group of Parliamentarians, pressmen, trade union leaders and writers: 'As for the problem of our rebels in the forest or in Uganda, and who are threatening to start trouble, and who have been making contacts with certain foreign organizations and governments, all that we say unto them is this:

    > We will construct – you destroy; we will build schools – you burn them down; we will build hospitals – you destroy them; we will build roads – you burn and break bridges. It shall be the people of the South to decide for themselves: who is building and who is destroying. In the end, it is they who will determine who shall be the political leaders: those who are destroying or those who are building. (id., p. 25).

13. For the details of the peace process leading to the Addis Ababa Accord, see Hizkias Assefa (1987) *Mediation of Civil Wars: Approaches and Strategies – the Sudan Conflict*, Boulder and London: Westview Press. See also Abel Alier (1990) *Southern Sudan: Too Many Agreements Dishonored*, Exeter: Ithaca Press, Chapters 4–8.

14. The most authentic source on this is Nimeiri himself in a conversation with the author.

15. Alier (1990) *The Southern Sudan: Too Many Agreements Dishonored*, Exeter, Ithaca Press, p. 95.

16. Ibid.

17. Ibid.

18. *Id.*, pp. 106–7.

19. Alier, p. 277.

Bibliography

Alier, Abel (1990) *The Southern Sudan: Too Many Agreements Dishonored*, Exeter: Ithaca Press.

Assefa, Hizkias (1987) *Mediation of Civil Wars: Approaches and Strategies – the Sudan Conflict*, Boulder and London: Westview Press.

Beshir, Mohamed Omer (1968) *The Southern Sudan Background to the Conflict*, London: C. Hurst and Company.

Daly, M.W. (1989) 'Islam, secularism, and ethnic identity in the Sudan,' in Gustavo Benavides and M.W. Daly (eds), *Religion and Political Power*, New York: State University of New York.

Hasan, Yusuf Fadl (1967) *The Arabs and the Sudan*, Edinburgh: Edinburgh University Press.

Rothchild, Donald (1991) 'Africa's interethnic conflicts: The linkages among demands require strategies and management of conflict,' in Francis Mading Deng and I. William Zartman, *Conflict Resolution in Africa*, Washington, DC: The Brookings Institution.

APPENDIX
The Southern Sudan Provinces Regional Self-Government Act 1972

An organic Law to organise self-government in the Southern Provinces of the Sudan.

In accordance with the provisions of the Constitution of the Democratic Republic of the Sudan hereinafter defined in this Act,

and

In realization of the memorable May Revolution Declaration of the 9th of June, 1969, for realization in the Southern Sudan of regional self-government within a united Socialist Union,

and

In accordance with the principle of the May Revolution that the Sudanese people shall participate actively in and supervise the decentralized system of the Government of their country,

and

In accordance with the provisions of Article 40 of the Republican Decree No. 1,

The President of the Democratic Republic of the Sudan hereby makes the following Act:

CHAPTER I: PRELIMINARY

1. This Act may be cited as 'The Southern Provinces Regional Self-Government Act, 1972', and shall come into force on 3rd day of March, 1972.

Definitions
2. In this Act unless the context otherwise requires the following words and expressions shall have the meanings hereinafter assigned to each respectively:

(i) 'Constitution' means the Republican Decree No. 5 or any other basic law replacing or amending it.

(ii)   'President' means President of the Democratic Republic of the Sudan.
(iii)   'Southern Provinces of the Sudan' means the provinces of Bahr El Ghazal, Equatoria and Upper Nile in accordance with their boundaries as they stood on 1 January, 1956 and any other areas that were culturally and geographically a part of the Southern complex as may be decided by a referendum.
(iv)   'People's Regional Assembly' means the Legislative body for the Southern region of the Sudan.
(v)   'High Executive Council' means the Executive Council appointed by the President on the recommendation of the President of the High Executive Council to supervise the administration and to direct public affairs in the Southern region of the Sudan.
(vi)   'President of the High Executive Council' means the person appointed by the President on the recommendation of the People's Regional Assembly to lead and supervise the executive organs responsible for the administration of the Southern provinces.
(vii)   'People's Assembly' means the National Legislative Assembly representing the people of the Sudan in accordance with the Constitution.
(viii) 'Sudanese' means any Sudanese citizen as defined by the Sudanese Nationality Act 1957 and any amendments thereof.

CHAPTER II: REGIONAL SELF-GOVERNMENT AND LANGUAGE

Regional self-government
3. The Southern Province of Sudan shall constitute a self-government region within the Democratic Republic of the Sudan and shall be known as The Southern Region.
4. The Southern Region shall have legislative and executive organs, the functions and powers of which are defined by this Act.

Language
5. Arabic shall be the official language for the Sudan and English the principal language for the Southern Region without prejudice to the use of any other language or languages which may serve a practical necessity for the efficient and expeditious discharge of executive and administrative functions of the region.

CHAPTER III: NATIONAL MATTERS NOT SUBJECT TO LEGISLATIVE AND EXECUTIVE JURISDICTION OF LEGISLATURE AND EXECUTIVE OF SOUTHERN REGION

6. Neither the People's Regional Assembly nor the High Executive Council shall legislate or exercise any powers on matters of national nature which are:

(i)   National defence
(ii)   External affairs

(iii)   Currency and coinage
(iv)   Air and inter-regional river transport
(v)   Communications and telecommunications
(vi)   Customs and foreign trade except for border and certain commodities which the Regional Government may specify with the approval of the Central Government
(vii) Nationality and immigration (Emigration)
(viii) Planning for economic and social development
(ix)   Educational planning
(x)   Public audit.

CHAPTER IV: LEGISLATURE

Legislature for the Southern Region
7. Regional legislation in the Southern Region shall be exercised by a People's Regional Assembly elected by Sudanese citizens resident in the Southern Region. The constitution and conditions of membership of the Assembly shall be determined by law.

Election of members
8. Members of the People's Regional Assembly shall be elected by direct secret ballot.

Additional members and other matters
9. (1) For the first Assembly the President may appoint additional members to the People's Regional Assembly where conditions for elections are not conducive to such elections as stipulated in Article 9, provided that such appointed members shall not exceed one quarter of the Assembly.
   (2) The People's Regional Assembly shall regulate the conduct of its business in accordance with regulations to be laid down by the Assembly during its first sitting.
   (3) The People's Regional Assembly shall elect one of its members as a Speaker, provided that the first sitting shall be presided over by the Interim President of the High Executive Council.

Legislative powers of the People's Regional Assembly
10. The People's Regional Assembly shall legislate for preservation of public order, internal security, efficient administration and the development of the Southern Region in cultural, economic and social fields and in particular in the following:
    (a) Promotion and utilization of regional financial resources for the development and administration of the Southern Region.
    (b) Organization of the machinery for regional and local administration.
    (c) Legislation on traditional law and custom within the framework of national laws.
    (d) Establishment, maintenance and administration of prisons and reformatory institutions.
    (e) Establishment, maintenance and administration of public schools at all

levels in accordance with national plans for education and economic and social development.

(f)   Promotion of local languages and cultures.

(g)   Town and village planning and the construction of roads in accordance with national plans and programmes.

(h)   Promotion of trade; establishment of local industries and markets; issue of traders licenses and formation of cooperative societies.

(i)   Establishment, maintenance and administration of public hospitals.

(j)   Administration of environmental health services; maternity care; child welfare; supervision of markets; combat of epidemic diseases; training of medical assistants and rural midwives; establishment of health centres, dispensaries and dressing stations.

(k)   Promotion of animal health, control of epidemics and improvement of animal production and trade.

(l)   Promotion of tourism.

(m)   Establishment of zoological gardens, museums; organization of trade and cultural exhibitions.

(n)   Mining and quarrying, without prejudice to the rights of the Central Government on the discovery of natural gas and minerals.

(o)   Recruitment, organization and administration of the services of the police and prisons in accordance with national policies and levels.

(p)   Land use according to national laws and plans.

(q)   Control of pests and plant diseases.

(r)   Development, use and protection of forest products and pastures according to national law.

(s)   Development and promotion of self-help schemes.

(t)   All other matters respecting which the President may authorize the People's Regional Assembly to legislate.

Request for facts and information
11. The People's National Assembly may make a request to be provided with facts and information concerning the administration of the Southern Region.

Relief of the President and members of the Assembly
12. (1) The People's Regional Assembly may, by a three-quarters majority and for specified reasons relating to public interest, request the President of the Republic to relieve the President or any member of the High Executive Council from office. The President shall accede to such request.

(2) In case of vacancy, relief or resignation of the President of the High Executive Council, the entire body shall be considered as having automatically resigned.

Postponement of coming into force of laws
13. The People's Regional Assembly may, by a two-thirds majority request the President to postpone the coming into force of any law which, in the view of the members, adversely affects the welfare and interests of the citizens of the Southern Region. The President, may, if he thinks fit, accede to such request.

Request to withdraw bills

14. (1) The People's Regional Assembly may, by a majority of its members, request the President to withdraw any bill presented to the People's National Assembly which in their view affects adversely the welfare, rights or interests of the citizens in the Southern Region, pending communication of the views of the People's Regional Assembly.

(2) If the President accedes to such request, the People's Regional Assembly shall present its views within 15 days from the date of accession to the request.

(3) The President shall communicate any such views to the People's National Assembly, together with his own observations if he deems necessary.

Communication of Acts and bills

15. The People's National Assembly shall communicate all bills and Acts to the People's Assembly for their information. The People's Regional Assembly shall act similarly.

CHAPTER VI: THE EXECUTIVE

Regional Executive Authority

16. The Regional Executive Authority is vested in a High Executive Council which acts on behalf of the President.

Specification of duties of Departments in the Southern Region

17. The High Executive Council shall specify the duties of the various departments in the Southern Region provided that on matters relating to Ministries and Departments of the Central Government it shall act with the approval of the President.

Appointment and relief of President of the High Executive Council

18. The President of the High Executive Council shall be appointed and relieved of office by the President on the recommendations of the People's Regional Assembly.

Appointment and relief of members of the High Executive Council

19. The High Executive Council shall be composed of members appointed and relieved of office by the President on the recommendation of the President of the High Executive Council.

Responsibility of the High Executive Council

20. The President of the High Executive Council and its members are responsible to the President and to the People's Regional Assembly for the efficient administration in the Southern Region. They shall take an oath of office before the President.

President and members of the High Executive Council may attend meetings of the Assembly

21. The President and members of the High Executive Council may attend

meetings of the People's Regional Assembly and participate in its deliberations without the right to vote, unless they are also members of the People's Regional Assembly.

CHAPTER VII: REGULATION OF RELATIONSHIP BETWEEN THE HIGH EXECUTIVE COUNCIL AND CENTRAL MINISTRIES AND THE ESTABLISHMENT OF A REGIONAL PUBLIC SERVICE

Regulation of relation
22. The President shall from time to time regulate the relationship between the High Executive Council and the central ministries.

Establishment of a regional public service
23. The High Executive Council may initiate laws for the creation of a regional public service. These shall specify the terms and conditions of service for the regional public service.

CHAPTER VIII: FINANCE

Imposition of duties and taxes
24. The People's Regional Assembly may levy regional duties and taxes in addition to national and local duties and taxes. It may make legislations and orders to guarantee the collection of all public monies at different levels.

Sources of revenue
25. (1) The source of revenue of the Southern Region shall consist of the following:
   (i) Direct and indirect regional taxes.
   (ii) Contribution from the People's Local Government Councils.
   (iii) Revenue from commercial, industrial and agricultural projects in the region in accordance with the National Plan.
   (iv) Funds from the National Treasury for established services.
   (v) Funds voted by the National Assembly in accordance with the requirements of the Region.
   (vi) The Special Development Budget for the Regional Assembly for the acceleration of the Southern economic and social advancement of the Southern Region as envisaged in the declaration of the 9th of June, 1969.
   (vii) Revenues to be determined in a special schedule attached to a Finance Law.
   (viii) Any other sources.
   (2) The High Executive Council shall prepare a budget to meet expenditure for the services of security, administration and development of the Southern Region according to national plans and programmes and it shall be presented thereby to the approval of the People's Regional Assembly.

CHAPTER IX: OTHER PROVISIONS

The People's Armed Forces

26. (1) Citizens of the Southern Region shall constitute a sizeable proportion of the People's Armed Forces in such reasonable numbers as will correspond to the population of the Region.
    (2) The use of the People's Armed Forces within the Region and outside the framework of national defence shall be controlled by the President on the advice of the President of the High Executive Council.
    (3) Temporary arrangements for the composition of units of the People's Armed Forces in the Southern Region are provided for in agreed arrangements.

Right of Veto

27. The President may veto any bill which he deems contrary to the provisions of the Constitution, provided the People's Regional Assembly, after receiving the President's view, may reintroduce the Bill.

Initiation of bills by the President and Members of Councils

28. The President and Members of the High Executive Council may initiate a bill in the People's Regional Assembly.

Initiation of bills by members of the People's Regional Assembly

29. Any member of the People's Regional Assembly may initiate any bill provided that financial bills shall not be presented without a sufficient notice to the President of the High Executive Council.

Duty of the Assembly to consolidate the unity of Sudan and respect the Constitution

30. The People's Regional Assembly shall strive to consolidate the unity of the Sudan and respect the Constitution.

Freedom of movement

31. All citizens are guaranteed the freedom of movement in and out of the Southern Region, provided restriction or prohibition of movement may be imposed on a named citizen or citizens solely on grounds of public health and order.

Guarantee of equal opportunity of education

32. (1) All citizens resident in the Southern Region are guaranteed equal opportunity of education, employment, commerce and the practice of any lawful profession.
    (2) The rights of citizens hereinbefore specified in subsection (I) hereof shall not be prejudiced because of race, tribal origin, religion, place of birth or sex.

Capital of Southern Region

33. Juba shall be the capital of the Southern Region and place of residence of the Executive and Legislature thereof.

AMENDMENTS OF THIS ACT

34. This Act shall only be amended by a majority of three-quarters of the People's National Assembly and the approval of a majority of two-thirds of the citizens of the Southern Region in a referendum to be carried out in that Region.

Made under my hand, at the People's Palace, this 3rd day of March, 1972.

Sigd.,

President of the Democratic Republic of the Sudan.

5 THE PUNJAB IMBROGLIO: THE PRELUDE TO THE ACCORD OF 1985

K.K. Panda

A matter of identity

Punjab has been one of the principal trouble spots of the Indian Union almost since independence. For a decade or more it has been a storm center. The background to the conflict and the causes of conflict in that state have been analysed in many books and articles[1] and the present chapter will not deal with the issues involved in any great detail. As would be appropriate to a chapter in a volume on Peace Accords and conflict resolution it will concentrate on issues that are relevant to an understanding of the causes and events that led to the Punjab Accord signed on 24 July 1985 by Rajiv Gandhi, then Prime Minister of India, and Harchand Singh Longowal, the leader of the moderate group in the Shiromani Akali Dal in Punjab.

Four distinct factors are discernible in the current crisis in the Punjab. These are, first of all, the political agendas of agitators spearheaded by the Shiromani Akali Dal and, second, of agitators led by more extreme communal and extremist groups among the Sikhs. Third, there are the secessionist activists whose aim is to establish an independent Sikh state with external assistance. Fourthly, the level of violence in the Punjab, which can only be understood by a recognition of the role played by politicized criminal elements, smugglers and other anti-social elements, and, in certain cases, ideologically committed groups bearing a distinct resemblance to Naxalites. Most of these issues will be dealt with in some detail later on in this chapter.

An essential preliminary to the discussion of the Punjab Accord is to understand the significance of the emergence and development of the concept of a separate Sikh identity. All writers on the Punjab crisis are agreed on the importance of this as a factor, just as they are agreed in tracing its roots back to the late 19th century heyday of the British raj. Both British writers and officials of this period and the early years of the 20th century contributed to this in their own way. Thus Cunningham's *History of the Sikhs* propounded the thesis that the Sikhs grew from 'a sect to a people' and 'from a people to a nation', while in 1911 D. Petrie then Assistant Director of the Criminal Intelligence Department of the Government of India argued that the 'Sikhs were encouraged to regard themselves as a totally distinct and separate nation'.

There is also no doubt that some Sikh groups were deeply influenced by Jinnah's agitation for the creation of a Muslim state to be carved out of the raj prior to the grant of independence to India. Thus, when the Cripps Mission was in India in 1942 a section of the Akali leadership called for the creation of 'Azad Punjab', which meant either an independent Sikh state or a political entity in which the Sikhs were a dominant element. The demand for a Sikh homeland was first raised by Master Tara Singh in 1946. It was formally propounded on 15 November 1948 when four demands were made. The first of these was the most important, the creation of a geographically compact, economically sound and financially viable Sikh or Sikh-dominated state. The fourth called for securing a contented Sikh community, which was to be achieved by the first, second and third demands. The second called for the eradication of causes of unrest and the restoration of communal harmony. There was no consensus among the Sikhs on these demands: while the Tara Singh faction was agitating in their favor, the Sant Fateh Singh faction was against them. The moderates among the Sikhs were in favor of a Sikh homeland within the Indian Union.

The partition of the raj was a traumatic experience for the people of Punjab and in particular the Sikhs. After the partition thousands of Sikhs fled from their homes which now formed part of Pakistan. The Akali leadership hoped that their demand for a special status for the Sikhs would be sympathetically received by the Constituent Assembly. But their demands met considerable resistance from the powerful Hindu elements in Punjab, and as a result the Akali proposals were rejected. The Akali representatives for their part did not sign the finalization of the Indian Constitution.

Thus the proceedings of the Constituent Assembly left the Sikhs dissatisfied, and the essential elements of their dissatisfaction could be traced back to the demands they placed before the Constituent Assembly, and which the Assembly, for the most part, rejected. One of the first of these issues to lead to contention in Punjab was language. By the early 1950s language-related agitation was causing serious concern for the stability of the Indian Union. The language controversies caused difficulties in Punjab as well although the real storm centers of language-related agitation were in other parts of India. The Akalis were agitating for the establishment of Punjabi as the official language of the state while the Hindus, with the Jana Sangh and the Arya Samaj taking the lead, were firmly opposed to it. The first post-independence census in India, in 1951, provided both sides, Sikhs and Hindus alike, with an opportunity for influencing the thinking of the people of the Punjab in regard to language. The Akalis, naturally enough, urged the people to identify Punjabi as their mother tongue, while the Arya Samajis, the Jana Sangh and a section of the Congress Party, campaigned among the Hindus of the Punjab urging them to insist on identifying Hindi as their mother tongue. The latter feared that a majority in favor of Punjabi would strengthen the Akalis in their agitation for a Sikh state within the Indian union. When the Akalis did launch an agitation for the re-drawing of the boundaries of Punjab on the basis of language, it confronted a powerful Hindu agitation against this, and a counter agitation to 'save Hindi'.

The report of the States Reorganization Commission (1956) was a great disappointment to the Akalis. The Commission refused to re-draw the boundaries of Punjab on the basis of language. Instead Punjab was recognized as a bi-lingual state. Almost all sections of the Sikhs refused to accept this decision and activists among them kept up an agitation to have it changed. They succeeded in 1966, after ten years of agitation but in the meantime, the pressures and counterpressures severely strained relations between the Sikhs and Hindus in Punjab. The Sikhs themselves were divided on the basis of moderates, activists and extremists.

The distribution of population in the Punjab state which emerged from the partition of the raj was such that it was impossible to create a Sikh majority state which did not have a large Hindu minority. Thus the second partition of Punjab which came about in 1966 caused as many problems as it settled. The present Punjab has both a Punjabi speaking majority as well as a Sikh majority, but there are now large numbers of Punjabi-speaking Hindus in neighboring states and, even more important, there are pockets of Sikhs in those states. Also the language agitation of the 1950s and 1960s in the pre-1966 Punjab state has left such distressing memories and created so much bitterness that in Haryana and large parts of Himachal Pradesh, which were originally parts of that state, a reaction has set in against Punjabi, and there is a refusal to accept it even as a second language.

The boundary changes of 1966 did lead to a period of stability within the new Punjab. It would be true to say that the demand raised by the Master Tara Singh faction for self-determination for the Sikhs lost much of its appeal after 1966. There was indeed a reduction of mistrust between the Sikhs and Hindus in the late 1960s and early 1970s. The

Akali Dal shared power with the Jana Sangh and the Communist Party of India in 1967 and with the Jana Sangh in 1969. In 1977 they shared power with the Jana Sangh dominated Janatha Party.

Power-sharing was not without its own problems. Not all Sikh groups were happy about it, despite recognizing the need for it on an electoral basis since the Sikhs enjoyed only a narrow majority within the Punjab. It was possible to build a coalition of forces which would leave some of the more aggressive Akali factions out in the cold. This began to happen in and after 1972 when the Congress won power in Punjab in its wave of electoral popularity after India's victory over Pakistan and the creation of Bangladesh. Giani Zail Singh the Congress Chief Minister, who later rose to be President of India, sucessfully exploited factionalism among the Akalis to maintain himself and his party in power. These political manoeuverings coincided with, and contributed to, a vigorous re-assertion of the Sikh identity. This re-assertion took many forms, including a revival of separatist agitation and, at a different level, a re-statement of the case for greater autonomy for a Sikh-dominated Punjab which was spelled out in the well-known Anandpur Sahib resolution of 1973. However, a consideration of the emergence of Sikh separatism, as follows, must necessarily precede an analysis of this resolution.

The demand for a separate Sikh state, 'Khalistan', emerged both within Punjab and outside it – especially among Sikh groups living in the United States, Canada and Great Britain. It was easier for these diaspora groups to raise this demand with impunity. The demand for 'Khalistan' was raised publicly in the West for the first time by Dr Jagjit Singh Chauhan, former Finance Minister of Punjab, at a press interview he gave in September 1971. Once the cry was raised in this form – and it received considerable publicity – it was taken up by others in the diaspora groups and by sections of the Akalis themselves. Very soon secessionism was an important factor in Sikh politics within Punjab and elsewhere in India, as well as among diaspora groups.

As with other separatist movements the root causes are a mixture of political and economic.[2] While the social and economic factors – dealt with by several scholars – are important enough, nevertheless one cannot underestimate the significance of political factors. Once the Congress governments at the center began the practice of using the powers of the presidency and of the governor of Punjab to dismiss Akali ministries, and exploiting divisions in the ranks of the Akalis to weaken the electoral base of the Akali moderates, the extremists among the Sikhs began to enjoy greater influence. Many of them were either separatists themselves or sympathizers and supporters of the separatists. With their influence on the increase the extremists began to use force against both the Hindus and moderate Akalis.

The Anandpur Sahib resolution

The working committee of the Shiromani Akali Dal under the leadership of Sant Harchand Singh Longowal adopted certain basic postulates of their political, social and economic program as the essential elements of the Sikh case for an autonomous Sikh state at Sri Anandpur Sahib. These basic postulates ranged from unexceptionable notions such as the need for 'human co-existence', human progress and the ultimate unity of all human beings with the Spiritual Soul, to the essentially political objective that the Shiromani Akali Dal be recognized 'as the embodiment of the hopes and aspirations of the Sikh Nation'.

The principal demand incorporated in the resolution was for a much greater degree of autonomy than the Punjab enjoyed as a constituent state of the Indian union. Indeed a case was made for a radical transformation of center-state relationships with a weak central government whose principal concerns were to be restricted to Defence, External Affairs, Communications and Currency. India's quasi-federal system would be converted into genuine federation in which Punjab like the other states of the union would be considerably stronger than under the existing system.

Like similar documents of its kind there is much ambiguity in the meaning of some of its clauses and there were, in fact, at least two versions of the resolution. Again, like so many similar documents, it sets out highly idealistic objectives which are intrinsically difficult to realize in practical life. Most of these idealistic expressions arose from the fact that the basic purpose of the Shiromani Akali Dal was considered to be that of propagating Sikhism and its code of conduct, of preserving the concept of a distinct and independent identity of the Panth, and of creating an environment in which the national sentiments of the Sikh Panth would have full expression. In the first part of the resolution an emphasis was placed on the Sikh religious heritage.

There was, as part of this, a reiteration of the concept of the oneness of God, of the grooming of religious preachers such as Ragis, Dhadis and poets for the propagation of Sikhism, and inculcation of the practice of 'Daswand' among the Sikhs. In addition to these an emphasis was placed on the streamlining of the Gurudwara administration, and a demand for the enactment of an All India Gurudwara Act in order to ensure that the administration of Gurudwaras could be improved, as well as for measures to facilitate easier if not free access to all Sikh shrines.

The Anandpur Sahib resolution also called for the alleviation of poverty and eradication of starvation; urged increased production; and advocated a 'just social order' in which all forms of discrimination on the basis of caste and creed would be eliminated; it also called for measures to remove illiteracy. All these were re-statements of policy objectives to which hardly anyone could take objection. They were accompanied by other demands of a more specific nature pertaining to improving the condition of the Sikhs or maintaining certain benefits that the Sikhs had enjoyed: thus a demand that there should be no discrimination against Sikh employees of the Central and State governments, was followed by an insistence that the traditional position of the Sikhs in all the defence services be maintained and the 'kirpan' be maintained as an integral part of the uniform of the Sikhs in the army. The resolution drew attention to the rehabilitation of ex-servicemen in civilian life and urged that this be given priority.

The clauses of the resolution which deal with economic policy and programs reveal an attempt to balance the conflicting interests of the various groups of Sikh society. Thus the resolution was of the view that unless proper economic policies were adopted the gulf between rich and poor in both urban and rural areas was bound to widen. It was very critical of the role of big traders, capitalists and monopolists in the economic development of the country. The resolution placed great emphasis on economic programs that could bring about a transfer of economic power from capitalists, monopolists and traders, to a wider section of the community ranging from small and middle-class farmers, to the working poor, landless agricultural labor, the backward castes in general and the scheduled castes. The resolution advocated a radical land reform scheme which would place a ceiling of 30 standard acres as the maximum, and distribute the excess over that ceiling on an equitable basis among poor farmers, landless tenant farmers and *harijans*. As the resolution saw it, meaningful land reform was crucially important for the improvement in the standard of living of all rural classes 'most particularly of the poor and the middle class farmers, as also the landless labourers'.

There were of course other proposals designed for the dual purpose of improving living standards and reducing the widening gap between rich and poor. The resolution urged the modernization of farming as one of these. It also stressed the importance of fixing prices of agricultural products on the basis of the returns of the middle-class farmers and the notification of prices of agricultural commodities by state governments before the sowing season. Reflecting the economic interests of Punjab as one of India's principal food surplus areas the resolution declared its opposition to the demarcation of food zones which acted as a barrier to the free movement of grain and other food commodities.

This insistence on the abolition of food zones was one of the few expressions in support of market forces that one saw in the resolution. Most of its clauses were in clear opposition to these and in support of an expanded public sector, and of active state intervention in the economy, whether it was through the establishment in rural areas of co-operative societies or agro-industries to provide some relief for the growing population pressures in the urban areas. The resolution urged the nationalization of all industries producing consumer goods for the mass market, and the placing of all major industrial ventures – which it defined as all industries with a capital of over Rs 10 million (Indian rupees) – under the state sector.

The resolution is suffused with a populist tone in many of its recommendations. There is something for everybody, and generally it involves additional expenditure by the state. The other feature is its parochialism. In a demonstration of its concern for the special problems of Punjab the resolution urged the need for a speedy completion of the Thein dam and the Bhatinda thermal plants, and called for the establishment of a nuclear power station in the state.

Its populism is also seen in a number of proposals, beginning with a call for a comprehensive revision of the nation's tax structure with the avowed objective of providing benefits for the poor and ensuring at the same time the eradication of the parallel black money economy. There was also the special emphasis it placed on full employment, progressive improvement in the standard of living of government employees, need-based wages for industrial workers, 'roofed accommodation for the rural and urban poor' and improved transport facilities for all sections of the population.

In the educational and cultural spheres the Shiromani Akali Dal 'aimed at grooming the Sikhs into a strong and sturdy nation, highly educated, fully aware of its fundamental rights, very well versed in various arts and ever ready to honour the more outstanding of its sons'. The resolution made a special plea for compulsory and free education at the primary and secondary levels with special arrangements for the education of the rural population and the poor; and urged that the Punjabi language be made a compulsory subject in schools up to the matriculation classes. In a gesture of support for the more orthodox groups in society the resolution urged that a ban be placed on the sale of liquors, and that the consumption of intoxicants and smoking in public places be prohibited.

Finally there were political goals embodied in the resolution, primarily the establishment of a political system in which the pre-eminence of the Khalsa could be ensured; and a special concern for the Punjabi speaking Sikh enclaves in Rajasthan and Haryana and Himachal Pradesh for whom it urged the creation of special administrative units that would help protect their identity. As for the wider Indian picture the resolution envisaged a recasting of the Indian constitution ' on real federal principles, with equal representation at the centre for all the states', and equal representation for all sections of the population in the central administration, the basis of such representation being determined by the number of seats each state held in Parliament. The resolution also commented on India's foreign policy but those proposals are less important than the ones discussed above in our analysis of the emergence of a distinct Sikh identity as a factor with significant political importance in the Punjab crisis.

The Punjab in turmoil

There is considerable controversy among scholars and others on the causes of the political instability in the Punjab in the 1970s. The situation was ironic, because Punjab continued to be the most prosperous state of the Indian union with a dynamic modern agricultural system that was a model to the rest of India. Some scholars have argued that the development and success of the green revolution contributed greatly to the social and political crisis in Punjab.[3] One cannot, however, underestimate the importance of the political factors that led to the crisis and helped to aggravate it to the point where the whole political process in Punjab has been jeopardized. The central government and the moderates in Punjab grappled unsuccessfully with extremist separatists within Punjab and other parts of India, as well as among the Sikh diaspora groups who were agitating for the establishment of a separate Sikh state, Khalistan.

Any objective analysis of the Punjab crisis would show that no systematic policy framework was ever attempted and formulated by the

Indian government on the basis of an analysis of the nature of the separatist movement, its strength, the forces behind it, and the linkages between various extremist groups and political organizations within the state. The absence of any announcement of measures – either long term and short term – to mitigate the grievances of the people, such as those outlined in the Anandpur Sahib resolution, helped to exacerbate the political crisis. Had there been any serious attempt to deal with some of the social and economic grievances identified in that resolution, it may have helped to bring peace to that troubled state. No such attempt was made. In addition the government, confronted by a serious situation in the early 1980s when Punjab had been converted into an arena of lawlessness, resorted to short-sighted political measures which only succeeded in intensifying political tensions and divisions within Punjab and rendering the state virtually ungovernable by the civil authorities. The factional politics of the state Congress leadership helped the extremists at the expense of the moderates.

In the meantime, diaspora groups continued their agitation for Khalistan and Dr Jagjit Singh was a key figure in these activities. He presided over the transmission of Shabad Kirtan on 2 March 1980 from the premises of the Golden Temple in Amritsar and in a symbolic and politically significant gesture he raised the Khalistan flag in front of the Gurudwara Kesgarh Sahib and announced his intention to hoist it in every district of Punjab. On 12 April 1980, Balbir Singh Sandhu, Secretary General of the National Council of Khalistan announced the formation of an 11 member Khalistan Council. The principal objectives of this council was to demand the creation of a sovereign Sikh state comprised of Punjab and the Sikh enclaves of Himachal Pradesh, Haryana and Rajasthan.

From that time onwards there was a succession of symbolic political gestures from the leaders of the Khalistan agitation which the Indian government regarded as gravely provocative. As a result, on 8 June 1980 Sandu issued a statement to the press at Jalandar announcing that the government of Khalistan would be proclaimed before the Akal Talchta at Amritsar on 16 June 1980. This statement was very critical of the Indian government which it charged with a systematic denial of the political and other rights of the Sikhs. It was also reported that on 16 June 1980 the International Council of Sikhs had announced the establishment of the republic of Khalistan with Dr Jagdit Singh as President, and that the new state would, for a start, have its own distinctive flag, issue its own currency, set up consulates in some Western countries and begin issuing passports. Within Punjab the Sikhs were inspired by these political gestures of the diaspora groups to set up 'Khalsa panchyats'. Within a month of all this the demand for Khalistan had been intensified to the point where the Indian state regarded it as a very serious challenge to its authority.

Within Punjab the initiative and control over the agitation for Khalistan were secured by extremist elements in the Akali Dal, and all this against a background of violence in which public men, journalists and other vocal elements in society as well as private individuals became the victims of the assassins' guns and bombs. When the elected government failed to control the situation, President's rule was imposed on Punjab on 6 October 1983. Punjab state was declared a disturbed area, and the police and paramilitary forces were given unprecedented powers to bring the situation under control. They did not succeed in that objective. Indeed repressive powers used in Punjab only strengthened the extremists among the Sikhs.

When the violence increased, the state administration under President's rule took the fateful decision, at the behest of the central government, to give active encouragement to Sant Jarnail Singh Bhindranwale, an extremist leader, in a calculated but short-sighted attempt to undermine the authority and influence of the Akali Dal leadership. This strengthened Bhindranwale who had a political agenda of his own, and continued with a systematic attempt to gain control of Sikh political agitation giving it a violent complexion.

He was in competition with the Akali Dali who responded to the Punjab crisis by sending the government a list of 45 demands as a prelude to a political agitation, the *Dharm Yudh Morcha* (1982–84). The 45 demands were part of an attempted negotiation process which was now linked to the *Dharm Yudh Morcha*. The original list was issued in September 1981; in October a revised list of 15 demands was issued. Both sets follow on the demands set out in the Anandpur Sahib resolutions.

By this time *Dharm Yudh Morcha* in combination with the demands of September–October 1981 had transformed the politics of the Sikhs and Punjab. The political agitation to recreate a Sikh nation had matured into a powerful and violent separatist movement. In Bhindranwale it had now a fiery leader whose political views and outlook had little in common with those of the bulk of the old style Akali leaders. He successfully undermined the latter, and in the process posed a more formidable challenge to the central government.

By the early part of 1984 Bhindranwale and his extremist associates had converted the Sikh holy of holies, the Golden Temple, into an armed camp. The Akali Dal was helpless in this regard, and although the central government could have stopped this process of converting a religious center into a fortified stronghold of extremists, it failed to do so. It too watched helplessly as the protege of one time Prime Minister Indira Gandhi now seemed set to take control of the Punjab. This failure to prevent the transformation of the Golden Temple into a convenient sanctuary was a major political mistake.

After giving repeated assurances that the army or police would not enter the Golden Temple to dislodge Bhindranwale and his associates, the government ordered the Indian army to attack the Golden Temple on 4 June 1984. Punjab was under curfew. Operation Blue Star led to a violent confrontation which resulted in heavy casualties.[4] The political fall-out was equally damaging, especially when it was linked to Operation Woodrose aimed at curbing terrorism in the rural areas of Punjab. Bhindranwale who was killed in the Golden Temple, with large numbers of his associates, was now a political martyr, and these events gave the extremists among the Sikhs a mass political base in the Punjab.

At a tragic personal level one of the victims of these developments was Mrs. Gandhi herself. Her assassination provoked the Delhi riot of 1984 as well as riots in other parts of the country in which thousands of Sikhs perished. These riots contributed greatly in legitimizing the secessionist activities of the Sikh extremists. With the great majority of the Sikh leadership in custody by this time, power went to the extremists.

The Punjab events helped in their own way in giving Rajiv Gandhi the massive victory that came his way at the general election of March 1985. The cry of 'the country in danger', and the necessity of protecting its unity and integrity was used to great effect. After securing his victory Rajiv Gandhi took positive steps to assuage the feelings of the Sikhs. Some of the Akali Dal leaders were released from detention and a public assurance was given on the early construction of the Thein Dam to augment the water supply to Punjab. A promise was also given to establish a factory to manufacture or assemble coaches. For his own part Sant Harchand Singh Longowal, who had earlier adopted a very belligerent attitude, became more conciliatory after his release.

The Punjab Accord – A fresh initiative

The young Rajiv Gandhi, at the peak of his popularity after his remarkable electoral victory, was intent on a dynamic approach to a settlement of some of India's most pressing ethnic problems. There was none more urgent than Punjab whose burgeoning political violence had consumed his mother's life. He began direct negotiations with Longowal on the framework of a settlement and after much hard bargaining they reached agreement and signed the Punjab Accord on 24 July 1985.[5] The Punjab Accord is discussed in greater detail in Gill's chapter in this book but we provide below a brief summary of its contents and a review of its significance.

The accord has 11 clauses of which the first promised compensation for innocent persons killed in recent events; and another clause conceded the Akali demand for an inquiry into the November 1984 riots in the wake of Indira Gandhi's death which had left thousands of Sikhs dead in Delhi and other parts of India. A Commission under Justice Ranganath Mishra of the Indian Supreme Court was appointed for this purpose. Most of the clauses of the accord dealt with issues that had troubled Punjab since the 1970s. Many of them had been identified in the Anandpur Sahib resolution of 1973 and in the Akali demands of August–September 1981. These included: the issue of recruitment to the armed services; the enactment of an All India Gurudwara bill; an equitable share of river waters; the fate of the Punjabi-speaking Sikh enclaves in neighboring states; and the fate of the city of Chandigarh which Akalis insisted should belong to Punjab. All of these were controversial, but especially the last three because neighboring states were also involved. The accord agreed that Chandigarh should be transferred to Punjab but Haryana was to be compensated for this with some Hindi-speaking areas of Punjab. These transfers were to be made on or before 26 January 1986, and the government of India agreed to appoint another commission to consider the views of Punjab and Haryana on the readjustment of their existing boundaries. Under clause 8 of the Punjab Accord, the issue of center-state relations, raised in the Anandpur Sahib resolution, was referred to the Sakaria Commission which had been appointed to make a comprehensive review of center-state relations in India.

The signing of the accord was received with much relief and great optimism. All that, however, proved to be very shortlived. Within a month of signing the accord Longowal was assassinated by Sikh extremists. The Indian Prime Minister did not permit the assassination of Longowal to deflect him from his objective of restoring stability to Punjab. Elections were called and, despite many threats, a very large turnout of voters gave the Akalis yet another chance to take control over the affairs of Punjab. The Congress I party suffered a setback.

As for the accord many of its clauses were honored, while others were not. These others were among the more significant ones dealing with the more sensitive issues including the transfer of Chandigarh to Punjab and this had disastrous consequences for the peace and stability of Punjab.[6] The levels of violence have kept increasing. All the while the country as a whole has continued its search for solutions to the problems posed by the spread of violence and the dangerous instability of Punjab. No viable solutions have yet been found.

Notes

1. See Henry Hayes (ed.) (1985) *The Sikh Question in India, 1942–1984*, London; Robin Jeffrey (1986) *What's Happening to India? Punjab, Ethnic Conflict, Mrs. Gandhi's Death and the Test for Federalism*, London: Macmillan; Rajiv A. Kapur (1988) *Sikh Separatism: The Politics of Faith*, London: Allen & Unwin.
2. Victor S. D'Souza (1982) Economy, caste, religion and population distribution: An analysis of communal tension in Punjab, *EPW*, 8 May, 783–92; Harish K. Puri (1983) The Akali Agitation: An analysis of socio-economic bases of protest. 22 January:113–18. See Murray J. Leaf (1985) The Punjab Crisis, *Asian Survey*, **25**(5), 475–89.
3. See, for example, Sucha Singh Gill and K.C. Singhal (1984) Farmers' agitation: Response to development crisis in agriculture, *EPW*, 6 October: 1728–32; Hardial Bains (1985) *The Call of the Martyrs: On the Crisis in India and the Protest Situation in the Punjab*, London.
4. The official version of these events is contained in *The White Paper on the Punjab Agitation* (Government of India, New Delhi, 1984). See also Kuldip Nayar and Khushwant Singh (1984) *Tragedy of Punjab: Operation Blue Star*, New Delhi: Vision Books.
5. For the text of the Punjab Accord see, *The Indian Express*, Chandigarh, 25 July 1985.
6. According to official sources as many as 15,000 Hindu families have migrated from Punjab to Delhi since 1986. See the Lok Sabha debates, New Delhi, 22 March 1990.

APPENDIX
Text of Punjab Accord

Following is the text of the memorandum of settlement:

1. *Compensation to innocent persons killed.*

1.1 Along with ex-gratia payment to those innocent killed in agitation or any action after 1.8.1982, compensation for property damaged will also be paid.

2. *Army recruitment.*

2.1 All citizens of the country have the right to enrol in the army and merit will remain the criterion for selection.

3. *Enquiry into November incidents.*

3.1 The jurisdiction of Mr Justice Ranganath Mishra Commission enquiring into the November riots of Delhi would be extended to cover the disturbances at Bokaro and Kanpur also.

4. *Rehabilitation of those discharged from the army.*

4.1 For all those discharged, efforts will be made to rehabilitate and provide gainful employment.

5. *All-India Gurudwara Act.*

5.1 The government of India agrees to consider the formulation of an All-India Gurudwara Bill. Legislation will be brought forward for this purpose in consultation with Shiromani Akali Dal, others concerned and after fulfilling all relevant constitutional requirements.

6. *Disposal of pending cases.*

6.1 The notifications applying Armed Forces Special Powers Act, Punjab will be withdrawn.
    Existing special courts will try only cases relating to the following type of offences:

(A) Waging war

(B) Hijacking

6.2 All other cases will be transferred to ordinary courts and enabling legislation if needed will be brought forward in this session of Parliament.

7. *Territorial claims.*

7.1 The capital project area of Chandigarh will go to Punjab.
    Some adjoining areas which were previously part of Hindi or the Punjabi regions were included in the Union Territory. With the capital region going to Punjab, the areas which were added to the Union Territory from the Punjab region of the erstwhile state of Punjab will be transferred to Punjab and those from Hindi region to Haryana. The entire Sukhna lake will be kept as part of Chandigarh and will thus go to Punjab.

7.2 It had always been maintained by Mrs Indira Gandhi that when Chandigarh is to go to Punjab some Hindi-speaking territories in Punjab will go to Haryana.
    A commission will be constituted to determine the specific Hindi-speaking areas of Punjab which should go to Haryana, in lieu of Chandigarh.

The principle of contiguity and linguistic affinity with a village as a unit will be the basis of such determination.

The commission will be required to give its findings by December 31, 1985 and these will be binding on both sides.

The work of the commission will be limited to this aspect and will be distinct from the general boundary claims which the other commission referred to in Para 7.4 will handle.

7.3 The actual transfer of Chandigarh to Punjab and areas in lieu thereof to Haryana will take place simultaneously on January 26, 1986.

7.4 There are other claims and counter-claims for readjustment of the existing Punjab-Haryana boundaries. The government will appoint another commission to consider these matters and give its findings. Such findings will be binding on the concerned States. The terms of reference will be based on a village as a unit, linguistic affinity and contiguity.

8. *Centre-State relations.*

8.1 Shiromani Akali Dal states that the Anandpur Sahib resolution is entirely within the framework of the Indian Constitution, that it attempts to define the concept of Centre-State relations in a manner which may bring out the true federal characteristics of our unitary constitution, and that the purpose of the resolution is to provide greater autonomy to the States with a view to strengthening the unity and integrity of the country, since unity in diversity forms the corner-stone of our national entity.

8.2 In view of the above, the Anandpur Sahib Resolution in so far as it deals with Centre-State relations, stands referred to the Sarkaria Commission.

9. *Sharing of rivers water.*

9.1 The farmers of Punjab, Haryana and Rajasthan will continue to get water not less than what they are using from the Ravi-Beas system as on 1.7.1985. Water used for consumption purposes will also remain unaffected. Quantum of usage claimed shall be verified by the tribunal referred to in para 9.2 below.

9.2 The claims of Punjab and Haryana regarding the shares in their remaining water will be referred for adjudication to a tribunal to be presided over by a Supreme Court judge. The decision of this tribunal will be binding on both parties. All legal and constitutional steps required in this respect will be taken expeditiously.

9.3 The construction of the SYL canal shall continue. The canal shall be completed by August 15, 1986.

10. *Representation of minorities.*

10.1 Existing instructions regarding protection of interests of minorities will be recirculated to the State Chief Ministers. (PM will write to all Chief Ministers).

11.   *Promotion of Punjabi language.*

11.1 The Central Government may take some steps for the promotion of the Punjabi language.

This settlement brings to an end a period of confrontation and ushers in an era of amity, goodwill and cooperation, which will promote and strengthen the unity and integrity of India.

6   THE PUNJAB ACCORD OF 1985 AND ITS FAILURE

Sucha Singh Gill

The roots of the crisis

At the heart of the Punjab crisis is a profound paradox: Punjab, the most prosperous state of the Indian union in terms of per capita income and infrastructure facilities, is also one of its most unstable and violence-ridden. Over the past two decades the crisis in the Punjab has eluded all efforts to manage or contain it. As the crisis unfolded revealing its many dimensions – all of them dangerous – there has been heavy loss of life and enormous damage to property. All of this has served to disrupt the entire social and political process of the state, apart from the spillover effect on its neighbors, not to mention the country at large. It has distorted the thinking processes of a whole generation of people and dulled their sensibilities with respect to the brutalities that the conflict has engendered. In a situation close to anarchy, the people at large are caught between the terror of extremist activists and the pressure of the state's (i.e., the central government's and not the Punjab state's) elaborate machinery of oppression.

The roots of this crisis go back well into the past. This chapter will only guide the reader's attention to the existing literature on the subject,[1] and take up the analysis of the problem as it unfolded in the 1980s. The previous chapter also provides information on this background, and especially on the 1960s and 1970s, including the well known Anandpur Sahib resolution of 1973. The Punjab peace accord of July 1985 signed by Rajiv Gandhi the then Prime Minister of India, and Sant Harchand Singh Longowal then president of Akali Dal and the virtual dictator of the Akali Dal *Dharm Yudh Morcha* was a significant attempt at a political settlement of Punjab's many-sided crisis.

The peroration of the accord provides an interesting glimpse of the optimism of those who negotiated it, and the sanguinity of their hopes for a future based on its successful implementation:

> This settlement brings to an end a period of confrontation and ushers in an era of amity, goodwill and co-operation, which will promote and strengthen the unity and integrity of India.

There was euphoria all round at the successful culmination of the negotiations on the accord. The press hailed it as a signal achievement, and the hope was expressed that it would bring peace to this trouble-torn state. Soon this euphoria evaporated and hopes were dashed when violence returned. Within a month of his placing his signature to the accord, Longowal paid for it with his life.

Before we turn to an analysis of the clauses of the accord and an examination of the causes for its failure, we need to take a brief look at the violence in the Punjab in the 1980s.

The *Dharm Yudh Morcha* of 1982, organized by Longowal, was an expression of the frustration and anger of large sections of the Akalis against the attempts of Congress I to exploit divisions among them for partisan and short-term political benefits. One of the most prominent Congress supporters who resorted to this as early as the 1970s was Congress Chief Minister Zail Singh who later became President of India. To compete successfully with the Akalis, Congress leaders gave their patronage to several extremist individuals and groups, and thus caused serious damage to the democratic process in the state. Among the most prominent of the extremist groups sponsored and originally protected by the Congress was the Damdami Taksal of Sant Jarnail Singh Bhindranwale. There were also the Nirankari (considered hostile to Sikhism by many Sikhs) and the Nihangs associated with Baba Santa Singh.

A prelude to the crisis of the 1980s was an event which occurred on 13 April 1978. This was a clash between Nirankaris on the one hand and the Damdami Taksal of Bhindranwale and the Akhard Kirtani Jatha on the other, in which several Sikhs were killed when Nirankaris opened fire on them. In retaliation terrorist groups associated with the Bhindranwale and the Athand Kirtani Jatha killed several Nirankaris in Punjab. The Nirankari chief, Baba Gurbachan Singh, was assassinated in Delhi on 24 April 1980. Following this, Nirankari missions in the state were under great pressure, and many if not most of them were compelled to close. Political leaders, public figures, journalists and communal Hindu leaders became the targets of these groups when they condemned the attacks on the Nirankari.

Despite this intensifying violence the Congress leadership in the state continued to encourage and patronize these extremist groups in their policy of exploiting factional politics to their own advantage. Moderate Akalis, and eventually the Congress itself, found their political base crumbling under pressure from the extremists who soon became powers to be reckoned with in Punjabi politics. Although the Congress has to take the largest share of the blame for this very short-sighted policy and the misguided tactics of factionalism, their major rivals in the mainstream of Sikh politics are not without blame themselves. Thus the Akali Dal itself, which had instigated mass political agitation since 1982 for the acceptance by the center of a charter of demands based on the Anandpur Sahib resolution, also permitted extremist and violent groups to emerge and grow under its wing in order to pressurize the center. The spate of violence increased considerably as a result – whether in the form of bank hold-ups or the robbery of individuals, or the murder of public persons, journalists and other vocal sections of the community as well as innocent persons. The state responded to this breakdown of law and order with an increasing resort to repressive measures. Ultimately when the elected government failed to bring the situation under control, it was dismissed from office and the state brought under President's rule on 6 October 1983. Punjab was declared a disturbed area and unprecedented powers of search were granted to the police and paramilitary forces, and along with this the normal restraints on opening fire on individuals or groups seen to be intent on disturbing the peace were considerably relaxed. The strengthening of these repressive measures did not much dampen violence in the state, but there was no mistaking the increase in the victimization of innocent individuals.

Bhajan Lal the Congress Chief Minister of the neighboring state of Haryana was also responsible for aggravating the sense of grievance of the Sikhs. 1982 was the year of the Asian Games in Delhi, a prestige event on which the central government had expended an enormous amount of money in building infrastructure. With the Punjab in a disturbed state there were rumors of the possibility of Sikh extremists staging demonstrations or indulging in some symbolic acts of violence to draw world attention to their cause. Thus unprecedented security measures had to be taken. Whatever justification there may have been for these, overenthusiastic supporters of the government used the opportunity to embarrass and harass Sikhs travelling to Delhi either to see the games or on general private business. Bhajan Lal was instrumental in this.

At the time of the 1982 Asian Games all Sikhs who passed through Haryana were subjected to gruelling searches and humiliating questioning by gangs mobilized by the Chief Minister, while the state police remained silent spectators on the scene. Sikhs of elite status ranging from judges of the High Court, senior lawyers, doctors, and professors to government officials of various grades, found this belittling security search a mortifying experience. But most of them fared better than humbler Sikhs who were harassed and publicly beaten on the roads and railway tracks. Thus the Asian Games contributed in their own way to the process of alienation of the Sikh community.

As we have seen, the imposition of President's rule in Punjab did little to restore law and order in the state. On the contrary the situation worsened. As the violence increased further the state administration under President's rule took what can only be described as a self-destructive act of monumental proportions, when they permitted armed extremists and terrorist groups led by Bhindranwale to convert the Golden Temple the holiest of Sikh shrines into an armed fortress, and a convenient sanctuary of its squads of killers.

The unfolding of the tragedy of Operation Blue Star is too well known to be referred to in any detail here.[2] But one point needs special mention. The day chosen for the army attack on the Golden Temple was the martyrdom day of the fifth Sikh guru, Arjan Dev. Ceremonies associated with this had attracted many pilgrims who were totally unconnected with the Akali Dal. There were also unarmed volunteers of the Akali Dal who were also present in the temple complex for the purpose of courting arrest. Both groups were caught in the crossfire as the armed militants battled it out with the army, and they were among the large number of innocent men, women and children who were killed or injured in the clash. The attack on the complex caused considerable damage to many buildings there. All of this contributed to the wave of anger in Punjab directed against the Indian government and Prime Minister Indira Gandhi.

The attack on the Golden Temple was followed by Operation Woodrose in the rural areas of Punjab aimed at eradicating terrorism there. That objective proved to be beyond the capacity of the security forces. It only served to strengthen the leaders among the extremists who successfully eluded capture. As the entire Sikh/Akali leadership had already been taken into custody the initiative in organizing protests in various forms against these measures was now taken by the extremist groups who were greatly strengthened as a result. Their popular support among the Sikhs grew wider and stronger.

The violence continued within Punjab and soon spread to other parts of the country. It began with the assassination of Prime Minister Indira Gandhi on 31 October 1984 by two of her Sikh guards at her residence in Delhi. Seen among the Sikhs as an act of revenge for the desecration of the Golden Temple by the army, it was viewed differently by others. In the wake of the assassination came a massacre of Sikhs resident in Delhi and other parts of India. Sikh-owned property, houses and shops were put to the torch and it is estimated that over 3,500 Sikhs were killed in Delhi alone, with large-scale killings in Kanpur, Patna and Bokaro. Anti-Sikh violence was reported at 43 places throughout India. Investigative reports made by Indian civil liberties and democratic rights organizations revealed that Congress politicians with the help of state machinery were responsible for organizing some of the anti-Sikh violence.

With the top Sikh leadership in custody, and Punjab state in the control of the army, there was no mass protest within the Punjab against the violence that had followed the assassination of the Prime Minister. Among the Sikhs in Punjab power was now very much in the hands of groups of armed extremists without a centralized command, and they indulged in violence against soft targets. The whole cycle of violence and repression served to thoroughly discredit the traditional Sikh leadership of Akali Dal, and strengthened the influence of the more militant among the Akali factions, the extremist groups in particular. At the general election of March 1985 the Punjab situation was made an election issue by the Congress under Rajiv Gandhi. The slogan of the unity and integrity of the country in jeopardy as a result of the violence in the Punjab paid rich dividends for Congress and helped it to secure an unprecedented electoral victory.

The prelude to the Punjab Accord

Soon after his election victory Rajiv Gandhi took a number of decisive steps to regain the initiative on the Punjab issue. He appointed a Cabinet committee to review the problems there, ordered the release of some of the principal Akali Dal leaders who had been detained since the time of Operation Blue Star, lifted the ban that had been placed on the All India Sikh Students Federation, one of the more militant Sikh organizations, and he appointed a new governor for Punjab, Arjun Singh. Several conciliatory gestures were made, and these were the prelude to beginning serious negotiations with Longowal on the essentials of a political settlement on Punjab. Eventually on 24 July 1985 a peace accord was signed by Rajiv Gandhi and Longowal. The negotiations were based on the Akali demands embodied in the Anandpur Sahib resolution of 1973, and, more important, the demands made in 1981 by the Akali Dal. We turn to a brief review of these latter demands.

Before the start of the political agitation named *Dharm Yudh Morcha*, the Akali Dal had submitted a list of 45 demands in September 1981.

These were later reduced to 15 demands in a revised list presented in October 1981. In the second list some of the demands of the first list were grouped together and placed in the generalized category. However one new demand – topical in nature – had been included. This related to the release of Sant Jarnail Singh Bhindranwale who had been arrested earlier. In the original list the demands were divided into four categories: (i) religious; (ii) political; (iii) economic; and (iv) cultural. These demands along with the Anandpur Sahib Resolution demonstrate clearly the political objectives of the Akalis and their view of the grievances – of the Sikh community in particular, and, more generally, those of Punjab state. Not surprisingly one of their principal demands was for more autonomy for Punjab in which 'the Sikhs should enjoy special rights as a nation'. Next they wished to have the Punjabi-speaking Sikh enclaves in some of the neighboring states included in Punjab. These were: the whole of the Union Territory of Chandigarh; parts of Himachal Pradesh; some parts of Haryana; and six *tehsils* of the Sriganganagar district of Rajasthan. Given the importance placed on water for Punjab's efficient agriculture there was a demand for transfer of control of dams and headworks of the principal irrigation schemes to Punjab and for provision to be made for a settlement of river water disputes in accordance with national and international laws.

As regards the economic development of the state in general, there was a focus on the protection of the interests of the farming community, but there was a special concern also for the interests of the educated unemployed youth and weaker sections of the population. The core of the Akali Dal perspective was the creation of a larger Punjab with special rights for, if not dominance of, the Sikhs; a state which enjoyed a much greater degree of autonomy, and with the power of the center reduced to jurisdiction over foreign affairs, defence, currency and communication including means of transport. Looking beyond their state the Akali Dal insisted that Gurudwaras outside Punjab be brought under the control of Punjab Sikhs through enactment of an All India Gurudwara Act.

These demands naturally put the Akali Dal in confrontation with others. First, its objective of restricting the jurisdiction of the government at the center to the four portfolios mentioned earlier, was certain to meet strong resistance in Delhi. In class terms these demands attracted the opposition of big business and the bureaucracy. In regional terms there was the opposition of the Hindi heartland from where the largest number of members of parliament are elected and the largest number of cabinet ministers come. In political terms it invited opposition from the Congress I which has remained in control of the center government most of the time since independence and the BJP which wants a strong center and looks at the issue of autonomy as an attempt to weaken the Hindu country.

Secondly, the Akali claims for some parts of the territory of neighboring states to be included in Punjab, as well as for a larger share of or exclusive control over river waters claimed by the neighboring states, provoked the opposition of these states. Since the major part of territory claimed and the issue of river water affects the state of Haryana (exclusively carved out of the erstwhile Punjab), more than others, it has been in the forefront of the opposition to the Akali demands.

Thirdly, the Akali Dal's insistence on a special, if not privileged position for the Sikhs in Punjab was certain to be opposed by the minority groups there, especially the Hindus. At the 1981 census the Sikhs constituted 60.75 per cent of the total population of the state while Hindus were 36.93 per cent followed by Christians and Muslims who were 1.1 per cent and 1 per cent respectively. The Hindus, the second largest religious community in the state, outnumber Sikhs in three of the 12 districts of the state and outnumber Sikhs in the total urban population. In 1981 the urban population of the state was 4,647,757 out of which the Hindus were 2,981,804 (64.15 per cent) and the Sikhs 1,542,623 (33.19 per cent). Hindus are not only in a majority in urban areas and in aggregate at three district levels, they are much more articulate, politically organized and influential in the administration. The influence on the English press is very substantial. The Congress I and BJP enjoy a large support base among them. Lastly, the demand of the Akali Dal that an all India Gurudwara Act be enacted bringing Gurudwaras outside Punjab under the control of Sikhs of Punjab tended to alienate a section of Sikhs who were already in control of these Gurudwaras. Thus while the objectives of the Akali Dal provoked the opposition of powerful sections in society in and outside Punjab, they did not attract support from other political parties and non-Sikh sections of the population. The Akali Dal's sectarian religious approach has the tendency to isolate it from secular forces as well as other political parties in the country.

The long drawn out struggle in Punjab has created a set of new demands relating to the victims of the crisis – the large number of innocent persons killed and injured in the violence on all sides of the divide and the many young women widowed and children made orphans. These victims belong to both major communities, Sikh and Hindu. The growing incidence of extortions at gunpoint has added to the uncertainties of life in Punjab. A large number of persons have been killed by security forces in contrived encounters, and thousands of youths have been tortured in police custody prior to their incarceration. In these instances the victims have been Sikh youths. We need also to take account of the death of security personnel at the hands of militants and the killing of militants during conflicts with the security forces whether these were bona fide conflicts or contrived ones, i.e., contrived by the security forces.

The deaths during Operation Blue Star, and in the wake of the assassination of Indira Gandhi had added to the toll. In addition to this there was the large-scale destruction of property of the state and of private persons. From the people of the Punjab there has been a demand for control of militant violence on the one hand and a call for an end to state repression on the other, and along with these a clamor for the punishment of those responsible for the killing of innocent people – particularly the massacres after the assassination of Indira Gandhi in November 1984.

One of the most significant developments from the cycles of violence in Punjab has been a proliferation of armed extremist organizations who are beyond the control of the leadership. These organizations are opposed to Akalis of all factions. They berate them as traitors to the Sikh cause. Their campaigns have substantially reduced the mass appeal and mobilizing capacity of the Akali Dals. As fervent advocates of separatism their goal is the establishment of Khalistan, an independent Sikh state. Inevitably, therefore, they were opposed to any political settlement which falls short of that.

The resolution of the Punjab crisis involved consultation with, if not the active support of, several contending parties: the Akali Dal/Dals; militant armed underground organizations; the central government; Congress I; and other opposition parties in Punjab; the neighboring states of Haryana, Rajasthan and Himachal Pradesh; urban Hindu organizations in Punjab; and Sikhs outside Punjab. The issues to be settled were: Akali demands; demands of Sikh militant organizations; and demands of Hindu organizations. Some of the issues had been lingering since 1966, while other issues have emerged as a result of the pattern of development on capitalist lines in Punjab,[3] and there are the new issues created by the long struggle between the contending parties.

The Punjab Accord

The Punjab Accord has 11 clauses.[4] Four out of the first six clauses deal with grievances of the Sikhs that had arisen during and out of the crisis of the 1970s and 1980s. The first clause has to do with payment of compensation to the innocent persons killed in agitation on or after 1 August 1982, and for property damaged or destroyed. Clause 3 relates to the institution of an inquiry into the November 1984 riots. The jurisdiction of the Commission to be appointed was widened to cover disturbances at Bokaro and Kanpur in addition to the disturbances at Delhi. Clause 4 deals with rehabilitation of Sikh soldiers discharged from the armed forces on account of their leaving their barracks following Operation Blue Star. Clause 6 referred to the disposal of pending cases against the persons arrested before and after Operation Blue Star and the withdrawal of the notification applying the Armed Forces Special Powers Act to Punjab. All such cases except (a) those relating to the waging of war against the state and (b) hijacking of planes, was to be transferred to the ordinary courts. Clause 2 promised that recruitment to the army would be made on the criterion of merit, for all the citizens in the country. Under clause 5 it was agreed that an All India Gurudwara Bill would be introduced after consultation with the Akali Dal and others concerned. Clauses 7, 8 and 9 which cover respectively territorial issues, center-state relations and sharing of river waters, dealt with the most sensitive issues, those which formed the core of the Akali demands. While Punjab's exclusive claims to Chandigarh were upheld it was agreed that Haryana would be compensated for this by the transfer of some Hindi-speaking territory from Punjab. The transfers were to be effected on or before 26 January 1986.

For a settlement of other territorial claims between Punjab and Haryana the central government agreed to appoint a commission of inquiry which would base its recommendations for re-adjustment of boundaries on linguistic affinity and contiguity and would use villages as units for this purpose. On the sharing of Ravi-Beas river waters between Punjab, Haryana and Rajasthan it was decided that the quantity of water available to them would be based on actual usage as of 1 July 1985. The claims of the respective states for water above and beyond this quantity were to be referred for adjudication to a tribunal presided over by a Supreme Court judge. The decision of this tribunal was to be given within six months and was to be binding for both parties. On the issue of center-state relations it was decided to refer the Anandpur Sahib resolution to the Sarkaria Commission which had already been set up to examine center-state relations in India as a whole. The clause 10 of the accord dealing with representation of minorities stated that existing instructions would be recirculated to Chief Ministers of states by the Prime Minister. The last clause stated that the Central Government would take steps to promote the Punjabi language. There was no indication of what these steps were to be.

From this brief summary of its contents it would seem that the accord as such touched only the fringes of the Akali demands and the long-term program of the party. It did not touch the controversial issue of the special rights of Sikhs in the state, much less the even more controversial one of a Sikh dominated Punjab. It completely ignored the issues of the pricing of agricultural produce, industrialization of the state and, even more important to Punjab, the transfer of control of dams and irrigation headworks to the state. Where some issues like recruitment in the army, an All India Gurudwara Act, center-state relations, representation of minorities and promotion of the Punjabi language are addressed, the references are vague assurances rather than a clear and specific acceptance of demands raised.

Only in regard to two issues was there any specificity. These are territorial issues (clause 7) and the sharing of river waters (clause 9). In both cases a time-bound implementation program was given. But in the process of drafting these clauses some serious complications were created. Clause 7 categorically states:

> The capital project area of Chandigarh will go to Punjab.... It has always been maintained by Smt. Indira Gandhi that when Chandigarh goes to Punjab some Hindi-speaking territories in Punjab will go to Haryana. A Commission will be constituted to determine the specific Hindi-speaking areas of Punjab which should go to Haryana in lieu of Chandigarh ... The actual transfer of Chandigarh to Punjab and areas in lieu thereof to Haryana will take place simultaneously on 26th January 1986.

It is further stated that for the determination of other territorial claims between Punjab and Haryana, the central government would appoint another Commission. Thus two Commissions were to be appointed, one for identifying Hindi-speaking areas in Punjab to be transferred as compensation for Chandigarh and the other for identifying Hindi-speaking areas in Punjab and Punjabi-speaking areas in Haryana for mutual transfer in the process of modification of boundaries. Similarly clause 9 of the accord states:

> The farmers of Punjab, Haryana and Rajasthan will continue to get water not less than what they are using from Ravi-Beas system as on July 1, 1985. Quantum of usage claimed shall be verified, the share in their remaining water will be referred for adjudication to a Tribunal presided over by a Supreme Court judge.

It is estimated that on this particular date Punjab used 6.4 million acre feet (MAF) while Haryana drew only 1.3 MAF. Earlier on Punjab's share had never been more than 4.22 MAF while Haryana's share was not less than 3.5 MAF.[5] Since these two issues directly affected Haryana, there was strong opposition to this clause of the accord from that state. The fact is that the accord did not provide an adequate base to satisfy all these parties. However, had clauses 7 and 9 been scrupulously implemented it could have increased the degree of understanding between parties concerned and created a more congenial atmosphere for resolving pending issues.

The implementation of the accord was bound to be difficult if not impossible the way it was arrived at. First, Haryana state which is directly and adversely affected by its implementation was not made a party in the negotiations or the signing of the accord. Secondly, Sikh militant armed groups were also not associated in the process. They killed Sant Longowal who signed the accord within a month labelling him a 'traitor' to the Sikhs and the accord a 'sell out' of Sikh interests.

After the signing of the accord a declaration was made that elections to Punjab Assembly would be held in September 1985. Despite Longowal's assassination Rajiv Gandhi honored the pledge to proceed with holding these elections by the due date. At these elections the Akali Dal (Longowal) captured power and its President, Surjit Singh Barnala was sworn in as Chief Minister.[6] Unfortunately, with the formation of the Akali Ministry in the state, the central government, under pressure from Congress I and opposition leaders in Haryana, began to drag its feet on the Chandigarh issue and Chandigarh was not transferred to Punjab on the specified date, 26 January 1985. This marked the beginning of a process of non-implementation of some of the crucial clauses of the accord, leading in turn to the abandonment of the accord.

In retrospect it seems that Rajiv Gandhi, after his convincing victory at the general elections of 1985, went ahead with the negotiation and signing of the Punjab Accord, ignoring the pressure of Haryana Congress I leaders, in order to buy peace with the Sikhs. After the signing of the accord, opposition in Haryana emerged led by an opposition leader Devi Lal who began organizing a *Nayay Morcha* on the pattern of the Akali *Dharm Yudh Morcha* in Punjab. As his movement evoked a strong response from the Haryana peasantry, Congress I leaders in that state led by Chief Minister Bhajan Lal became nervous and exerted pressure on Rajiv Gandhi to retrace his steps. At the same time, after the assassination of Sant Longowal, Surjit Singh Barnala who succeeded him appeared to have consolidated his position in the early stages, but his position within the party was eroded as a result of factionalism, chiefly the combined opposition of the former Chief Minister, P.S. Badal and the SGPC[7] Chief G.S. Tohra within the Akali Dal while extremist groups stepped up their violence, accompanied by mass mobilization by the United Akali Dal led by Baba Joginder Singh, father of the late Sant Jarnail Singh, Bhindranwale, from outside. The weakened position of the pro-accord elements within Akali Dal proved to be a handicap for them in mounting sufficient pressure on Rajiv Gandhi to honor his obligations under the accord. As a result an opportunity to begin an era of peace and cooperation was lost.

The narrow sectarian party politics also undermined the credibility of the Prime Minister himself and the central government. The Commissions appointed for settlement of territorial and river water disputes gave every impression of succumbing to pressure from the Congress I leadership at the national level. The resulting loss of credibility in the judiciary completed a dismal picture in a situation that deteriorated to the point where no Akali leader worth the name was prepared to engage in a dialogue with the central government to revive the lost momentum of the accord. Instead the Akalis preferred a dialogue with underground militant organizations who were engaged in fearful internecine rivalries themselves. The Akalis were not interested any longer in referring contentions to any Commission. What they sought were immediate unilateral announcements of acceptance of pending demands.

In the meantime violence was the order of the day through the late 1980s and into the 1990s.[8] Punjab has seen the rise and fall of fortunes of the Congress I and Akali Dals as political parties and governing parties, and also of many individuals as political leaders and governors of the state. With the assassination of Rajiv Gandhi in May 1991 even the memory of the accord which he negotiated with such hope may fade away.

Notes

1. See, Paul R. Brass (1974) *Language, Religion and Politics in North India*, Cambridge: Cambridge University Press; Robin Jeffrey (1986) *What's Happening to India? Punjab, Ethnic Conflict, Mrs. Gandhi's Death and the Test for Federalism*, London: Macmillan; Rajiv A. Kapur (1986) *Sikh Separatism: The Politics of Faith*, London: Allen & Unwin; Sucha Singh Gill and

K.C. Singhal (1984) Historical Roots of Punjab Problem, *EPW* 7 April; Sucha Singh Gill (1988) Contradictions of Punjab Model of Growth and Search for Alternatives, *EPW*, 15 October.

2. Mark Tully and Sathis Jacob (1985) *Amritsar: Mrs. Gandhi's Last Battle*, London:Hamish Hamilton; Lt. Gen. (Retd.) J.S. Aurora (1984) Assault on the Gold Temple, in Amarjit Kaur, *et al.* (eds), *The Punjab Story*, Delhi.

3. See my article, Contradictions of Punjab model of growth and search for alternatives, *EPW*, 15 October 1988; see also Sucha Singh Gill and K.C. Singhal (1984) Farmers' agitation: Response to development crisis of agriculture, *EPW*, 6 October.

4. For the text of the Punjab Accord, see *The Indian Express*, Chandigarh, 25 July 1985.

5. The question of sharing surplus Ravi-Beas (rivers flowing through Punjab territory) water is a most difficult one. This water is to be distributed between the states of Punjab, Haryana and Rajasthan. All these states are facing acute shortages of water for irrigation purposes. Along with surface water, Punjab has gone in for use of ground water resources in a big way. As a consequence, the water table in the state is falling at an alarming rate. Seventy-five per cent of the development blocks in the state have exhausted their capacity for further increase in tubewells and pumpsets. There is a greater need of the state to have a larger share if not exclusive right to the river waters. The same is true of Haryana and Rajasthan. This is necessitated by the present green revolution cropping pattern requiring more and more irrigation in the semi-arid climatic zone. With the present cropping pattern it is very difficult if not impossible to get these states to agree on the issue.

6. For the election see, Gopal Singh (ed.) (1987) *The Punjab Today*, New Delhi, especially M.S. Dhami, Shifts in the party support base in 1985 Punjab assembly elections: A preliminary analysis, pp. 286–304 in this volume.

7. This was the Shiromani Gurudwara Prabundhak Committee.

8. See Pramod Kumar (1991) Punjab: No alternative to Political Struggle. *Mainstream*, XXIX (24), 6 April. It is estimated that the number of persons killed *in Punjab* since 1981 is between 14,000 and 18,000. See the *Tribune*, Chandigarh, 6 January 1992, and the *Indian Express*, Chandigarh, 5 January 1992.

7 THE MAKING OF THE INDO-SRI LANKA ACCORD THE FINAL PHASE: JUNE–JULY 1987

K.M. de Silva

Introduction

The Indo-Sri Lanka Accord signed on 29 July 1987 was over three years in the making. Earlier phases in the negotiating process have been reviewed elsewhere[1] and only some of their salient features will be summarized in this brief but essential introduction to this chapter. Three distinct phases in the negotiations can be identified: the first, from the end of July 1983 to the assassination of the Indian Prime Minister, Mrs Indira Gandhi, in November 1984; the second, which began in early 1985 under her son and successor as Prime Minister, Rajiv Gandhi, ends in the first quarter of 1986; and the third began in early 1986 and came to an end in June 1987.

We need to begin with Mrs Gandhi's well-timed initiative to secure for India the role of sole mediator in a complex ethnic conflict in a small neighboring state. She chose the chaotic situation in Sri Lanka that resulted from the anti-Tamil riots of late July 1983 as the opportune moment to make her move. The Sri Lanka government faced widespread criticism for its mishandling of the riots and was thus in no position to refuse this offer to mediate – an offer that is best described as one that could not be refused – from its powerful neighbor.[2] Mrs Gandhi chose as her special envoy to Sri Lanka for these negotiations a trusted confidant and able diplomatist, G. Parathasarathy. His task was to reconcile the demands of the Tamil minority for a substantial measure of regional autonomy with the need to preserve the territorial integrity of the island state. The spokesmen for the Tamil minority, the mainstream Tamil United Liberation Front (TULF) at this stage, insisted that the unit of devolution should be a province (there are nine in the island) and not a district (there are two or three in each province and the Northern province has four) as it had been since the establishment of the District Development Councils (DDCs) in 1981, and over and beyond that a larger Tamil ethno-region be created through the amalgamation of the Northern and Eastern provinces.

Parathasarathy's negotiations yielded a document which bore the unusual title of 'Annexure C' incorporating these among other proposals. Opinions differ as to the authorship of this document but it would appear that President Jayewardene was actually involved in its drafting. President J.R. Jayewardene, placed this document, along with other proposals, for debate at a conference of political parties and other groups called the All Party Conference (APC). While 'Annexure C' did not get much support at this conference a complex set of proposals, based on the consensus that emerged on the devolution of power at its discussions, was presented by the government. Nevertheless the talks broke down by the end of the year. The TULF rejected these proposals and when that happened the government withdrew its own support for them.[3]

It was left to Rajiv Gandhi to revive the mediatory process, and in a more cordial atmosphere – so far as the Sri Lankan government saw it – than before. Instead of continuing with the negotiations that had been stalled at the end of 1984, it was decided to make a fresh start, with Romesh Bhandari India's Foreign Secretary, the head of the foreign service establishment, serving as the principal negotiator.[4] Bhandari persuaded the Sri Lankan government to agree to widening the range of participants in the negotiating process by bringing in Tamil separatist activist groups who were now more representative of Tamil opinion than the TULF. These groups and the TULF participated in two rounds of negotiations with representatives of the Sri Lanka government, held at Thimpu, the capital of Bhutan, with Bhandari serving as mediator. These talks held in July and August 1985 failed, but negotiations continued thereafter in Delhi between Bhandari and other Indian officials with the Sri Lankan delegates to the Thimpu talks. This time only the TULF was consulted.

The Delhi negotiations were much more fruitful and agreement was reached on the framework of devolution of power in Sri Lanka. Two key factors, both important concessions made by the Sri Lankan government, were: recognition of the province as the unit of devolution; and a substantial strengthening of the powers granted to these provincial units. The agreement which came to be known as the Delhi Accord was initialled on 30 August. This draft accord became the basis of all future negotiations between the two governments on Sri Lanka's ethnic problems in so far as these concerned the Tamil minority. None of the Tamil groups would support the accord because the most powerful of them, the Liberation Tigers of Tamil Eelam (LTTE), were opposed to anything short of a separate Tamil state, and were intent on imposing their will on all their rivals in this regard. This latter included the TULF who had been consulted in regard to the principles and details of the Delhi Accord. By December 1985 they too had repudiated it.[5]

The third phase in India's mediatory role began in the first quarter of 1986, and one of the principals in it was Bhandari's successor as Foreign Secretary, A.P. Venkateswaran, who endeavored to make the Delhi Accord more acceptable to the Tamil groups active in separatist agitation in Sri Lanka by refining it to fit the mold of an Indian model – the states in India's quasi-federal system. There was another significant departure. For the first time the leadership in the mediation process was delegated to Indian politicians, P. Chidambaram, a young Congress politician from Tamil Nadu and Natwar Singh, Rajiv Gandhi's Minister of State for External Affairs. Together they visited Sri Lanka three times in 1986 in an effort to persuade President Jayewardene and his cabinet to proceed beyond the Delhi Accord in so far as the powers conceded to the provinces was concerned. The Sri Lanka government, for its part, accepted the adoption of the Indian state system as a model although this was never made explicit. With the consent of the other Tamil groups, the TULF was pushed forward as the lead team for the Tamils on negotiations with the Sri Lanka government and other Sri Lankan parties in the Political Parties Conference (PPC) which began its discussions in July 1986. This time the negotiations were a great success, and a consensus emerged on the nature of the devolution package for Sri Lanka.[6]

There were two insuperable difficulties. The LTTE rejected these proposals as inadequate; the TULF for its part continued to insist on the creation of a Tamil ethno-region encompassing the Northern and Eastern provinces. The PPC consensus did not extend beyond a system of provincial councils to this larger and more controversial entity and one which all Sinhalese parties rejected.

The proposals agreed to in September 1986 formed the basis of negotiations between President Jayewardene and Prime Minister Rajiv Gandhi when they met in Bangalore at the summit of the South Asian Association for Regional Cooperation (SAARC) on 17 and 18 December. The Delhi Accord of 1985 and the refinements of it negotiated in 1986 were formally approved, and a timetable was set for the signing of the Accord by the two governments in January 1987. However the political future of the multi-ethnic Eastern province remained an intractable problem.

Chidambaram and Natwar Singh visited Colombo on 24 November and again on 18–19 December in a futile bid to make a breakthrough on this. Two proposals were made, one a trifurcation of the province into Tamil, Sinhalese and Muslim areas, with the Tamil unit linked to the Northern province through a narrow land corridor. When every group in the island refused to accept this, the Indian negotiators made a second proposal, to excise the Ampara district (largely Muslim and Sinhalese) or failing that the largely Sinhalese Ampara parliamentary electorate from the Eastern province. Not a single group would agree to this. Thus by the end of the year, a carefully negotiated settlement was held up by the refusal of the Tamil groups to abandon their insistence on a larger Tamil ethno-region linking the Northern and Eastern provinces.[7]

All these negotiations took place against the background of regular outbursts of ethnic violence, especially in the north and east of the island, and clashes between the security forces and Tamil guerrillas and terrorist groups. Greatly improved relations between the two countries after Rajiv Gandhi became Prime Minister of India did not extend to any serious efforts to prevent the use of Indian territory by guerrillas and terrorists for attacks on a friendly neighbor, much less to close down these facilities and camps despite the assurances given to President Jayewardene in Delhi in June 1985. Nor, more importantly, did the supply of arms through Indian agencies to the various Tamil separatist groups stop. Rajiv Gandhi, so much less dependent on a southern political base than his mother, and intent on taking a more even-handed approach than her to the problems posed by Sri Lanka's ethnic conflicts, found his options for leverage more limited than he would have liked them to be. And the constraint lay in the ethnic politics of Tamil Nadu and the public support the Sri Lankan Tamils enjoyed there. The Tamil guerrillas and terrorist groups continued to have training facilities and bases in Tamil Nadu and ready access to sophisticated weapons and money.[8]

The Tamil separatist groups in Sri Lanka all had their supporters among the political parties of Tamil Nadu, government and opposition parties alike. They were barely able to avoid being drawn into the internecine warfare that became a prominent feature of the parties of the Tamils of Sri Lanka. Although the bloodiest of these encounters took place in Jaffna as the LTTE fought its way to a position of pre-eminence, the conflict spilled over occasionally to Tamil Nadu as well, and every so often compelled one or the other of the prominent Tamil Nadu parties to back one side or the other, often in a desperate attempt to keep the peace among their proteges and to prevent any single group from totally eliminating all the others. Just as often, efforts would be made to bring them together in a single umbrella organization, but all such efforts failed.[9] The Indian government for its part steered clear of these divisive and self-destructive antagonisms so common to exile groups, but one of its intelligence arms, the Research and Analysis Wing (RAW), sought to exploit these divisions for the benefit of what it perceived to be India's national interest. In general the Indian government showed a preference for the TULF, the mainstream party, whose strength – such as it was – lay in Delhi rather than in Jaffna or elsewhere.

The Sri Lanka government could do little about the internecine warfare of the Tamil groups in Jaffna however fearsome they were and despite the heavy toll of life. When clashes occurred between the Tamil separatist groups and the security forces, there was serious concern about these because of their potential for eroding the government's base of political support. These political difficulties were aggravated when the Tamil guerrillas and terrorists turned their guns on unarmed Sinhalese civilians in the remoter parts of the north-central and eastern regions, or on specially chosen symbolic targets such as the ancient city of Anuradhapura where, in May 1985, 150 civilians were killed in one raid, and attacks were made on religious sites in that city venerated by the Buddhist population as among the holiest in the Buddhist world.

It was only in the last weeks of 1986, during and after the Rajiv Gandhi–J.R. Jayewardene talks in Bangalore, that the Indian government began to take measures to make it difficult for these Tamil groups to operate from Tamil Nadu with the freedom they had been accustomed to. At this point the LTTE leadership, including its leader V. Prabhakaran, decided to move back to Jaffna from Tamil Nadu. Their arrival in Jaffna triggered off a series of events that culminated in the first episode in the Indian government's direct intervention in Sri Lankan affairs as an overt supporter of the Sri Lankan Tamil cause.[10]

It would appear that the LTTE leadership was intent on disrupting the agreement that the two governments were on the verge of signing. To do this they hit upon the notion of a unilateral declaration of independence for the north of the island. In an attempt to pre-empt such a declaration the Sri Lanka government sent troop reinforcements into the Northern and Eastern provinces with instructions to clear these areas of the LTTE and other separatist groups. Contrary to expectations the LTTE did not put up much of a fight. Instead they fled to the Jaffna peninsula in considerable disarray.

The Indian government, much perturbed by these developments, and obviously concerned about the reaction of Tamil Nadu to this weakening of the LTTE, began to put diplomatic and political pressure on the Sri Lankan government to abandon these military moves, and to resume the search for a political solution. As a result of these, and especially the public expressions of displeasure from New Delhi, relations between the two governments were strained through much of February and March 1987.

On 14 March 1987 another Indian emissary, Dinesh Singh, a Minister of State, arrived in Colombo for discussions with President Jayewardene in the hope that the political process could be revived. In response the Sri Lankan government offered the Tamil separatist activists a cease-fire for the duration of the national holidays in the period from 12 April to about 20 April. The LTTE spurned this offer and responded with the Good Firday bus massacre where 130 persons were mowed down by automatic weapons on the road from Trincomalee to Colombo. The Eelam Revolutionary Organization Students (EROS) group, the LTTE's allies followed this up with a bomb explosion in Colombo's main bus station a few days later, in which over 150 persons were killed.

Faced with a serious erosion of political support as a result of these outrages, the government decided to make an attempt to regain control of the Jaffna peninsula. 'Operation Liberation' which began on 26 May 1987 in the Vadamarachchi division in the north-eastern part of the peninsula was directed at preventing the hitherto easy movements of men and *matériel* from Tamil Nadu. It was also chosen as a target because Prabhkaran's home town was located there. By the end of May, Sri Lankan forces had gained control of this area. The LTTE, the most formidable Tamil separatist group, had suffered a serious setback, and in a region they had long dominated.

At this point India moved swiftly to prevent the subjugation of the Jaffna peninsula by the Sri Lankan forces. There was first a well-publicized monetary grant of US $3.2 million from the Tamil Nadu government to the LTTE and its allies. The Indian government, for its part, escalated the level of its own involvement in the Sri Lanka imbroglio when it announced that it would be sending shipments of food and petroleum products to Jaffna which, it claimed, was facing a severe shortage of these items through a blockade by the Sri Lankan forces. Despite the refusal of the Sri Lanka government to accept this offer, or concede the need for it, a first shipment, in a flotilla of about 20 Indian fishing vessels, was dispatched on 3 June 1987. It was turned back by the Sri Lanka navy. When this happened, the Indian Air Force in a blatant violation of international law and of the Sri Lankan airspace, used five Indian Antonov-22 transport planes escorted by four Mirage-2000 combat planes to drop food and medical supplies in Jaffna on the following day, 22 tons in all. All these constituted an unmistakable demonstration of Indian support for the Tamil separatist movement in Sri Lanka. The Indian supply of food to Jaffna continued over the next few weeks by sea with the formal but clearly reluctant agreement of the Sri Lankan government. The result was that, by the end of June, Indo-Sri Lankan relations were mired in mutual recrimination and deep suspicion. And the island's ethnic conflict seemed headed for prolonged and debilitating deadlock.

This limited demonstration of Indian power against a small neighbor had achieved a number of objectives which those who planned these operations had set themselves. It had stopped any expansion of the Sri Lanka army's campaign in the Jaffna peninsula after the Vadamarachchi expedition; it had saved the LTTE from any further weakening of its military strength; and above all it had reduced the Sri Lanka government to political impotence in regard to its initiatives on the Tamil problem.[11]

Early initiatives–June 1987

The renewal of the negotiating process in June 1987 led eventually to the belated signing of the accord which the two governments had originally scheduled for January 1987. The main phases in this, outlined below, form a classic study in the demonstration of the limits of a small power's initiatives when it confronts a regional power intent on imposing its will on it. All the initiatives now lay with the regional power, India.

What happened over the next four weeks was a superb demonstration of the 'art of ambivalence' which the high priest of the extension of India's power, K. Subhramanyam, has spoken of in relation to Pakistan.

> The art of ambivalence is to let the people know that one has the capability, then to deny that the capability is backed by intention to do what one can, to drop hints that it may have to be done under certain contingencies, then more hints that such a course has been imposed upon the party by external circumstances, then again to deny the development, inspire those not in authority to disclose the possibility of it, allow discussions to take place on the general assumption of the capability, once again officially deny it, release some partial but inadequate information about the capability, carry out actions which tend to reinforce the suspicions, issue statements that confirm interest in dispelling any suspicion yet vehemently deny having embarked on the course of action.[12]

Within a fortnight of the Indian 'food-drop' there were talks once more of a negotiated settlement of the Sri Lanka conflict through Indian mediation. Those who had some inkling of these early moves would not take them too seriously. They had heard of peace moves so often and just as often these had come to nothing. How was it possible to expect something more fruitful after the Indian humiliation of Sri Lanka, and the resultant bitter anti-Indian feeling in the country? The general belief was that Sri Lanka would be under tremendous pressure to make more concessions to the Tamil separatists.

On 12 June 1987 Gamini Dissanayake, Minister of Lands, Land Development and Mahaveli Development received what turned out to be the first of three feelers.[13] It came in the form of a letter from N. Ram the influential Associate Editor of the well-known Madras-based Indian newspaper, the *Hindu*. Dissanayake had come to know Ram during his visits to India as Chairman of the Board of Control for Cricket in Sri Lanka. Ram and his newspaper had taken an active interest in Sri Lanka's Tamil problem ever since it became a major divisive issue in the region, and had been in touch with many of the principal figures in the negotiations between the two countries, including President Jayewardene himself. Given Ram's easy access – at that time – to Rajiv Gandhi the presumption was that the contents of the letter had been discussed with the Indian Prime Minister himself, and had his approval. The letter outlined a set of proposals for a possible settlement of the Sri Lankan crisis through Indian mediation. These were: first, the Sri Lanka government would not re-open military operations in the Jaffna peninsula; second, the Sri Lanka government would remove all embargoes then in force for the transport of food and other essentials to Jaffna, and would restore telecommunications facilities; third, the government and the LTTE should agree to attend appropriate talks with Indian mediation. The talks should be held at any agreed venue. Some agreement should be reached about a broad recognition of Tamil rights in a pluralistic society, and the devolution of authority to a Tamil-dominated ethnic area/areas, within the framework of Sri Lanka's independence and territorial integrity, and with appropriate safeguards for other ethnic groups in that area. Finally, and most important of all, India would play a mediatory role in all discussions, and would underwrite the implementation of any agreement reached.

Ram's letter was one of the important early phases in the train of events that led to the signing of the Indo-Sri Lanka Accord in July 1987. The letter was transmitted to President Jayewardene. He looked upon it as a possible breakthrough in the situation of deadlock after the Indian airdrop and as a means of using Indian power to check the LTTE's political ambitions in Sri Lanka. That was the only option available to him after Prime Minister Rajiv Gandhi had demonstrated India's perception of the permissible limits of Sri Lanka's military action in re-imposing control over the Jaffna peninsula. The Indian High Commissioner, J.N. Dixit was given a mandate to begin negotiations within the framework of the principles enunciated in Ram's letter.

After these negotiations had commenced, and were proceeding apace, they received a setback because of a stiff official response from India to an announcement by the Sri Lanka government that local government elections would be held in Sri Lanka along with by-elections to 16 vacant parliamentary seats in the Northern and Eastern provinces. The TULF who held these seats vacated them after the passage of the 6th amendment to the constitution in 1983, which placed a ban on the advocacy of separatism as a political objective, and required all MPs to take an oath to uphold Sri Lanka's unitary constitution.

While the local government elections could have gone ahead if the government really persisted with them, it seems unlikely that the by-elections could have been held in the Northern and Eastern provinces in the context of the prevailing situation, with the LTTE riding high because of the newly established rapport with the Indian government and with the TULF unlikely to contest in the face of the opposition of the LTTE and of the Indians. The Indian riposte which came on 1 July surprised President Jayewardene. It took the form of a personal and confidential message from Rajiv Gandhi to him, delivered by High Commissioner Dixit at the President's private residence in Ward Place at 7:30 in the evening.[14] It read as follows:

1. While there is no intention at all to interfere in the internal affairs of Sri Lanka, the Government of India has taken note of recent formal decisions taken by [sic] Sri Lankan government to hold bye-elections to 16 vacant Parliamentary seats from the North and the East of Sri Lanka and to hold elections to Municipal Councils, Urban Councils and Pradeshiya Sabhas.

   It is the Government of India's assessment that going in for these elections without resolving the ethnic problem on the basis of a durable framework of compromises by peaceful means, will only prolong the ethnic crisis of Sri Lanka, including the violence which characterizes this crisis.

   To India this also implies that the processes that we have followed since 1983 to evolve a compromise are no longer valid. The Government of India has also taken note of the views expressed by all other important political Parties in Sri Lanka opposing these proposed elections. In this context, the President may carefully consider the implications of holding these elections unilaterally and then take a final decision.

2. India suggested that relief supplies to Jaffna may continue for some more time in response to genuine needs of the people there. The relief operations have also helped in bringing down the temperature and reducing violence in the peninsula. The time so gained can be utilized for positive purposes.

3. The government of India believes that a peaceful political solution to the ethnic problem is possible if the Sri Lankan government evolves a genuine solution which would meet the basic concerns of the Tamils. If the Sri Lankan government has any further ideas in this regard, India would be willing to co-operate on the basis of such ideas to evolve a compromise with the Tamils. Prime Minister would like to have His Excellency President Jayewardene's reactions to this suggestion if any.

It was a blatant act of interference in Sri Lanka's internal affairs and it rattled President Jayewardene, who could not reconcile its tone and contents with the feeler sent through M. Ram, and the negotiations that had begun on that basis. On 2 July he gave an interview to the late Professor Edward Azar, the Lebanese-American head of the Center for International Development and Conflict Management at the University of Maryland who was then on a brief visit to Sri Lanka. President Jayewardene was in a very thoughtful and reflective mood on that occasion, deeply disturbed by the very muted criticisms of the Indian actions from the Western powers, especially the US. Naturally, Indo-Sri Lankan relations figured very prominently in the discussions of which Azar kept a comprehensive record.[15] Two brief extracts from that document are quoted below. They have a particular poignancy and sadness in the light of recent events – the assassination of Rajiv Gandhi by the LTTE.

India says the ball is in our court. However I am not sure to whom to throw it back. In this, India is engaged in threatening the future of Sri Lanka and perhaps the region. Unless India acts positively, the future of Sri Lanka will witness hard times but so will the future of India. You can not play with fire without worrying about the spread of it to beyond what you control.

The second extract reads thus:

. . . Sri Lanka wonders who is helping increase the level of victimization and violence. India may be weakening itself by helping those who would destabilise Sri Lanka . . .

The Sri Lankan government returned the ball to the Indian side of the court. It took the form of a telegram dated 6 July in which President Jayewardene explained Sri Lanka's views. This important note is quoted in full below.

There is reference in your note about the elections we propose to hold in the North and East. These elections are necessary to enable people to express their views. These will in no way mitigate against a political settlement. Once a political settlement is arrived at, if necessary, these election results can be reviewed.

To postpone elections would be to continue the freeze placed on democracy in the Northern Province. This is exactly what the LTTE/EROS wants to ensure.

We note that during the period of relief supplies the LTTE has activated their sea movements from India and consequent to that they have attacked our Army establishments. The LTTE have done this despite their [sic] own cessation of hostilities during the period of relief. Do you expect the Sri Lanka Government to remain inactive in the face of such threats [?].

We stand committed in making every effort to resolve this matter politically. We believe that the TULF and also the other terrorist groups which have lost their military power may want to do so but on our present information it is quite clear that the LTTE and probably the EROS do not want anything other than a Separate State. Recent LTTE settlement [sic] confirm their intransigence. We are convinced that the LTTE will come for talks only when, like the other terrorists groups, their military power is sharply reduced. We seek your co-operation to do so.

However, we are prepared to discuss the following ideas to resolve the current problem within Sri Lanka:

(a) Specific discussions regarding alleged grievances of the Tamil community covering the whole of Sri Lanka, particularly those matters referred to in the UNP Manifesto of 1977.

(b) The establishment of Provincial Councils set out in June 1986 and the improvement and adjustment made thereafter.

(c) A setting up of the Boundary Commission to determine the boundaries of the Northern and Eastern Provinces in order to elevate [sic][16] the fears of all communities.

(d) Setting up of Inter Provincial Councils enabling cooperation between different Councils on any matter of the devolved subjects. We are prepared to discuss further details of the modalities of Inter Provincial Councils.

(e) The wishes of all the communities in the Northern and Eastern Provinces must be considered and there must be accommodation of their views.[17]

Throughout this period there appeared to be no sign of improvement in relations. Indeed Sri Lanka was intent on boycotting a SAARC ministerial meeting scheduled for early July in Delhi, and it required considerable persuasion from Pakistan and Bangladesh to get the Sri Lanka government to send its Foreign Minister A.C.S. Hameed, to attend this meeting. Yet a dramatic change occurred between 7 and 15 July 1987. What happened to bring about this change? One factor was, probably, President Jayewardene's note of 6 July. Secondly, it would appear that the Indians, and Dixit in particular, had received a signal from the LTTE just at this time offering to accept the 18–19 December 1986 proposals if an amalgamation of the Northern and Eastern provinces was incorporated into them.[18] Once this 'signal' was received messages flashed between Colombo and New Delhi and both leaders felt that this would help break the deadlock.

President Jayewardene seized the opportunity to lay down his own conditions. He indicated that the offer contained in his note of 6 July was '... conditional to an acceptance of the Proposals from 4.5.86 to 19.12.86, and the relevant proposals finalized on [sic] 30.8.85 to 13.9.85'. It was, in short, an insistence on the continuity of the negotiating process that had been interrupted by the Sri Lankan campaign against the LTTE, and the Indian government's actions of early June 1987.

In addition to this he insisted that if any Tamil separatist group refused to accept this settlement:

a) Government of India [would] co-operate directly with the Sri Lanka Government to implement these proposals;

b) ... [and] ensure that the Indian Navy co-operates with the Sri Lankan Navy in preventing Tamil separatist activities from affecting Sri Lanka.

c) ... [would] deport from India, Sri Lanka citizens who are taking part in terrorist activities or advocate separatism.

d) ... [and would] expedite the repatriation from Sri Lanka of Indian citizens to India who are resident here simultaneously with the return of Sri Lanka refugees from Tamil Nadu.

The fifth condition laid down by President Jayewardene was that if

... the Sri Lankan Government requests the Government of India to afford it military assistance to implement these proposals, the Government of India will co-operate by giving such assistance as requested.[19]

Reactivating negotiations, July 1987

The negotiations went on, with greater confidentiality than in the recent past. Sometime after 9 July, Rajiv Gandhi confirmed that India was intent on helping to break the deadlock in the negotiations on a settlement of Sri Lanka's ethnic conflict, and that he would force the Tamil separatists to accept a settlement on the basis of the agreements reached between the governments of India and Sri Lanka between May and December 1986. The gist of the offer was as follows: if the Sri Lanka government would agree to an amalgamation of the Northern and Eastern provinces on a *temporary* basis, India would impose a settlement on the Tamils. If the LTTE would not agree, the settlement would still go ahead and they would be forced to comply.

To the skeptics in the government this offer was no more than a trap, one more humiliation Rajiv Gandhi seemed intent upon heaping on Sri Lanka. However, a small group within the government was inclined to consider the offer as an important breakthrough to a negotiated settlement. The leadership was taken, as usual, by President Jayewardene, and he had the support of Gamini Dissanayake, the Minister of Lands, Land Development and Mahaveli Development, and Ronnie de Mel, Minister of Finance. The President came up with the suggestion that the temporary amalgamation should have a time limit, and that a referendum be held in the Eastern province to decide whether or not the people there wished to continue the link with the Northern province. The Indians agreed to this suggestion with remarkable alacrity.

In agreeing to an amalgamation of these two provinces, even on a temporary basis, President Jayewardene was taking a calculated risk. He himself had gone on record in the past – from as long ago as 1957 and frequently in the early 1980s – as being strongly opposed to the concept of a Tamil ethno-region encompassing the Northern and Eastern provinces. He was aware that neither the Sinhalese nor the Muslims who together constitute 60 per cent of the population of the Eastern province would willingly accept its merger with the overwhelmingly Tamil Northern province. There was, of course, the escape clause of a referendum which President Jayewardene hoped would mollify critics of this proposal within the government and in the country at large. Against this he saw, as he thought, the great advantages of getting the Indian government to underwrite a settlement of the Sri Lanka dispute.

By mid-July through its envoy in Colombo, the masterful J.N. Dixit, the Indian government indicated that they would indeed underwrite such a settlement. They requested as a quid pro quo an agreement between the two countries that would satisfy some of the foreign policy concerns of India in regard to Sri Lanka.

By now Rajiv Gandhi was tired of Prabhakaran and the LTTE, and he felt that it was time for a decisive move. He had made up his mind that he would proceed with implementation of any deal he would make with President Jayewardene, with the LTTE's acquiescence if possible, or without the LTTE if necessary. Indeed he had decided that he would impose it on the LTTE and use force for that purpose. He was therefore responsive to the last point in President Jayewardene's undated note, referred to earlier, namely, that in case

... the Sri Lanka Government requests the Government of India to afford it military assistance to implement these proposals, the Government of India will co-operate by giving such assistance as requested.

The Sri Lanka government, then made a crucial decision in insisting that any agreement reached must be between the two governments, not between the Sri Lanka government and the LTTE. India readily agreed to this, and proceeded to add that if this were indeed to be so, then her own foreign policy interests must be part of the agreement. These were to include: Trincomalee and other ports; foreign communications centers based on Sri Lankan soil;[20] the training of Sri Lankan troops; and the foreign military presence in Sri Lanka (i.e., Israelis and British mercenaries).

President Jayewardene, was by then so deeply disappointed with the failure of the US and other Western powers to condemn the Indian food-drop, that he was willing to accept these restraints on Sri Lanka's freedom of action if it meant that Indian support could be secured to effectively curb the Tamil separatist movement.[21] The agreement that emerged was so framed, however, that the existing arrangements in regard to these issues would not be immediately disturbed.[22]

Once agreement was reached on the broad principles of the accord, both parties set to work on the details. These latter were hammered out in the course of discussions between Dixit and Gamini Dissanayake, with the President's approval and encouragement. Much of the drafting was done by Dixit and Gamini Dissanayake at the Bullers Road office of the Mahaveli Development Authority in Colombo.[23] The President himself vetted each successive preliminary draft until agreement was reached on an acceptable final version.[24]

In preparing these drafts of an agreement, Gamini Dissanayake and the officials who helped him in this business, ensured that the concept of a traditional homeland of the Tamils should not be endorsed. They hit upon the phrase 'historical habitations', a phrase which was intended to mean 'where the Tamils had lived', and which they felt did not have the separatist political connotations of the term 'traditional homelands'.[25]

A draft of the Accord was ready by 15 July for discussion by the Cabinet at its meeting of 16 July. Dixit was invited to meet members of the Cabinet on two occasions, 16 July and 27 July 1987, to explain the implications of the draft as the Indian government saw it and especially to explain the nature of India's commitment and her interests.[26] On both occasions the Cabinet moved to the conference room of the old Senate building in Republic Square when Dixit spoke to its members. The discussions were not in the cabinet room proper.[27] Dixit recalled that on the first occasion – 15 July – the most critical comments came from Ministers Gamini Jayasuriya (Agriculture), M.H. Mohammed (Transport), and Ranjith Atapattu (Health). Lalith Athulathmudali (Minister of National Security), was skeptical about the agreement from the outset. However, despite these critical comments from important Cabinet ministers there was no formal opposition from any of them, much less from the Cabinet as a whole, to President Jayewardene proceeding with the negotiations.

Once Rajiv Gandhi secured support for the main outlines of the Accord from the Sri Lankan President, he moved very swiftly. He proposed that the Accord be signed in Colombo on 25 July (Saturday). President Jayewardene had to hold him back until 29 July (Wednesday). The Sri Lankan President needed to gain the formal support from the Cabinet, from the Executive Committee of the UNP and above all the Prime Minister who was out of the island and was due to return on 25 July.

The Cabinet was due to meet again on 27 July. By then the news of the impending signing of an agreement between Sri Lanka and India had leaked out; several rather garbled versions of its contents were being spoken of in the press. The news that Rajiv Gandhi would be in the island to sign an agreement could not be kept a secret for long. When the Cabinet met on 27 July Dixit was called in once again for discussions, to answer questions relating to the proposed accord directed at him by its critics. This time the critics included R. Premadasa, the Prime Minister who had just returned from an overseas visit. Lalith Athulathmudali remained the principal critic. Dixit recalled visiting Athulathmudali around 25 July intent on securing the latter's support for the agreement, but the latter remained skeptical. His main objection was that the Accord seemed more concerned with Indo-Sri Lanka relations than with Sri Lanka's ethnic conflict.[28]

The Cabinet meeting of 27 July took place against a general background of violent opposition to the accord led by the proscribed JVP, in association – willing or not – with the SLFP, and a large mass of *bhikkhus*. Indeed the signs seemed so unpropitious that even President Jayewardene began to worry about the situation. But he went ahead with arrangements for the signing of the agreement since it was clearly impossible to put it off now that the Indian Prime Minister was scheduled to arrive in the island for the official signing. Although the resounding endorsement of the Accord which President Jayewardene hoped the Cabinet would give him on 27 July was not forthcoming, the Cabinet, as a whole, gave him authority to proceed with the signing of the Accord on the scheduled date, i.e., 29 July.

For Gandhi the compelling force behind the pressure for the signing of an accord was, first, the need to gain some political 'triumph' to overcome the damaging effects of his many recent electoral failures. Second, there was the need also to arrive at a settlement while the charismatic Tamil Chief Minister, M.G. Ramachandran was still alive. Ramachandran's health was failing rapidly. In India as in Sri Lanka the general belief, at that time, was that Ramachandran's death would leave a huge vacuum in Tamil Nadu politics, and the struggle to fill it would lead to instability and chaos. Third, the Indian government was visibly tired of its mediatory role in the Sri Lanka Tamil problem, and wanted to get it over with, by converting it into a Sri Lankan rather than an Indian or Tamil Nadu problem. Fourthly, there was the need to reach a settlement while President Jayewardene was still in control of things in Sri Lanka. The Indians believed, with good reason, that neither the Prime Minister R. Premadasa, nor Mrs Bandaranaike, as potential successors to President Jayewardene would have the same strong commitment to the package of proposals for a settlement of Sri Lanka's ethnic conflict which had been negotiated through 1984 to 1987.

The Sri Lanka President for his part was just as anxious to reach an understanding with the Indian government. The next presidential election was scheduled for the period 4 December 1988 to 3 January 1989, while the parliamentary elections could be held at any opportune moment up to August 1989. An agreement with the Indian government on the basis of the terms negotiated between the middle of 1985 and mid-July 1987, would give his government time to begin the reconstruction and rehabilitation of the Northern and Eastern provinces and to stimulate economic growth in other parts of the island in time for the elections. Moreover his principal military advisers in Colombo were urging the need for a political settlement. They argued that the successful Vadamarachchi expedition should not blind the government to the realities of the military situation. The manpower resources of the Sri Lankan forces were inadequate for the purpose of holding the areas recently re-captured from the LTTE in the Jaffna peninsula. Thus the options, as they saw it, were either an honorable settlement underwritten by India or damaging reverses at the hands of the LTTE in territory in which the latter held most of the advantages.[29]

The principal document and an appendix (referred to as an annexure) of the Indo-Sri Lanka Accord faithfully embodied the proposals agreed between the two governments since the middle of 1985, while India's security concerns were contained in a letter from the Indian Prime Minister to the Sri Lankan President and the latter's rather brief response to it. The first clause (with its five subclauses) of the principal document was in the nature of a preamble about the nature of the Sri Lankan polity and its '... multi-ethnic, multi-lingual, and multi-religious plural society...' The substance of the Accord lay in its second clause, or part, with its 18 subclauses, beginning with 2.1 to 2.7 which dealt with the temporary amalgamation of the Northern and Eastern provinces, and the referendum that would be held in the Eastern province.

Subclause 2.9 was also important. It read as follows:

> The emergency will be lifted in the Eastern and Northern Provinces by August 15, 1987. A cessation of hostilities will come into effect all over the island within 48 hours of the signing of this Agreement. All arms presently held by militant groups will be surrendered in accordance with an agreed procedure to authorities to be designated by the Government of Sri Lanka.
>
> Consequent to the cessation of hostilities and the surrender of arms by militant groups, the Army and other security personnel will be confined to barracks in camps as of 25 May 1987. The process of surrendering arms and the confining of security personnel moving back to barracks shall be completed within 72 hours of the cessation of hostilities coming into effect.

In subclause 2.14 the Indian government agreed 'to underwrite and guarantee the resolutions, and co-operate in the implementation of the proposals'. The next subclause, 2.15, stated

> These proposals are conditional to an acceptance of the proposals negotiated from 4.5. 1986 to 19.12.86. Residual matters not finalized during the above negotiations shall be resolved between India and Sri Lanka within a period of

six weeks of signing this agreement. These proposals are also conditional to the Government of India co-operating directly with the Government of Sri Lanka in their implementation.

There was next the vitally important question, so far as the Sri Lankan government was concerned, of what would be done in case 'any militant groups operating in Sri Lanka' did not accept the proposals of the Accord. This was dealt with in subclause 2.16 which stated that 'These proposals are also conditional to the Government of India taking the following actions if any militant groups in Sri Lanka do not accept this framework of proposals for a settlement . . .' Five conditions were laid down, four of them based on those insisted upon by President Jayewardene in his telegram to Prime Minister Rajiv Gandhi on 6 July 1987. It included the condition that:

In the event that the Government of Sri Lanka requests the Government of India to afford military assistance to implement the proposals the Government of India will co-operate by giving to the Government of Sri Lanka such military assistance as and when requested.

The annexure to the agreement had six clauses all of which clarified issues dealt with in the main document. We need to focus attention on the sixth clause:

The President of Sri Lanka and the Prime Minister of India also agree that in terms of paragraph 2.14 and paragraph 2.16(c) of the Agreement an Indian peace-keeping contingent may be invited by the President of Sri Lanka to guarantee and enforce the cessation of hostilities if so required.

India's security concerns were outlined in Prime Minister Rajiv Gandhi's letter to the Sri Lankan President. The latter's own response to this letter was unusually brief. It merely said:

This is to confirm that the above correctly sets out the understanding reached between us.

The employment, by Sri Lanka, of foreign military and intelligence personnel was the first of these issues identified; it was followed by three others. India sought assurances that Trincomalee or any other ports in Sri Lanka would not be made available for military use by any country in a manner prejudicial to her interests; and that the restoration and operation of the Trincomalee oil tank farm would be undertaken as a joint venture between India and Sri Lanka. There was, finally, a call for a review of Sri Lanka's agreements with foreign broadcasting organizations to ensure that any facilities set up by them in Sri Lanka are used solely as public broadcasting facilities and not for any military or intelligence gathering purposes.

Of these, the second was a restatement of an obvious Indian concern. Sri Lanka, for her part, would not, at any cost, want to get involved in any military use of these ports by others – especially any military use directed against India. But the first of these directly concerned Sri Lanka's own interests and was seen by critics of the accord as a constraint on *her* choices in security. The references were directly to an Israeli presence in the island, and to British mercenary groups engaged in training Sri Lankan forces. The resort to these was forced upon Sri Lanka by Indian pressure on Great Britain, and other countries likely to be of assistance to Sri Lanka, preventing the establishment of training facilities for Sri Lankan forces in the island. The Indian offer to provide training facilities and military supplies for Sri Lankan security forces was regarded as one-sided when the threat to Sri Lankan security was, and still is, seen to come from India alone. Throughout this period Pakistan had provided both training facilities and *matériel*, and China was the main supplier of arms. A reading of the operative clause in the letter, clause 3(ii), would show that it did not actually place an embargo on the provision of training facilities by other nations.

The opposition parties in the island, and the JVP in particular, sensed much more accurately than the government the public mood of hostility to an agreement with India so soon after the humiliation inflicted on Sri Lanka in early June. The Accord ignited massive protests in the country in the last week of July. The intensity of the opposition was partly a reflection of an innate hostility to Indian pressure, partly a rejection of the more controversial features of the Accord such as the amalgamation of the Northern and Eastern provinces; and the provision for the entry of an Indian peace-keeping force. There was also an antipathy if not antagonism to Rajiv Gandhi himself because of the violation of Sri Lankan airspace which had occurred just six weeks earlier.

Although the Cabinet had approved the signing of the Accord at its meeting of 27 July, the divisions in its ranks on this issue, were public knowledge, especially the opposition of the Prime Minister, and of Lalith Athulathmudali. Opponents of the Accord, outside of the ranks of the government, were greatly encouraged by this latter development, and sought to exploit it to their advantage in gathering support for the extra-parliamentary agitation they were organizing. Sinhalese newspapers, and broadsheets gave extensive coverage to the divisions in the

Cabinet, and used it very effectively in whipping up opposition to the Accord.

From 23 July or so there was mounting tension in the city of Colombo and its suburbs as *bhikkhus* gathered in force to protest against the Accord. They had the support of the SLFP and other political groups as well as Buddhist lay organizations. As we have seen, the Prime Minister was out of the island on a visit to Britain and Japan and only returned on 25 September. Just as his absence during these critical negotiations with India fueled speculation about his own views on the Accord, his arrival was anxiously awaited by opposition critics of the Accord in the expectation that, given his general anti-Indian views, he would oppose it at the crucially important Cabinet meeting scheduled for 27 July. The Cabinet usually met on Wednesday mornings but because the Indian Prime Minister was expected to arrive in Colombo on 29 July to sign the Accord – 29 July was a Wednesday – the Cabinet meeting was advanced to Monday 27 July.

Even as the Cabinet met on 27 July violence broke out in Colombo when the police broke up an opposition rally held in one of the most crowded parts of the city, in close proximity to the main bus station and railway station. It soon spread into the suburbs and the main towns of the south-west of the island and developed into the worst anti-government riots in the island's post-independence history. The government's thinly spread security forces and the police took from three days to a week to quell the riots.

When Prime Minister Rajiv Gandhi arrived in the island on 29 July to sign the Accord, the security services and the police were still engaged in preventing the mobs from entering the city of Colombo intent on demonstrating their opposition to the accord. Never had a peace accord been signed in less propitious circumstances.

Several critics of the Accord within the Cabinet absented themselves from the signing ceremony at the President's house – the Prime Minister and Lalith Athulathmudali being among the more prominent among them – thus providing critics of the accord further evidence of divided counsels at the highest levels of government. The former was absent at all the social occasions associated with the Indian Prime Minister's visit, and the latter was also absent on some.

Rajiv Gandhi himself narrowly escaped serious injury, if not death, when an enraged sailor swung his rifle butt at him at the guard of honor ceremony prior to his departure from Colombo on 30 July. Pictures of the assault on the Indian Prime Minister were flashed around the world in newspapers and television screens. One other picture also in evidence, showed one of the more prominent critics of the accord, a lawyer and Buddhist activist, seeking to restrain a young *bhikkhu* in a violent mood, at a protest meeting in Colombo on 27 July. The two pictures together conveyed a vivid impression of the passions that tore the country apart that fateful week and nearly took the life of Rajiv Gandhi, as the LTTE succeeded in doing four years later. Rajiv Gandhi left behind him on this occasion a ghost city and an imperilled government.

Indian negotiations with the LTTE – Delhi July 1987

Prior to Rajiv Gandhi's visit to Sri Lanka, leaders of the five main Tamil separatist groups had been flown to New Delhi for negotiations with the Indian government. The Indian High Commission in Colombo and in particular the High Commissioner J.N. Dixit played a prominent role in getting them across from Jaffna to India. The first stage was a helicopter flight to Palaly airport (the Jaffna airport) from where they were whisked across to India. The Tamil groups were kept, heavily guarded, at the government-owned Ashok Hotel in New Delhi located near the diplomatic enclave there. The initial reaction of the separatist groups was hostile. A Reuter report carried by the government controlled *Daily News* in Colombo on 28 July stated that the Tigers in particular refused to agree. Not that the others were more enthusiastic. The LTTE's main sticking point was at having to lay down arms within 72 hours of the signing of the accord.[30]

Gandhi summoned the ailing Tamil Nadu Chief Minister, M.G. Ramachandran to Delhi to talk to the LTTE. But he had not been able to persuade Prabhakaran to accept the Accord by the time Rajiv Gandhi left for Colombo.

On his return to Delhi on 31 July Rajiv Gandhi was informed that Prabhakaran had at last agreed to accept the Accord. There was still considerable reluctance, but he had agreed. A very relieved Gandhi informed President Jayewardene on 2 August 1987 of these new developments.[31] That document read as follows:

1. In light of offers conveyed through Dixit on 1st August about interim administrative arrangements in the North-Eastern Province to be created, and offers concerning employment of Tamil separatist cadres after they surrender their arms, Prabhakaran, leader of the LTTE has:

   (a) *agreed to participation in the implementation of the agreement;*

(b) *agreed to the surrender of arms*; and

(c) Prabhakaran would like to be in Jaffna personally to organize surrender of arms.

2. In the interest of conciliation and peaceful implementation of the Accord, Prabhakaran will be airdropped at Jaffna by the evening of today, 2nd of August. Prabhakaran has agreed to the following schedule for the surrender of arms, etc. as given by Government of India:

August 2 evening — Arrive in Jaffna

August 3 noon — Indian Army to fan out into all parts of the Jaffna peninsula, including Jaffna city.

LTTE to publicly announce surrender of arms to the press on the same day.

August 4 and 5 — Surrender of arms by LTTE. Events to be witnessed by the Press and TV.

August 5 — President Jayewardene may kindly announce the decision, in principle, to set up an interim Administration in the North-Eastern Province before Provincial Council elections. Details to be worked out in consultation with Government of India.

3. I would like to assure you that if Prabhakaran goes back on his word in any manner or fails to organize surrender of arms, *the Indian Army will move to disarm LTTE by force.*

4. In the light of the above, time limit for the surrender of *arms will have to be extended from 1530 hours of August 1 to the evening of August 5th: another 48 hours extension is envisaged.* Cease-fire will be maintained by the Indian forces.

5. *I request that no publicity should be given to these arrangements till the late afternoon of 3rd August. The above arrangements can be announced on the 3rd August afternoon.*

There was considerable speculation in Sri Lanka at this time and later on about the reasons behind Prabhakaran's change of heart. There was little doubt that some arm twisting had been done by the Indian government. But suspicions remained that there was something more sordid if not sinister – the payment of a large sum of money as well.[32]

It would be evident after all this hard bargaining and from Rajiv Gandhi's message to President Jayewardene on 2 August that he (Gandhi) had few illusions about the LTTE and the prospects of a peaceful implementation of the Accord. His fears in this regard would have been strengthened by the initial reaction of the Indian High Commission in Colombo and its senior officials as they read Prabhakaran's speech to the citizens of Jaffna at Sudamalai on 5 July as the text of it came in from Jaffna through the High Commission telex in Colombo.[33] They realized at that time that he was intent on making trouble for both Sri Lanka and India, and advised the Indian government to take early action to restrain the LTTE, but Delhi was not inclined to take such firm measures so early.[34]

The arrival of the Indian Peace-Keeping Forces (IPKF)

As for the Indian Peace-Keeping Force (IPKF) India had originally had in mind a relatively small contingent. The increase in numbers and the urgency with which they were dispatched to the island was largely in response to the Sri Lanka government's own request. President Jayewardene was anxious to get Sri Lankan troops out of Jaffna as quickly as possible to meet the threat to security from the JVP.[35] Thus India moved troops in almost immediately after the signing of the accord at the request of the Sri Lanka government and Rajiv Gandhi's own assessment of the measures necessary[36] to help the Sri Lanka government to resist if not survive the powerful and violent opposition that the signing of the accord had triggered. Talking to the Sri Lankan President and the Ministers who gathered to sign the Accord, and as reports of rampaging mobs in the suburbs of Colombo came in, Rajiv Gandhi had concluded that the local police force just could not cope with civil disturbances of this magnitude. There was a clear need to move some of the army units based in Jaffna to Colombo almost immediately – and this could only be done by bringing an Indian force to Jaffna to keep the peace there. He recalled in April 1990 that he had resolved that under no circumstances would Indian troops be sent to the Sinhalese areas. The question that Gandhi was confronted with was how quickly this could be done. President Jayewardene urged that the Indian force be moved in almost immediately and Gandhi himself called the Defence Ministry in New Delhi from Colombo to see if this could be done. He was advised that it could not be done immediately but certainly it could be done within 24 hours and this is what eventually happened. To Rajiv Gandhi, the situation in Colombo seemed so bad that he decided to move a destroyer of the Indian Navy to the Colombo harbor, just in case the situation got out of hand and the President and his Ministers needed to be evacuated.

Between 29 July and 1 August more than half the Sri Lankan troops in the Jaffna peninsula were airlifted to Colombo in Indian airforce transport planes. Their presence and that of the Special Task Force of the Police helped quell the riots much more expeditiously than seemed likely at first.

At the time he sent the Indian troops into Jaffna, Rajiv Gandhi thought they would return home very quickly having accomplished the tasks set out for them.

The implementation of the accord – the early stages

Although many risks were expected in any progress toward the stabilization of the Accord (given the opposition of the SLFP, and the proscribed but nevertheless powerful JVP, and of a section of the government), the early indications seemed encouraging. True the original timetable for the surrender of weapons and the disarming of the warring factions was not adhered to, but the LTTE began a symbolic – although visibly reluctant – handing over of arms. The smaller separatist groups joined the process and were readier to hand over their weapons to the IPKF.

The Sri Lankan security forces in the Northern and Eastern provinces returned to their barracks and the paramilitary forces there were disarmed as part of the Sri Lankan government's obligations under the Accord. Although the Indian intervention prevented the completion of the campaign to seal off the coast of the Jaffna peninsula which had begun in late May 1987 with the Vadamarachchi campaign, the Sri Lankan security forces were willing supporters of the political settlement set out in the Indo-Sri Lanka Accord. Surprisingly there had been little or no consultation with them on the military aspects of the implementation of the accord. The accord, in fact, imposed severe restrictions on the Sri Lankan forces in the north and east of the island. They were clearly unhappy at the use of the term 'confined to barracks' because of its pejorative connotations. In normal army tradition it denotes a punishment.

Rajiv Gandhi and his advisors had banked on a speedy disarming of the Tamil separatists, including the LTTE, and a speedy departure of the IPKF.[37] Their hidden timetable for a departure by the end of 1987 or early 1988, was based on intelligence assessments provided by RAW. These latter proved to be fundamentally flawed, but that was all the provision the Indian government had for its contingency planning.[38]

When things began to go wrong, they went disastrously wrong within a few weeks, the IPKF was confronted with a task for which it was ill-prepared because neither political objectives, nor the chain of command were really clarified for purposes of a long military campaign against a defiant LTTE.

The information at Rajiv Gandhi's disposal when he embarked on his Sri Lankan intervention was clearly defective. First, he was, he stated in 1990, quite insistent from the outset that the IPKF would not be sent to Sinhalese areas. Was he unaware that the Trincomalee district had a substantial Sinhalese population, as did the Ampara district? Moreover, the IPKF had necessarily to go through the Sinhalese districts of the North Central province in travelling from the Northern province to the Eastern province. Second, many of the senior officials in Delhi's South Block persisted in regarding the Muslims as Tamils merely because they spoke Tamil. This was based on South Indian experience, but they did not know, or ignored, the fact that the Sri Lankan situation was totally different. Thirdly, although RAW had armed and financed various groups and individuals among the Tamil separatists, they had neglected to keep essential data on their protégés, with the result that when the IPKF really needed to crack down on the more recalcitrant among them the information at their disposal was very inadequate. The deficiencies in the material at the IPKF's disposal were best illustrated by the fact that they were using 1937 ordinance maps of Jaffna, when any self-respecting intelligence operative could easily have secured more up-to-date maps in Colombo.[39] No wonder Rajiv Gandhi, for one, reflecting on these events in 1990 as Leader of the Opposition, was bitterly critical of RAW and its role in Sri Lanka.

The problem, however, was the LTTE. For most of August 1987 the Indian High Commission in Colombo, and the dynamic J.N. Dixit who was by now both High Commissioner *de jure* and proconsul *de facto*, were engaged in exasperating and long drawn out negotiations with the LTTE to get them to stick to the promise extracted from them in Delhi, to support the Accord. From the outset both Rajiv Gandhi and Dixit realized that this was a very difficult task. Once back in Sri Lanka Prabhakaran shifted ground. The LTTE leadership did not change their basic aim, to secure recognition of its claim to be sole spokesmen for the Tamils of Sri Lanka, and they regarded the Indo-Sri Lanka Accord as essentially an obstacle to their objective of establishing a separate state.

They kept up the pressure on their Tamil rivals in the north and east of the island. The bloody encounters with them became more frequent. No amount of cajoling by the Indian High Commissioner and his staff could bring the LTTE to an acceptance of the need and accommodate their rivals in political activity rather than to turn their guns on them.

More important was the complex question of the Interim Administration of the amalgamated Northern and Eastern province on the setting up of which the Indian government had extracted a promise from its Sri Lankan counterpart. Although the composition of the Council had not been settled before the accord was signed it was treated as an essential and urgent necessity for its effective implementation. There were two problems here: first, the relative strength of the Tamil groups within it; and secondly, the question of leadership of that council.

While the Sri Lanka government was committed to the principle of such an Interim Council, it was also intent on seeing that the LTTE would not have a majority on it, and that there was a balance between representation for the Northern and Eastern provinces respectively. While the second of these did not present any great difficulties from the LTTE, the first clearly did, and they were intent on securing not merely an influential position in it, but a numerical majority and a clearly dominant position.

By the first week of September the handing in of arms by the Tamil separatist groups, and in particular the LTTE, had become more sporadic. It was clear that only a fraction of the arms in their possession had been surrendered by the LTTE. The LTTE had already clashed with the IPKF, who were inclined to ignore the incident in the cause of a peaceful settlement. The implementation of the Accord was impeded by further and bitter factional fighting among the Tamil separatist groups (involving the LTTE in particular). The LTTE turned their guns on their Tamil rivals once more and killed over 150 of them while the IPKF did little or nothing to prevent these killings.

The Indian government for its part seemed intent on moving slowly in collecting weapons from the Tamil activist groups, and above all else was anxious to get the LTTE to enter the arena of democratic politics. On 20 September the Indian government sent President Jayewardene a note on the composition of the Interim Council for the Northern and Eastern provinces. Its principal feature was that it gave the LTTE a majority (7 out of 12) in that body as well as having a say in the nomination to the post of chief administrator there. Although this was a clear departure from the understanding reached with him, President Jayewardene gave his consent to this new arrangement on 25 September. The document read as follows:[40]

1. On the basis of latest discussions with the LTTE and other Tamil groups,

the Government of India puts forward the following proposals for the composition of the Interim Administrative Council:

The Council may consist of:
- Chief Administrator   – 1 (one of the nominees of the LTTE)
- LTTE members   – 5
- TULF members   – 2
- Muslims   – 2 (one of the Muslims may be LTTE nominee)
- Sinhalese   – 2

2. The Chief Administrator and the 5 LTTE nominees may be chosen out of a list of nominees already available in the President's Secretariat.

3. Mr Soosaithasan and Mr Sampanthan may be nominated as TULF members of the Council.[41]

4. Out of the two Muslims, President may kindly choose one of the Muslim nominees of the LTTE. The second Muslim may be chosen in discretion.

5. The two Sinhalese may be nominated in discretion (Mr Lionel Fernando is acceptable to the Tamils).[42]

6. President may kindly consider giving up the idea of nominating Co-Administrator initially.

7. In the orders detailing the terms of reference of the Interim Administrative Council, President may consider transferring power envisaged in paragraphs 10.1 and 10.2 of the Bangalore proposals.

In the meanwhile, the Government of India is immediately approaching the LTTE to simultaneously fall in line on various matters step-by-step.

The Interim Administrative Council may be announced, if possible, in the coming 24 to 36 hours, so that it politically neutralises attempts of the LTTE to misinform the Tamil population about various developments.

It is the Government of India's assessment that either the LTTE will join the Interim Government and give a momentum to the peace process or if they do not join after the announcement of the Interim Government by His Excellency, it will start the process of their political marginalization.

The official announcement of the Sri Lanka government's acceptance of this new arrangement was made on 28 September. The Sri Lanka government had made yet another concession under Indian pressure. But every concession led to more demands by the LTTE.

By the middle of September it was very evident that the LTTE was looking for an opportunity for a dramatic demonstration of their opposition to the Indo-Sri Lanka Accord and a confrontation with the Indians. On 15 September Thileepan a prominent LTTE activist – he was chief of the LTTE's political wing in Jaffna – began what he called 'a fast unto death'. He put up five demands, two of which dealt with the settlement of Sinhalese peasants in the Eastern province, and release of prisoners. At first the fast was regarded as a ploy to divert attention from the LTTE's attack on other Tamil groups in Batticaloa which took place two days earlier.[43] But Thileepan was in earnest, and did fast himself to death.

His death was soon overtaken by a more significant event which gave the LTTE the opportunity it was looking for. On 4 October the Sri Lanka Navy intercepted a boat carrying a group of LTTE men off Point Pedro. It contained 17 men, including some of the most prominent LTTE leaders. One of them was Pulendran who had led the group that had butchered 150 men, women and children in the Good Friday bus massacre of 1986, at a time when the government had declared a unilateral cessation of hostilities. In addition the boat carried arms in contravention of the accord. The Sri Lanka government insisted that the captured men be brought to Colombo for interrogation. Dixit was not in Sri Lanka at this stage. There was a sharp difference of opinion between the IPKF man on the spot in Jaffna and the Sri Lankan army representative who insisted on carrying out his instructions which were to take the group to Colombo. At the time of their capture these young men did not have the cyanide capsules for which the LTTE is well known. But while in custody these capsules were apparently smuggled in to them. They preferred to commit suicide by swallowing them rather than face interrogation in Colombo.[44] Some died immediately; others lingered on to die a slow death. The death toll from this mass suicide was 12. Their deaths gave the LTTE the excuse to do what they had always intended to do. They turned their guns on the Sinhalese in Jaffna (the few who remained) and in the Batticaloa and Trincomalee districts, in a deliberate attempt to destabilize the Eastern province.

The LTTE's aim was to drive the Sinhalese out of the Trincomalee district, and to cause so much confusion and panic that the Sinhalese in the Eastern province would flee to the south of the island. They had in mind the referendum to be held to decide whether the joinder between the Northern and Eastern provinces would be made permanent and were intent on reducing the number of Sinhalese voters. The LTTE caused enormous damage to Sinhalese property in the town, apart of course from killing a large number of men, women and children.

The IPKF contributed to this process of destabilization in two ways: first, they committed a serious blunder in sending a Madrasi regiment to Trincomalee, who being Tamils largely, fraternized with the LTTE; secondly, and even more important, they made no attempt to intervene when the peace was broken. Indeed there is evidence that some of the IPKF soldiers participated in the burning and looting of houses, and the harassment of the beleaguered Sinhalese.

The attacks on the Sinhalese in Trincomalee town and district, and elsewhere in the Eastern province created a huge political problem for the government. Fleeing refugees made their way to towns in the north-central and central regions, and some even took trains to Colombo. There was, for a few days, the prospect of a Sinhalese backlash in the rest of the island. The JVP and SLFP either singly or in concert were fanning the flames of discontent.

The massacre of about 200 Sinhalese eventually led to a toughening of the Indian attitude. On October 4, President Jayewardene announced that he would be compelled to order the IPKF out of Trincomalee if law and order were not restored immediately, and to call upon Sri Lankan forces to keep order there.

The LTTE had hoped for a clash between the IPKF and the Sri Lankan armed forces in Trincomalee. Such a conflict may have erupted if the Madrasi regiment had not been ordered out of Trincomalee, and if the IPKF had not begun to check the LTTE's depredations. Fortunately for both countries the clash did not take place.

In the meantime urgent discussions between President Jayewardene and Prime Minister Gandhi brought into force part of the hidden agenda of the peace accord, that Indian troops would eventually be used against the LTTE. The Indian Defence Minister, K.C. Pant, was despatched to Colombo. With practically world-wide condemnation of the LTTE, and severe criticism of India for its failure to maintain the peace, the Indian government at last decided to disarm the LTTE, and to destroy it as a political force.

There was thus an ultimate irony: the Indian government which intervened to prevent the destruction of the LTTE by the Sri Lankan army earlier in the year, were now destroying it themselves; the Indian government which objected to the Sri Lankan army taking Jaffna city were doing it themselves, and in that process inflicted much heavier casualties and far greater hardships on the people of the Jaffna peninsula than anything done so far by the Sri Lankan security forces. The Indian government which accused the Sri Lanka forces of violation of human rights in their confrontation with the Tamil separatist groups now found themselves facing similar charges and with even greater frequency.

India's national pride was at stake, through this defiance of India by the forces of Tamil separatism in Sri Lanka, and so the LTTE had to be taught a lesson, one that had long-term implications; and not for the LTTE alone but also for Tamil separatism in South India. This was namely that the Indian government would not put up with it and would crush it if it got out of hand. Indeed it was meant for *all* separatist forces in India. If a slogan had to be coined for this, it would be autonomy 'yes' but separatism, 'never'.

Accordingly the IPKF now moved in to disarm the LTTE and, when faced with resistance from the latter, launched a major attack on the LTTE strongholds in the Jaffna town and peninsula in the second week of October. Despite stiff resistance from the LTTE which necessitated the deployment of thousands of reinforcements, the LTTE's hold on the peninsula was eventually broken. Both parties, the Indian army and the LTTE suffered heavy casualties, but those who suffered most were the people of Jaffna and the Jaffna peninsula as the Indian army set about its business of defeating the LTTE with a heavy-handed professionalism. There was no Indian *coup de grâce* either. The LTTE survived a bruising defeat. Their harried forces escaped, or were allowed to escape, to the jungles south of the Jaffna peninsula[45] from where they continued their resistance against the Indian forces for more than two years. The short, sharp campaign that Rajiv Gandhi planned turned out to be India's longest war.

Quite apart from the miscalculations that bedeviled India's military intervention in the north and east of Sri Lanka, India's mediation in Sri Lanka's protracted ethnic conflict suffered from two built-in flaws. First of all, there was a confusion of objectives, in particular, the inherent contradiction between *realpolitik* that conditioned the thinking of many of those involved in fashioning of Indian policy on Sri Lanka, and the peacemaking, peace-keeping and peace-building roles that are essential to the integrity of a genuine effort at mediation. Secondly, the complex history of India's diplomatic endeavours in the Sri Lanka imbroglio demonstrates one important theme in third party mediation: namely, that a mediator who keeps on extracting one important concession after another from one party – in this case the Sri Lanka government – without compensating concessions of similar value from the other, or others, eventually undermines the viability of the whole mediation process. Thus the Indian pressure which compelled the Sri Lanka government to agree to the merger – on a temporary basis – of the

Northern and Eastern provinces, proved to be a serious error of judgement that jeopardized the successful selling of the accord to the normally skeptical Sinhalese electorate who were inclined, at the best of times, to be suspicious of Indian intentions.

Notes

1. See my article (1992) The prelude to the Indo-Sri Lanka Accord of July 1987, in *Ethnic Studies Report*, X(1), January–June 1992.
2. For the background to these developments, see S. Ratnatunga (1988) *Politics of Terrorism: The Sri Lanka Experience*, Canberra, pp. 318–31.
3. *Ibid.*, pp. 331–57.
4. K.M. de Silva, The prelude to the Indo-Sri Lanka Accord of July 1987, *op. cit.*
5. *Ibid.*
6. *Ibid.*
7. *Ibid.*
8. *Ibid.*
9. S. Ratnatunga, *Politics of Terrorism*, *op. cit.*, pp. 243–66.
10. These events are reviewed in K.M. de Silva, The prelude to the Indo-Sri Lanka Accord of July 1987, *op. cit.*
11. *Ibid.*
12. K. Subrhamanyam (1984) Pakistan's nuclear capability, in V.D. Chopra (ed.) *Studies in Indo-Pakistan Relations*, New Delhi: p. 132. I owe this reference to Professor Howard Wriggins who has used it in another context altogether.
13. Gamini Dissanayake, interview with the author, 23 September 1989.
14. This note is in the J.R. Jayewardene Mss.
15. A copy of it is available with the present author who was present throughout the interview with Azar.
16. An obvious mistake. It should have been alleviated.
17. This document is in the J.R. Jayewardene Mss.
18. J.N. Dixit, interview with author, 3 April 1989.
19. This document is in the J.R. Jayewardene Mss. The copy in the J.R. Jayewardene Mss does not bear a date. This message was probably relayed to New Delhi through Dixit.
20. The reference was clearly to the Voice of America relaying station. Negotiations had been concluded for an extension of the lease, and an expansion of the facility.
21. President Jayewardene's deep disappointment with the US in particular, was made clear in his interview with Edward Azar, referred to earlier. In an interview with Howard Wriggins, Ronnie de Mel, the former Finance Minister made this point very strongly. Ronnie de Mel's interview was on 21 July 1990.
22. J.N. Dixit, interview with author, 3 April 1989.
23. J.N. Dixit's and Gamini Dissanayake's interviews with the author referred to earlier.

24. There are several such preliminary drafts in the J.R. Jayewardene Mss.

25. Gamini Dissanayake, interview with the author, 23 September 1989.

26. Dixit, interview with author, 3 April 1989.

27. Gamini Dissanayake, interview with author, 23 September 1989.

28. Dixit, interview with author, 3 April 1989.

29. This paragraph is based on several official documents in the J.R. Jayewardene Mss, including a report to the Cabinet by General Cyril Ranatunge on 12 August 1987. Ranatunge was in overall charge of the operations against the LTTE forces.

30. Lalith Athulathmudali explained this to me on more than one occasion. He added that he had told Dixit on a later occasion that the surrender of arms would only succeed if Prabhakaran who was then in Delhi was kept there or elsewhere in India until arms were surrendered.

31. There is a copy of this important telegram in the J.R. Jayewardene Mss. The underlining of some of the passages in the text appears to have been done in Colombo at the President's office, very probably by President Jayewardene himself.

32. These suspicions were confirmed in early 1988 when an enterprising Indian journalist revealed that Prabhakaran had insisted on receiving a large sum of money estimated at Indian rupees 100 million (about $7.5 million at the prevailing rate of conversion) and was assured that he would receive it. Indeed a first installment had been paid before the LTTE turned their guns on the Indian Peace Keeping Force. A full and more candid explanation was provided on 6 April 1988 by K. Natwar Singh, Minister of State for External Affairs to the Lok Sabha, the lower house of the Indian Parliament on this embarrassing transaction.
    The text of Natwar Singh's speech was published in Colombo by the Indian High Commission on 6 April 1988. PR/23 of 6 April 1988.

33. Prabhakaran's speech (in an English translation) was carried in full, in the *Hindu*, 6 August 1987.

34. Dixit's interview with the author, *op. cit.*

35. *Ibid.*

36. Rajiv Gandhi, interview with the author, 23 April 1990.

37. See his comment, 'It should be a short, sharp exercise and our boys should be back home soon', in the *Far Eastern Economic Review*, 31 August 1987. He made the same point in his interview with the author, 23 April 1990.

38. Rajiv Gandhi, interview with the author, 23 April 1990.

39. See S. Bhaduri and Afsir Karim (1990) *The Sri Lankan Crisis*, Lancer Paper I, New Delhi: Lancer International, p. 65 for a discussion of this.

40. This document is in the J.R. Jayewardene Mss.

41. Soosaithasan and Sampanthan had been TULF MP's for Mannar and Trincomalee, respectively, in the period 1977–1983. They were widely regarded as moderates.

42. Lionel Fernando had been a very popular Government Agent (Chief Administrative Officer) of Jaffna in the early 1980s.

43. One of the most comprehensive and objective accounts of politics in Jaffna during this period is provided in R. Hoole *et al.*, (1990) *The Broken Palmyra. The Tamil Crisis in Sri Lanka – An Inside Account*, Sri Lanka Studies Institute, Claremont, CA, revised ed. The Thileepan fast is discussed in pp. 170–74.

44. *Ibid.*, pp. 187–94.
45. These were the areas from which they had been driven out by the Sri Lankan army earlier in the year.

APPENDIX
Draft framework of terms of accord and understanding

System of government

The principal Agencies, apart from the Central Government, for the exercise of the powers of government within the framework of the Constitution as amended will be:

(a) the Provincial Council in each province,
(b) the District Council in each administrative district, and
(c) the Pradesheeya Sabha with representation at the village level in each AGA Division.

2. The existing provincial boundaries will constitute the limits of the area of authority of the Provincial Council, without prejudice to the power of Parliament to alter them.

3. The existing district boundaries will constitute the limits of the area of authority of the District Council, without prejudice to the power of Parliament to alter them.

4. There shall be an Authority for the Port of Trincomalee and its environs for the purpose of its administration and economic development. The area of such authority shall be excluded from the area of authority of any Provincial Councils or District Council established. (The area of authority to be discussed).

Establishment of Provincial Councils

5. A Bill for the amendment of the Constitution to enable the creation of Provincial Councils and the devolution of powers on them shall be enacted by Parliament by 2/3rd majority. Thereafter, Parliament will pass an Act, directly conferring on the Provincial Councils the requisite legislative powers. Such power shall not be revoked or altered in any manner except by an Act of Parliament passed by a two-thirds majority after consultation with the Provincial Council or Councils concerned.

6. The process and procedures for the amendment of the Constitution and the enactment of the Act of Parliament will be commenced by the Government of Sri Lanka within 30 days of the Agreement.

7. The constitutional amendment contemplated in para 5 shall be of such a nature as would not require its approval at a referendum.

Devolution of powers

8. The powers to be devolved on a Provincial Council will be specified in the Act referred to in para 5 above.

   The more important powers to be devolved on a Provincial Council are specified in the Annexe I hereto.

Legislative powers

9. Subject to the provisions of the Constitution as amended in regard to the exercise of legislative powers, Provincial Councils will have powers to enact laws on subjects specified in the Act of Parliament, which will be operative within the Province.

Executive powers

10. The President shall appoint as a Chief Executive of a Provincial Council one of the members who in the President's opinion is most likely to command the confidence of the council. The Chief Executive will be entitled to choose the Executive Committee from among the members of the Provincial Council.

10. (*a*) The members of the Executive Committee will be appointed by the President on the recommendation of the Chief Executive and executive powers will be delegated to the Chief Executive and other Members of the Executive Committee.

10. (*b*) The powers that may be delegated to the Chief Executive (and members of the Executive Committee) will be specified in the Act referred to in para 5 above. Such executive powers shall include all areas of legislative powers delegated to the Provincial Council.

10. (*c*) The Chief Executive and members of the Executive Committee need not be Members of Parliament. If they are not Members of Parliament, they will not be accountable in or to Parliament. However, in that event, they will be responsible to the President in respect of matters for which the President would be responsible to Parliament, and to the Provincial Council in respect of all other matters.

Financial powers

11. The Provincial Councils shall have the power to levy taxes, cess or fees and to mobilise resources through loans, the proceeds of which will be credited to a Consolidated Fund set up for that particular Council to which will also be credited grants, allocations or subventions from the Republic. Financial resources will be apportioned to the Provinces on the recommendations of a representative Finance Commission appointed from time to time by the President.

11. (*a*) In respect of loans or grants, any foreign loans or grants would require the sanction of the Government of Sri Lanka in accordance with national policy.

11. (*b*) The nature of taxes to be levied by the Provincial Councils will be defined by Parliament by law.

Elections

12. Elections will be held in respect of each Province on the proportional representation system on the basis of Administrative Districts for the constitution of a Provincial Council. The number of members to be elected to each Provincial Council will be determined according to the population and area of each district within that Province.

Membership of Provincial Council

13. The members of the Provincial Council shall be the members elected from the Province as set out in para 12 above. Every Member of Parliament elected from the Province shall be entitled to be an ex-officio member of the Provincial Council if he so elects within a specified period. No vacancy shall be deemed to have been created if an MP ceases to be a member of the Provincial Council by reason of his failure to elect.

    The number of ex-officio members shall not exceed the number of elected members of the Council.

14. Where the President is satisfied that the affairs of any Provincial Council are not being carried on in accordance with the provisions of the Constitution or of any other law, he may take such measures or pass such orders as he may deem fit to ensure that they are so carried on, including an order for the dissolution of the Council and for taking such consequential measures as he may deem necessary. Every such order dissolving a Council shall be operative for a period of six months at a time but not exceeding one year in all provided however that Parliament approves of such action within two months of making of the order of dissolution.

15. Parliament shall by law provide that a Provincial Council be established in any Province, if more than half the number of Development Councils, constituted under Act No. 35 of 1980 within that Province by a resolution passed by a simple majority decide to constitute themselves a Provincial Council, at meetings held immediately after the date of coming into force of the said amendment to the Constitution and the said Act of Parliament.

15. (*a*) If the majority of such Development Councils do not determine to function as part of a Provincial Council, a Provincial Council shall not be constituted for or function in respect of that Province.

15. (*b*) In such event, the existing District Development Councils shall be deemed to be District Councils established under the Act of Parliament referred to in para 5 and shall continue to function in respect of each of the Districts in the Province, having the powers, duties and functions set out in the Development Councils Act No. 35 of 1980, as amended from time to time.

15. (*c*) *Provided that*, where in any Province more than half the number of Development Councils in that Province have ceased to exist or are not functioning on the date of this Agreement, a Provincial Council shall be deemed to be established on the coming into force of the said amendment to the Constitution and the said Act of Parliament.

16. (*a*) Where a Provincial Council has been constituted and is functioning, the members elected in respect of more than one half the number of Districts within that Province together with any ex-officio members thereof, sitting separately by virtue of their election from that District, may by a simple majority decide that such district shall cease to be part of that Provincial Council and withdraw therefrom.

16. (*b*) For the purposes of this paragraph the members of a Development Council constituted under Act No. 35 of 1980 shall be deemed to be members elected under this law.

16. (*c*) In that event, a Development Council shall be deemed to be constituted under the Development Councils Act No. 35 of 1980 for each such District and will function as such Council.

17. *Other subjects (for discussion)*

17. (1) *Minorities Commission* – This would be envisaged as an institutional mechanism safeguarding the rights and interests of linguistic and other minorities as equal citizens of Sri Lanka.

17. (2) *National Policy on Employment* – The policies of the Government of Sri Lanka in regard to employment would be non-discriminatory.

17 (3) *Tamil Office or Ministry* – There already exists a Ministry for Hindu Religious Affairs. The scope, functions and nature of such a Tamil Office can be examined if specifically desired.

17. (4) *Minorities representation in Armed Forces* – Recruitment to the Armed Forces to be carried out so as to ensure that the Armed Forces reflect the ethnic ratio as far as possible within a specified time frame.

18. *Persons of recent Indian origin in Sri Lanka*
Of the total of 600,000 persons of Indian origin to whom, under the provisions of the Indo-Sri Lanka Agreements of 1964 and 1974, the Indian Government agreed to grant citizenship there were only 505,000 (approx.) applicants for Indian citizenship leaving a balance of 95,000 (approx.) unaccounted for who would, therefore, continue to be 'Stateless'.

The Sri Lanka Government proposes to grant citizenship to this 95,000 when all persons of Indian origin who have applied for Indian citizenship have been granted such citizenship and are repatriated.

Initialled by

> R. Mathai – Deputy Secretary
> Ministry of External Affairs
> New Delhi
> 30.8.85.

> E.F. Dias Abeyesinghe – Secretary of the Sri Lanka Delegation.
> 30.8.85
> 8.50 p.m.

New Delhi.

ANNEXE I

The Provincial Councils shall exercise powers and shall have responsibility for subjects including:

(i)   internal law and order to the extent defined in the Paper I appended.
(ii) land settlement within the Province to the extent defined in the Paper II appended.
(iii) Agriculture and industry to the extent set out in the appended Papers III and IV.
(iv) Education and Culture. A brief statement on Education is appended at V, and on Culture at VI.

The aforesaid list of subjects and functions is not exhaustive, and additional subjects will be finalised later.

For the removal of doubts the subjects and functions that would be exclusively reserved for Parliament are specified in Annexe 2.

There would be provision for establishment of a Provincial or District Service and for secondment of public officers from the Central Government Public Service.

INDO-SRI LANKA AGREEMENT TO ESTABLISH PEACE AND NORMALCY IN SRI LANKA

The Prime Minister of the Republic of India, His Excellency Mr. Rajiv Gandhi and the President of the Democratic Socialist Republic of Sri Lanka, His Excellency Mr. J.R. Jayewardene having met at Colombo on July 29, 1987.

Attaching utmost importance to nurturing, intensifying and strengthening the traditional friendship of India and Sri Lanka and acknowledging the imperative need of resolving the ethnic problem of Sri Lanka, and the consequent violence, and for the safety, well-being and prosperity of people belonging to all communities in Sri Lanka.
Having this day entered into the following Agreement to fulfil this objective.

1.1 *desiring* to preserve the unity, sovereignty and territorial integrity of Sri Lanka;

1.2 *acknowledging* that Sri Lanka is a multi-ethnic and a multi-lingual plural society consisting, inter alia, of Sinhalese, Tamils, Muslims (Moors), and Burghers;

1.3 *recognising* that each ethnic group has a distinct cultural and linguistic identity which has to be carefully nurtured;

1.4 *also recognising* that the Northern and the Eastern Provinces have been areas of historical habitation of Sri Lankan Tamil speaking peoples, who have at all times hitherto lived together in this territory with other ethnic groups;

1.5 *Conscious* of the necessity of strengthening the forces contributing to the unity, sovereignty and territorial integrity of Sri Lanka, and preserving its character as a multi-ethnic, multi-lingual and multi-religious plural society, in which all citizens can live in equality, safety and harmony, and prosper and fulfil their aspirations;

2. *Resolve that:*

2.1 Since the Government of Sri Lanka proposes to permit adjoining Provinces to join to form one administrative unit and also by a Referendum to separate as may be permitted to the Northern and Eastern Provinces as outlined below:

2.2 During the period, which shall be considered an interim period (i.e.) from the date of the elections to the Provincial Council, as specified in para 2.8 to the date of the referendum as specified in para 2.3, the Northern and Eastern Provinces as now constituted, will form one administrative unit, having one elected Provincial Council. Such a unit will have one Governor, one Chief Minister and one Board of Ministers.

2.3 There will be a referendum on or before 31st December, 1988 to enable the people of the Eastern Province to decide whether:

(A) The Eastern Province should remain linked with the Northern Province as one administrative unit, and continue to be governed together with the Northern Province as specified in para 2.2, or
(B) The Eastern Province should constitute a separate administrative unit having its own distinct Provincial Council with a separate Governor, Chief Minister and Board of Ministers.

The President may, at his discretion decide to postpone such a referendum.

2.4 All persons who have been displaced due to ethnic violence, or other reasons, will have right to vote in such a referendum. Necessary conditions to enable them to return to areas from where they were displaced will be created.

2.5 The referendum, when held, will be monitored by a committee headed by the Chief Justice, a member appointed by the President, nominated by the Government of Sri Lanka, and a member appointed by the President, nominated by the representatives of the Tamil speaking people of the Eastern Province.

2.6 A simple majority will be sufficient to determine the result. of the referendum.

2.7 Meeting and other forms of propaganda, permissible within the laws of the country, will be allowed before the referendum.

2.8 Elections to Provincial Councils will be held within the next three months, in any event before Dec. 31, 1987. Indian observers will be invited for elections to the Provincial Council of the North and East.

2.9 The emergency will be lifted in the Eastern and Northern Provinces by Aug. 15, 1987. A cessation of hostilities will come into effect all over the island within 48 hours of the signing of this agreement. All arms presently held by militant groups will be surrendered in accordance with an agreed procedure to authorities to be designated by the Government of Sri Lanka. Consequent to the cessation of hostilities and the surrender of arms by militant groups, the army and other security personnel will be confined to barracks in camps as on May 25, 1987. The process of surrendering of arms and the confining the security personnel moving back to barracks shall be completed within 72 hours of the cessation of hostilities coming into effect.

2.10 The Government of Sri Lanka will utilise for the purpose of law enforcement and maintenance of security in the Northern and Eastern Provinces the same organisations and mechanisms of Government as are used in the rest of the country.

2.11 The President of Sri Lanka will grant a general amnesty to political and other prisoners now held in custody under the Prevention of Terrorism Act and other emergency laws, and to combatants, as well as to those persons accused, charged and or convicted under these laws. The Government of Sri Lanka will make special efforts to rehabilitate militant youth with a view to bringing them back to the mainstream of national life. India will cooperate in the process.

2.12 The Government of Sri Lanka will accept and abide by the above provisions and expect all others to do likewise.

2.13 If the framework for the resolution is accepted, the Government of Sri Lanka will implement the relevant proposals forthwith.

2.14 The Government of India will underwork and guarantee the resolutions, and co-operate in the implementation of these proposals.

2.15 These proposals are conditional to an acceptance of proposals negotiated from 4.5.1986 to 19.12.1986. Residual matters not finalised during the above negotiations shall be resolved between India and Sri Lanka within a period of six weeks of signing this agreement. These proposals are also conditional to the Government of India co-operating directly with the Government of Sri Lanka in their implementation.

2.16 These proposals are also conditional to the Government of India taking the following actions if any militant group operating in Sri Lanka do not accept this framework of proposals for a settlement, namely:

(A) India will take all necessary steps to ensure that Indian territory is not used for activities prejudicial to the unity, integrity and security of Sri Lanka.

(B) The Indian Navy/Coast Guard will co-operate with the Sri Lanka Navy in preventing Tamil militant activities from affecting Sri Lanka.

(C) In the event that the Government of Sri Lanka requests the Government of India to afford military assistance to implement these proposals the Goverment of India will co-operate by giving to the Government of Sri Lanka such military assistance as and when requested.

(D) The Government of India will expedite repatriation from Sri Lanka of Indian citizens to India who are resident there concurrently with the repatriation of Sri Lankan refugees from Tamil Nadu.

(E) The Government of India and Sri Lanka, will co-operate in ensuring the physical security and safety of all communities inhabiting the Northern and Eastern Provinces.

2.17 The Government of Sri Lanka shall ensure free, full and fair participation of voters, from all communities in the Northern and Eastern Provinces in electoral processes envisaged in this agreement. The Government of India will extend full co-operation to the Government of Sri Lanka in this regard.

2.18 The official language of Sri Lanka shall be Sinhala. Tamil and English will also be official languages.

3. This agreement and the annexure there-to shall come into force upon signature.

In witness whereof we have set our hands and seals hereunto. Done in Colombo, Sri Lanka, on this the twenty ninth day of July of the year one thousand nine hundred and eighty seven, in duplicate, both texts being equally authentic.

Rajiv Gandhi
Prime Minister of the Republic of India

Junius Richard Jayewardene
*President of the Democratic
Socialist Republic of Sri Lanka*

ANNEXURE TO THE AGREEMENT

1. His Excellency the Prime Minister of India and His Excellency the President of Sri Lanka agree that the referendum mentioned in paragraph 2 and its sub-paragraphs of the Agreement will be observed by a representative of the Election Commission of India to be invited by His Excellency the President of Sri Lanka.

2. Similarly, both Heads of Government agree that the elections to the Provincial Council mentioned in paragraph 2.8 of the Agreement will be observed by a representative of the Government of India to be invited by the President of Sri Lanka.

3. His Excellency the President of Sri Lanka agrees that the Home Guards would be disbanded and all para-military personnel will be withdrawn from the Eastern and Northern Provinces with a view to creating conditions conducive to fair elections to the Council.

   The President, in his discretion, shall absorb such paramilitary forces, which came into being due to ethnic violence into the regular security forces of Sri Lanka.

4. The Prime Minister of India and the President of Sri Lanka agree that the Tamil militants shall surrender their arms to authorities agreed upon to be designated by the President of Sri Lanka. The surrender shall take place in the presence of one senior representative each of the Sri Lanka Red Cross and the Indian Red Cross.

5. The Prime Minister of India and the President of Sri Lanka agree that a joint Indo-Sri Lankan observer group consisting of qualified representatives of the Government of India and the Government of Sri Lanka would monitor the cessation of hostilities from 31 July, 1987.

6. The Prime Minister of India and the President of Sri Lanka also agree that in terms of paragraph 2.14 and paragraph 2.16(c) of the Agreement, an Indian Peace Keeping contingent may be invited by the President of Sri Lanka to guarantee and enforce the cessation of hostilities, if so required.

PRIME MINISTER OF INDIA

NEW DELHI

July 29, 1987,

Excellency,

Conscious of the friendship between our two countries stretching over two millenia and more, and *recognising* the importance of nurturing this traditional friendship, it is imperative that both Sri Lanka and India reaffirm the decision not to allow our respective territories to be used for activities prejudicial to each other's unity, territorial integrity and security.

In this spirit, you had, during the course of our discussions, agreed to meet some of India's concerns as follows:

(i) Your Excellency and myself will reach an early understanding about the relevance and employment of foreign military and intelligence personnel with a view to ensuring that such presences will not prejudice Indo-Sri Lankan relations.

(ii) Trincomalee or any other ports in Sri Lanka will not be made available for military use by any country in a manner prejudicial to India's interests.

(iii) The work of restoring and operating the Trincomalee Oil tank farm will be undertaken as a joint venture between India and Sri Lanka.

(iv) Sri Lanka's agreement with foreign broadcasting organizations will be reviewed to ensure that any facilities set up by them in Sri Lanka are used solely as public broadcasting facilities and not for any military or intelligence purposes.

In the same spirit, India will:

(i) Deport all Sri Lankan citizens who are found to be engaging in terrorist activities or advocating separatism or secessionism.

(ii) Provide training facilities and military supplies for Sri Lankan security forces.

India and Sri Lanka have agreed to set up a joint consultative mechanism to continuously review matters of common concern in the light of the objectives stated in para 1 and specifically to monitor the implementation of other matters contained in this letter.

Kindly confirm, Excellency, that the above correctly sets out the agreement reached between us.

Please accept, Excellency, the assurances of my highest consideration.

Yours Sincerely,
Rajiv Gandhi)

His Excellency
Mr. J.R. Jayewardene,
President of the Democratic Socialist Republic of Sri Lanka, Colombo.

PRESIDENT OF SRI LANKA

July 29, 1987

Excellency,

Please refer to your letter dated the 29th of July 1987, which reads as follows:

"Excellency,
Conscious of the friendship between our two countries stretching over two millenia and more, and recognizing the importance of nurturing this traditional friendship, it is imperative that both Sri Lanka and India reaffirm the decision not to allow our respective territories to be used for activities prejudicial to each other's unity, territorial integrity and security.

2. In this spirit, you had, during the course of our discussions, agreed to meet some of India's concerns as follows:

   (i)   Your Excellency and myself will reach an early understanding about the relevance and employment of foreign military and intelligence personnel with a view to ensuring that such presences will not prejudice Indo-Sri Lanka relations.
   (ii) Trincomalee or any other ports in Sri Lanka will not be made available for military use by any country in a manner prejudicial to India's interests.
   (iii) The work of restoring and operating the Trincomalee Oil tank farm will be undertaken as a joint venture between India and Sri Lanka.
   (iv) Sri Lanka's agreements with foreign broadcasting organisations will be reviewed to ensure that any facilities set up by them in Sri Lanka are used solely as public broadcasting facilities and not for any military or intelligence purposes.

3. In the same spirit, India will:

   (i)   deport all Sri Lankan citizens who are found to be engaging in terrorist activities or advocating separatism or secessionism.
   (ii) Provide training facilities and military supplies for Sri Lankan security forces.

4. India and Sri Lanka have agreed to set up a joint consultative mechanism to continuously review matters of common concern in the light of the objectives stated in para 1 and specifically to monitor the implementation of other matters contained in this letter.

5. Kindly confirm, Excellency, that the above correctly sets out the agreement reached between us.

Please accept, Excellency, the assurances of my highest consideration.

Yours sincerely,
Sd/-
(Rajiv Gandhi)

His Excellency
Mr. J.R. Jayewardene,
President of the Democratic Socialist Republic of Sri Lanka,
Colombo

This is to confirm that the above correctly sets out the understanding reached between us. Please accept, Excellency, the assurances of my highest consideration.

Sd/-
(J.R. Jayewardene)
President

His Excellency
Mr. Rajiv Gandhi,
Prime Minister of the Republic of India,
New Delhi

8 FRIENDS AND FOES OF THE INDO-SRI LANKA ACCORD

S.W.R. de A. Samarasinghe and Kamala Liyanage

The Indo-Sri Lanka Accord (1987) was a 'failed' attempt on the part of Sri Lanka's President J. R. Jayewardene and India's Prime Minister Rajiv Gandhi to resolve Sri Lanka's internationalized and protracted Sinhalese-Tamil ethnic conflict.[1] In retrospect, it failed largely because it focused too much attention on the 'international' aspects of the conflict and too little attention on the domestic aspects which were far more complex and intractable than the former. This chapter seeks to: review the support for the Accord and the opposition to it generated in Sri Lanka; to evaluate that experience in terms of some basic principles of ethnic conflict resolution; and to draw the implications of those events for the peaceful resolution of the conflict in the future. To place this in an appropriate context, we provide a brief outline of the key features of the Sri Lankan ethnic conflict on the eve of the signing of the Accord on 29 July, 1987.[2] Those events had a powerful influence on the responses to the Accord among large sections of the population, especially the Sinhalese. We believe that an examination of the responses to this Accord will be of very great value in fashioning future efforts at a resolution of this conflict, and especially in the mechanics of the negotiation process.

Nature of the conflict: c. July 1987

Certain key features of the ongoing Sinhala-Tamil ethnic conflict had a direct bearing on both the specifics of the Accord as well as the response that it evoked in Sri Lanka. First, it had developed into what the late Edward Azar[3] has described as a 'protracted' conflict. The conflict had persisted and developed over at least three decades. Starting around 1955-6 it was marked by periodic outbreaks of ethnic riots thereafter, the worst of which was in July 1983. From the early 1980s armed conflict between government security forces and Tamil militants gradually escalated and turned into a full–scale civil war by the mid-1980s. By that time the protagonists had taken strongly entrenched positions. For example, the Tamil groups, from the relatively moderate Tamil United Liberation Front (TULF) to the militant Liberation Tigers of Tamil Eelam (LTTE), were uncompromising in their claim that the Northern and Eastern provinces together constituted the 'homeland' of the Tamils and that the Tamils were a 'distinct' people with an inherent right to self-determination and nationhood. The overwhelming majority of the Sinhalese and the Sri Lankan government were equally adamant in refusing to concede any of these demands.

Second, as protracted ethnic conflicts often do, the Sri Lankan conflict had also moved beyond the domestic arena and had been internationalized.[4] In particular, India played an increasingly important role in that process of internationalization.

Thirdly, a series of events immediately preceding the Peace Accord had served to antagonize the Sri Lankan government and to create a strong anti-Indian mood among the Sinhalese general public. A military campaign (the 'Vadamarachchi' operation) started by the government security forces in May–June 1987 scored some resounding successes in the Jaffna peninsula. When there was a reasonable prospect of the security forces marching into Jaffna, the LTTE stronghold, the Indian government intervened and warned the Sri Lankan government not to do so. A public message to that effect was delivered by a display of Indian military superiority; India air-dropped food in Jaffna in violation of Sri Lankan airspace and sovereignty. In less than two months of this the Indo-Lanka Accord had been signed.

The Sri Lankan public were taken aback by the speed with which the two governments reached an accommodation on a resolution of Sri Lanka's ethnic conflict. To many it seemed as though the Indian government was merely continuing its aggressive support of the Tamil cause in Sri Lanka, this time through a peace accord. For most of the Sinhalese, India's role in this conflict was seen to be far too partisan for her to play the role of mediator. Their depth of feeling was best symbolized by two separate incidents. One was the fact that the President's own son – who played an important back-room advisory role in the prosecution of the government military campaign against the Tamil separatists – boycotted the tea party given by the President in honor of the visiting Indian Prime Minister Gandhi. The second was the sympathy and even approval shown by a large section of the Sinhalese public for the action of the naval rating who assaulted the Indian Prime Minister with his rifle butt when the former inspected an honor guard at his departure ceremony.

Supporters

In general the supporters of the Accord were less vociferous than its opponents. One reason was that they were in a numerical minority, at least in the Sinhalese and Muslim communities. Another reason was that the supporters of the Accord were threatened with physical violence by the Janatha Vimukthi Peramuna (JVP) in the south and by the LTTE in the north.

The official viewpoint of the ruling United National Party (UNP) was expressed by President Jayewardene at the press conference following its signing. He asserted that Sri Lanka had no option but to deal with India in the manner that it did through the Accord.[5] There were several reasons for President Jayewardene to take this position. First, Sri Lanka could not destroy the Tamil Nadu bases of the militants that acted as the nerve centre for their armed campaign against the Sri Lanka government. Second, the flow of Sri Lankan Tamil refugees to Tamil Nadu caused by the war provided an excuse for Tamil Nadu politicians to apply pressure on Delhi to interfere in the Sri Lankan problem, usually in favour of the separatists. Thirdly, Jayewardene quite rightly concluded that, influenced partly by the appalling violence and partly by the propaganda of the separatists and that of India, international opinion on Sri Lanka was relatively unfavourable. The way to improve international opinion was to make a settlement with India's involvement. The irony of this situation was that whereas India perceived President Jayewardene to be pro-American, he received almost no backing from the Americans or the other Western powers in dealings with India on the ethnic issue. This diplomatic isolation strongly influenced President Jayewardene's decision to go ahead with the Accord. Thus it was a case of using the Indians to the best possible advantage of Sri Lanka under unfavorable and difficult circumstances.

The Accord received strong support from the left parties both in the south as well as in the north. Of course the results of numerous elections, both national and local, held in the past 15 years had clearly demonstrated that these parties were electorally marginal and had very limited popular support. Nevertheless, for the government even this limited degree of support for the Accord helped break its sense of isolation on this issue and was thus a source of strength and encouragement. The formation of the southern-based United Socialist Alliance (USA) in 1987 comprising the Lanka Sama Samaja Party (LSSP), the Communist Party (CP), the Nawa Sama Samaja Party (NSSP) and the Sri Lanka Mahajana Pakshaya (SLMP) was to some extent prompted by the shared view held by these parties that devolution of power through a system of provincial councils was desirable. They also believed that the Accord would help restore peace and democratic processes in the country.[6] All of them, but more particularly the NSSP, had strong reservations about the presence of the Indian Peace Keeping Force (IPKF) in the north-east.[7]

The left-oriented Tamil militant groups, People's Liberation Organization of Tamil Eelam (PLOTE) and the Eelam People's Revolutionary Liberation Front (EPRLF) indulged in armed conflict against Sri Lankan security forces until the Accord was signed. However, after July 1987 they opted to co-operate with the Sri Lanka government and India to implement the Accord. Two other Tamil separatist groups, the Tamil Eelam Liberation Organization (TELO) and the Eelam National Democratic Liberation Front (ENDLF) which was an ally of the EPRLF, also decided to extend their support to the Accord. The two centrist Tamil parties the Tamil United Liberation Front (TULF) and the Tamil Congress (TC) as well as the Ceylon Workers' Congress (CWC) that represented the plantation Tamils also welcomed the Accord. They viewed it as a 'reasonable alternative' to a separate Tamil state, 'Eelam', and expected India to exert pressure on Sri Lanka to implement it effectively.[8] In general, a substantial section of the Tamil public opinion was very supportive of the Accord. This was not surprising because it was the Tamil population in the north-east that suffered most from the ongoing civil war. The cessation of hostilities and the prospect of peace brought a sense of relief to them.

Open support for the Accord from the Sinhalese and Muslim communities was limited. A few pressure groups representing liberal opinion welcomed the Accord. For example, a small group of prominent academics, professionals and intellectuals issued a press statement approving it.[9] Two other similar groups, the Movement for Inter Racial Justice and Equality (MIRJE)[10] and the Committee for Rational Development,[11] also made press statements welcoming the Accord.

Those supporting the Accord were motivated by a variety of factors. In so far as the government and the ruling UNP, and especially its leadership were concerned, they desperately wanted a settlement of the conflict that had, by then, precipitated a major political, economic and a diplomatic crisis. Politically, the government was under severe pressure in the Sinhalese areas of the country especially from the militant JVP which increasingly resorted to violence against it.[12] Economically, the war had a severe debilitating affect on development. The share of annual government expenditure on the security services had gone up from 4.9 per cent (Rs 1.5 billion) of current government expenditure in 1982 to 20.7 per cent (Rs 20.7 billion) in 1987.[13] The adverse impact on tourism, foreign investment and the production activity in the war zone had slowed down the annual economic growth rate which was down from an average of over 5.0 per cent in the early 1980s to less than 3.0 per cent by 1986–7.[14] Diplomatically, Sri Lanka's relations with India in the early and mid-1980s resembled a political roller-coaster ride. The Jayewardene administration felt that India was undermining Sri Lanka's territorial integrity through the covert, and occasionally overt, support given to Tamil separatists. Moreover, the international community, with a few exceptions such as Pakistan and China, showed little or no sympathy for Sri Lanka's predicament *vis-à-vis* India. The leading Western countries who had very considerable leverage on Colombo on account of Sri Lanka's heavy dependence on foreign economic assistance, insisted that the Jayewardene administration must seek a peaceful solution to the conflict with India's help.

In general, all the political parties, pressure groups and sections of the public that welcomed the Accord were primarily attracted by the prospect for peace. However, many had some reservations about one or the other specific features in it. Government ministers had an opportunity to air their views on the subject at a cabinet meeting on 12 August summoned specifically to discuss the Accord and its external implications. Several senior members of the government including the Prime Minister R. Premadasa and the Minister for National Security Lalith Athulathmudali were unhappy that India had dictated terms to Sri Lanka. Premadasa argued that the constitution did not permit the holding of a regional referendum as proposed in the Accord. He strongly opposed the presence of the IPKF. However, the Prime Minister was willing to support any legislation to implement the Accord provided such legislation were approved by the Supreme Court as being in accordance with the constitution. It was reported that Premadasa had urged President Jayewardene to persuade Gandhi to delay the latter's visit.[15] In any event, in a symbolic act of disapproval, Premadasa, who was number two in the government, boycotted the Accord signing ceremony.

The Minister for National Security Athulathmudali was probably the most consistent critic of the Accord in the cabinet. He had been carefully excluded from the actual drafting, with the responsibility being taken by his 'rival' Gamini Dissanayake in association with J. N. Dixit the Indian High Commissioner (Ambassador) in Colombo. Athulathmudali asserted that in so far as the Accord dealt with issues such as language rights and devolution of power designed to meet the demands of the Tamil minority, it merely embodied decisions that had been taken much earlier, which, in fact, formed part of a *modus vivendi.* What was new in it were the concessions made by Sri Lanka to meet India's security concerns. To register his protest against it Athulathmudali boycotted the Accord signing ceremony. However, only one senior cabinet minister, Agriculture Minister Gamini Jayasuriya who is a prominent Buddhist lay leader, resigned from the government on the issue. One M.P., Asoka Somaratne, who represented an electorate in the southern province where anti-Accord feelings were particularly intense, resigned from his seat in parliament later in September before legislation to implement it were presented. In general the ruling party backed President Jayewardene's decisions on the Accord.

Among the Tamils, those who supported the Accord viewed it as a reasonable framework for further negotiation leading to a peaceful settlement of the conflict. The recognition of the Northern and Eastern provinces as areas of 'historical habitation of Sri Lankan Tamil speaking peoples', the ('temporary') merger of the north-east, the acknowledgement that Sri Lanka was a 'multi-ethnic, multi-lingual and multi-religious plural society', the acceptance of Tamil as an official language and the withdrawal of the Sri Lankan army to barracks constituted an acceptable package as an alternative to Eelam. However, every Tamil group wanted a permanent merger of the north-east and were unhappy about a referendum to decide it.[16] In general, the supporters of the Accord felt that having India underwrite it was a positive element that virtually guaranteed its proper implementation. The presence of the IPKF was also seen as a positive element. This, however, soon changed when hostilities broke out between the IPKF and the LTTE in October. Indeed many Tamil civilians[17] and even the LTTE[18] criticized the IPKF for behaving in a manner much worse than the predominantly Sinhalese Sri Lankan forces ever behaved in the pre-Accord days.

Opponents

It is probably fair to assert that the majority of the Sinhalese were opposed to the Accord. Among the mainstream Sinhalese political parties, the opposition was led by Mrs Sirimavo Bandaranaike's Sri Lanka Freedom Party (SLFP), the major opposition party in the south.

A number of minor parties, most notably the Mahajana Eksath Peramuna (MEP) and the Eksath Lanka Janatha Pakshaya (ELJP) also voiced their opposition.

It should be noted that the critics of the Accord welcomed some of its clauses. For example, the SLFP leader Mrs Bandaranaike had no objection to the cessation of hostilities and the surrender of arms by the separatist groups.[19] The party's position on devolution was ambivalent. They were apparently prepared to accept devolution provided it was based on socio-economic need rather than on ethnic division. However, the important point is that the SLFP was not willing to support many of the principal clauses.

The strong opposition expressed by two groups proved to be critical in forming public perceptions of the Accord and especially in shaping the events in the aftermath to it. One were the *bhikkhus* (members of the Buddhist order). The first protest meeting against the Accord was one that was held by *bhikkhus* on 23 and 24 July. On 27 July about 3000 *bhikkhus* met in Colombo and vowed to frustrate the plans of the government. Leading *bhikkhus* and lay Buddhist groups and organizations were among the most vocal opponents. The principal *bhikkhus* of the main Buddhist sects were practically unanimous in condemning the Accord. Some of them subscribed to the view that it was a 'conspiracy' against the Sinhalese-Buddhists.[20] Most of them preferred peaceful opposition to violent outbursts, but they proved incapable of restraining some of the younger or more radical *bhikkhus*.

The Maubima Surakime Viyaparaya – MSV (The Movement to Protect the Motherland) established in July 1986 one year before the Accord led the campaign of the *bhikkhus* against it. The MSV in its formative stages enjoyed the active support of the leaders of the SLFP, MEP and JVP. However, in November 1986 the movement split into two with the radical element constituting the parent organization and the less radical element forming the Maubima Surakime Sangamaya – MSS (Association for the Protection of the Motherland). The MSV retained the support of the MEP and JVP and the MSS enjoyed the support of Mrs Bandaranaike and the SLFP. It was the MSV that emerged as the fulcrum for unrest and agitation when the Accord was announced. They were already fairly well prepared for this purpose having formed, probably with the blessings of the JVP, 'one hundred-man units' in villages to 'defend' the motherland. Young *bhikkhus*, many of whom were undergraduates, played a very prominent role in the protest campaign inspired by the MSV and even had a hand in the violence that erupted.

The second group that had a critical influence on post-Accord events was the Janatha Vimukthi Peramuna (JVP). The JVP was proscribed by the government in 1983 and had operated ever since as a clandestine organization. The party from its very inception in the late 1960s viewed India as a country with expansionist designs on its neighbours, Sri Lanka included. In training sessions for party cadres the JVP devoted one out of five lectures to this theme.[21] For the party, the Accord provided unimpeachable evidence of Indian expansionism. Given this ideological orientation, the public antipathy to the Accord was cleverly exploited by the JVP to mount a vicious and brutal anti-government campaign.

The Sinhalese critics of the Accord were generally in agreement regarding several features in it that they found objectionable. These were:

1. All these groups condemned the government for the apparent haste and secrecy with which it was formulated and signed, without due consultation and debate.[22] Though not entirely accurate, this was the popular perception. The fact is that while the negotiations in the final stages of the Accord were shrouded in secrecy, several of its key clauses had been agreed upon several years earlier, beginning in about 1984 with discussions and negotiations involving the parties concerned: notably the government, opposition political parties, Tamil groups and the Indian government. We refer in particular to the All Party Conference (APC) of 1984, the 'Delhi Accord' of 1985,[23] and the Political Parties Conference of 1986. For example, a proposal to establish provincial councils was incorporated in the Delhi Accord. Thus, it was not entirely accurate to accuse the government of haste at arriving at some of the key clauses.

2. They felt that Sri Lanka had compromised its sovereignty and independence by agreeing to a number of conditions that advanced India's security interests and limited Sri Lanka's freedom to decide on its foreign policy.[24] For example, in an Annexure to the Accord the Sri Lankan President accepted a proposal from the Indian Prime Minister Gandhi that 'Trincomalee or any other ports in Sri Lanka will not be made available for military use by any country in a manner prejudicial to India's interests'. Critics argued that this was a one-sided agreement which did not require India to reciprocate by giving similar assurances. What they had in mind was the fact that Tamil militant groups were freely based in Tamilnadu to organize and conduct their military activities against Sri Lankan government

forces. Moreover, it was pointed out that this clause violated a fundamental right of a sovereign state to take any steps it deems fit including permitting foreign powers to use facilities in the country for military purposes, if such were in one's own best interest.[25]

3. The merger of the Northern and Eastern provinces was condemned as an undemocratic move that undermined the rights of the Sinhalese and Muslim residents in the Eastern province.[26] The merger was viewed as an unprincipled capitulation to Indian pressure and an acceptance of the Tamil claim that the north-east constituted a 'Traditional Tamil Homeland'. The historical[27] and demographic[28] basis for this claim is weak and neither the Sinhalese nor the Muslims were willing to concede the point. In clause 1.4 of the Accord[29] its framers used the phrase 'areas of historical habitation' instead of 'traditional homeland' to describe the Northern and Eastern provinces. However, critics have argued that this was mere word play and that in substance the Tamils have been granted a 'homeland'.[30] Indeed much of the intensity in the agitation against the Accord stemmed from opposition to the merger of the two provinces.

4. The Accord was faulted, especially by its constitutional lawyer critics, for making provision to hold a referendum only in the Eastern province to decide the future of the temporary merger. In their view it was a national issue that required a national referendum.

5. The presence of the IPKF was vehemently opposed by almost every critic of the Accord. Some argued that the President had no powers under Sri Lankan law to invite foreign troops to the country.[31] In any event the IPKF was a symbol of Indian domination of Sri Lanka and most could not see any positive results emerging from what was frequently described as an 'occupation army'.

6. The critics believed that the Accord and the events involving India that immediately preceded it prevented the Sri Lankan security forces from defeating the Tamil separatists in war.

7. Some opposed the devolution of power, based on the principle of ethnic division under the proposed provincial council (PCs) system. It was also argued that PCs were superfluous in a small country such as Sri Lanka and would waste scarce resources.

The Muslim community in general and the Eastern province Muslims in particular opposed the Accord from the very beginning. The Accord was the principal precipitating factor that led to the formation of the Sri Lanka Muslim Congress (SLMC) in 1988.[32] It took a strong anti-Accord position in response to the concerns of the Eastern province Muslims and developed a strong electoral base in the area.[33] Even senior Muslim leaders in the government, such as the Transport Minister, M. H. Mohammad, expressed their strong dissatisfaction with the Accord for the manner in which the interests of the Muslim community were disregarded.[34] First, the Accord had not recognized the Muslims as a separate community but appeared to have grouped them with the Tamils as a part of the 'Tamil-speaking' community. Secondly, they wanted a separate administrative unit for the Muslims in the Eastern province and objected to the merger that reduced them to a politically impotent minority in the new region.

As K. M. de Silva shows in his chapter in this book, the LTTE accepted the Accord only under pressure from India and with great reluctance. In a post-Accord rally in Jaffna the LTTE leader Prabhakaran declared that 'he was forced to tow New Delhi's line and wanted to avoid a confrontation with the Indian army'. However, he added that he was still committed to a separate Tamil state 'without which there will be no lasting peace'.[35] Prabhakaran felt that he was not adequately consulted on the framing of the Accord and gave four principal reasons for objecting to it. First, the Accord, in his view, justified 'illegal Sinhala colonization' by stating that the 'Northern and the Eastern Provinces have been areas of historical habitation of Sri Lankan Tamil speaking peoples, who have *at all times* [authors' emphasis] hitherto lived *together in this territory with other ethnic groups* [authors' emphasis]'. Second, the Tamils were not recognized in the Accord as a distinct and separate nation. Third, Prabhakaran wanted an immediate permanent merger of the two provinces. Fourthly, he objected to the Accord calling for the surrender of arms by the separatist groups without a parallel withdrawal of the Sri Lankan forces from the two provinces.[36] The LTTE was also unhappy that the Accord would prove to be an obstacle to its objective to become the sole representatives of the Tamils.

Anti-accord campaign

The opposition of the LTTE to the Accord eventually led to a war between the group and the IPKF. The war itself is outside the scope of this chapter and will not be discussed here. The opposition to the Accord in the south had two facets, one peaceful and one violent. The SLFP summoned a central committee meeting of the party on 22 July to discuss its response to the impending Accord. The party decided to launch a mass campaign of agitation through public rallies, *bodhi poojas* (Buddhist ceremonies of religious worship) and the hoisting of black flags. The party also resolved to exert pressure on (government) members of parliament to desist from supporting the Accord and from voting for it in parliament. For example, the SLFP tried to exploit the dissention that was apparent in government ranks by declaring that it would back Prime Minister Premadasa if he were to maintain his opposition to the Accord.[37]

The *bhikkhu* organization MSV summoned a *Sangha Sabha* (a meeting of the *bhikkhus*) in Colombo on 27 July under the chairmanship of the Ven Palipane Chandananda, one of the most senior and respected *bhikkhu* leaders of the country. The leaders of the opposition political parties that opposed the Accord including Mrs Bandaranaike were present at this meeting. The plan of action proposed to the assembly by the leaders of the movement was not significantly different to that proposed by the SLFP at the latter's central committee meeting. However, the more radical *bhikkhus* in the gathering led by representatives of the Deshapremi Shishya Viyaparaya (Patriotic Students Movement) affiliated with the JVP deplored the 'tame' speeches from the platform and demanded more militant action including a 'fast unto death'.

The protest marches and rallies organized by the MSV, SLFP and other mainstream opposition political parties that took place in Colombo and elsewhere on 28 July took a violent turn. In Colombo at least three buildings, including one that housed a government ministry and another that housed a state-owned newspaper office, were set on fire. Scores of buses, trucks and cars were also gutted. Police opened fire after a section of the crowd went on a rampage and at least 19 people were killed and some 120 injured. On 29 July, the day the Accord was signed, mobs, estimated to be at least 10,000 in total, gathered in the outskirts of Colombo defying a 24-hour curfew. Their objective was to converge on the area where the President's House was located, their intention being to make a last ditch attempt to stop the signing of the Accord that was scheduled to take place that morning. The police prevented the marchers from reaching the President's House or its vicinity. However, they committed a spate of acts of violence that caused extensive damage to private and public property. Similar incidents of public disorder and violence were reported from almost all the provincial towns in the Sinhalese areas. During the period 28 July to 2 August, over 2,500 acts of violence were reported including at least 20 deaths and over 150 injuries. In addition, about 1,000 vehicles and over

700 buildings destroyed or damaged.[38] Much of this violence was attributed to the involvement of the JVP in the *satyagraha* (demonstrations). However, that round of protest soon subsided and one could say that the first stage of protest against the Accord came to an end. The second stage of protest that followed had two facets. One was the mainstream opposition campaign against the Accord that continued along peaceful lines through debates in parliament and public rallies and meetings. The other was the violent campaign of the JVP launched under the aegis of a front organization appropriately named Deshapremi Janatha Viyaparaya – DJV (Patriotic People's Movement). The principal tactic of the JVP campaign was to use violence against members of the government. The most dramatic incident was a grenade and gun attack on a meeting of the government parliamentary group held in the parliamentary premises on 18 August to discuss the Accord. The assailants succeeded in killing one Junior Minister and injuring several other members of the government including the Minister for National Security Lalith Athulathmudali. Had the JVP succeeded on that occasion in reaching its main targets, primarily the President and senior members of the government, it would have precipitated a major political crisis and probably destroyed the Accord as well. The government responded to the JVP campaign by strengthening security of the ministers and MPs.

The third stage of the anti-Accord campaign began with the passage of the 13th amendment to the constitution in November 1987 that gave legislative teeth to the various provisions of the Accord including the creation of provincial councils and making Tamil an official language. Prime Minister Premadasa piloted the legislation through parliament. Only two government MPs, both representing electorates in the Southern province, defied the government whip and abstained from voting during the second reading of the bill. However, even they voted with the government in the third reading. The nine SLFP MPs and the lone MEP MP in parliament abstained from voting and walked out of parliament at the time the vote was taken. However, the amendment was passed in parliament. It was challenged in the supreme court as being unconstitutional but that was approved by the justices by a very narrow margin of five to four.

The JVP continued its campaign of agitation and violence until it was brutally put down by the security forces in late 1989 and early 1990. However, after August 1987 its campaign was increasingly directed at toppling the government and capturing power. The Accord and especially the presence of the IPKF were exploited systematically by the

JVP for this purpose. The JVP escalated its campaign of terror – especially against government MPs who did not enjoy the same degree of state security service protection as ministers. The objective was to prevent the enactment of legislation to implement the Accord. One government MP thought it more prudent to resign his seat in parliament rather than vote for the 13th amendment.

The SLFP and other opposition parties opposed to the Accord continued their peaceful protest by refusing to cooperate with the government to implement the Accord. For example, the SLFP decided to boycott the elections for the provincial councils held in 1988. However, the government went ahead with the implementation of the clauses of the Accord pertaining to devolution and language. Notwithstanding such efforts, the Accord failed to bring peace and a lasting solution to the conflict.

Evaluation

The anti-Accord campaign of the Sinhalese opposition – both mainstream and JVP – was not entirely sustained by anti-Accord feelings among the public. It also reflected the frustration of the youth over growing unemployment, the dissatisfaction of many sections of the community about certain anti-democratic measures (e.g. the 1982 December Referendum that extended the life of the 1977–83 parliament) taken by the government and the deteriorating economic conditions. As for the LTTE, its leadership was apparently not willing to settle for anything short of a separate state – Eelam. However, even if the Sinhalese had no other major grievances and the LTTE had given up its goal of Eelam, the fact was that the Accord itself had some inherent defects and limitations that doomed it.

First, a major problem concerned India's role as a mediator. Her credibility as a mediator was seriously flawed because neither the Sinhalese nor the Tamils viewed India as a neutral player. As some theorists suggest, it may be possible to have an effective and successful intermediary who is also partisan.[39] In practice, however, at least in the Sri Lankan case it proved to be unhelpful. The Sinhalese did not trust India because of its record of helping Tamil separatists. Some Tamils, especially the LTTE, also did not fully trust it because India's actions were viewed not as that of a disinterested mediator, but that of a participant in the conflict with its own interests to protect.

A second flaw of the Indo-Sri Lanka Accord was that it was a bilateral agreement between one party to the conflict and the mediator – to the exclusion of the second party to the conflict, the Tamil separatists, especially the LTTE. India did try to use its leverage to persuade the LTTE to adhere to the Accord. For example, LTTE was given a substantial cash grant as a part of the deal. Prabhakaran was held under virtual house arrest in Delhi until he agreed to accept the Accord. However, such leverage proved to be an insufficient substitute for bringing in the LTTE as a party to the Accord.

Third, the Sri Lanka case illustrates the importance of timing to any attempt to solve a complex and emotion-ridden ethnic conflict. The events immediately preceding the Accord were such that the Sinhalese were in no mood to accept a settlement that apparently humiliated them. This despite the fact that with the exception of the temporary merger all the other provisions of the Accord that applied to the domestic issue (though not the Indian foreign policy concerns) had been more or less accepted by at least some segment of the public over the preceding three years.

Fourth, both India and Sri Lanka as the implementors of the Accord failed to adequately take into account the complex political and psychological reality that lay behind the protracted conflict and to address them effectively. India failed to understand the sensitivity of the Sinhalese to 'Indian intervention' in Sri Lanka. The only way that they could have won the confidence of the Sinhalese would have been by effectively disarming the Tigers. Had that been done India would have been in a strong position, both morally and politically, to insist on the strict implementation of the Accord, especially with respect to devolution. The Indians also underestimated the military strength of the LTTE and the depth of public support that the latter seems to enjoy in the north.

The Sri Lankan government for its part could have been more sensitive to the concerns of the Tigers who were looking for an excuse to sabotage the Accord. That opportunity was given on 4 October when the administration insisted on bringing 17 LTTE men arrested by the Sri Lankan Navy to Colombo. The men committed suicide rather than come to Colombo to face interrogation and trial. The LTTE used the incident as an excuse to turn their guns on the few Sinhalese who still remained in Jaffna and the Sinhalese community in Trincomalee and elsewhere in the north-east. Then the Indians were forced to intervene and launch a military campaign against the LTTE. That effectively ended the peace that lasted no more than about two months.[40]

Conclusions

Although the Accord failed to settle the Sinhalese-Tamil conflict and restore peace in Sri Lanka, it has contributed to the long-term settlement process of the conflict and eventual peace in several ways. First, it has provided a basic framework for a settlement. For example, it recognized the legitimacy of the Tamil concerns. It made provision for language rights and devolution. It formally established the principle that Sri Lanka is a multi-ethnic society.

Second, it clearly identified the constraints that have to be overcome to achieve a lasting political solution. For example, the opposition to the Accord from the Muslims and the Sinhalese in the Eastern province was a clear indication that the complex demography of that province must be taken into account in any future settlement.

Thirdly, the problems that India faced as a mediator highlighted the constraints that any future third-party mediator in the Sri Lankan conflict would face. On balance the events of the latter part of 1987 reviewed here seem to suggest that the most fruitful course of action for a peaceful settlement may be bilateral negotiations between Colombo and the LTTE. That way there is a reasonable chance of mobilizing more public support for an accord than that ever enjoyed by the Indo-Sri Lanka Accord.

Notes

1. For the specific clauses of the Accord see Appendix II to chapter 7 of this book.
2. For a general account of Sri Lanka's ethnic conflict see S.W.R. de A. Samarasinghe (1990) The dynamics of separatism: The case of Sri Lanka, in Ralph R. Premdas, et al. (eds) *Secessionist Movements in Comparative Perspective*, London: Pinter Publishers, pp. 48–70.
3. Azar, Edward E. (1990) *The Management of Protracted Social Conflict*, Hampshire, England: Dartmouth.
4. K.M. de Silva (1991) Indo-Sri Lanka relations, 1975–89: A study in the internationalization of ethnic conflict, in K.M. de Silva and R.J. May (eds) *Internationalization of Ethnic Conflict*, London: Pinter Publishers, pp. 76– 106; Shelton U. Kodikara, Internationalization of Sri Lanka's ethnic conflict: The Tamilnadu factor, in K.M. de Silva and R.J. May (eds), Ibid, pp. 107–14; S.D. Muni, Indo-Sri Lanka relations and Sri Lanka's ethnic conflict, in K.M. de Silva and R.J. May (eds), Ibid, pp. 115–124.
5. *The Observer* (Colombo) (1987) 16 August.
6. *Ceylon Daily News* (Colombo) (1988) 29 July.
7. The Peace Accord – A view from Tamil Left, (1988) *Lanka Guardian* (Colombo), II, 1, 23–25 May.

8. *The Island* (Colombo) (1988) 31 July.
9. *Lanka Guardian* (Colombo) (1987) **10**, 8, 15, 15 August.
10. *Lanka Guardian* (Colombo) (1987) **10**, 15, 6, 1 December.
11. *Lanka Guardian* (Colombo) (1987) **10**, 5, 6, 1 December.
12. C.A. Chandraprema (1991) *Sri Lanka: The Years of Terror – The JVP Insurrection of 1987–89*, Lake House, Colombo.
13. Central Bank of Sri Lanka, *Review of the Economy*, 1987.
14. One study has estimated the total economic cost of political violence over the period 1983–88 at Rs 138.6 billion (US $4.2 billion) or almost three times the cost of the Accelerated Mahaweli River Diversion Project (John Richardson and S.W.R. de A. Samarasinghe (1991) Measuring the economic dimensions of Sri Lanka's ethnic conflict in S.W.R. de A. Samarasinghe and Reed Coughlan (eds), *Economic Dimensions of Ethnic Conflict*, London: Pinter Publishers, pp. 194–223).
15. *The Daily Telegraph* (London) (1987) 29 July.
16. *Tamil Times* (London) (1987) **VI**, 10, 5 August.
17. An unholy war, *Tamil Voice International* (1988) **1**, **1**, 3, 15 January.
18. *The Island* (Colombo) (1988) 12 July, p. 4.
19. Sirima on Indo-Lanka Accord *Lanka Guardian* (Colombo) (1988) **10**, 19, 7, 1 February.
20. Some of the information on the attitude of the *bhikkhus* towards the Accord was gathered by the authors in a series of interviews with *bhikkhu* leaders.
21. R. Wijeweera (1975) 'Speech to the criminal justice commission, in Robert Blackburn (ed), *Explosion in a Sub-Continent*, London: Penguin.
22. The following is an English translation of a handbill that was distributed by the SLFP inviting people to a Public National Prayer in Colombo on 28 July morning.

> 65 Rosmead Place
> Colombo 7
>
> Dear Patriots,
> The rumor that has now spread is that on Wednesday July 29 a *secret* [authors' emphasis] agreement will be signed in *haste* [authors' emphasis] making our Sri Lanka a subject state of India.
> At this moment as Sri Lankans it is our prime duty to protect our motherland. Join the National Prayer to be held on Tuesday July 28 at 8 am at the Viharamahadevi Park, Colombo to compel the government to desist from this great betrayal.
>
> Sgnd. Sirimavo Bandaranaike

(Note by the Authors: In the handbill that was distributed the venue of the Prayer Meeting was changed by freehand from the Viharamahadevi Park to the Colombo Fort Railway Station.)
23. See Appendix I to Chapter 7 of this book.
24. *The Sunday Times* (Colombo) (1987) 30 August.
25. S.L. Gunasekera *Indo-Lanka Accord: An Analysis*, Colombo: Mahajana Publications (undated).
26. According to the 1981 population census, the ethnic composition of the population in the east was as follows: Tamil 4.2 per cent, Muslim 32.2 per

cent, Sinhalese 24.9 per cent. In a merged north-east the respective percentages would be 68.7 per cent, 17.6 per cent and 13.2 per cent.
27. K.M. de Silva (1987) *The Traditional Homelands of the Tamils of Sri Lanka: A Historical Appraisal*, ICES Occasional Papers, No 1, International Centre for Ethnic Studies, Kandy, Sri Lanka.
28. G.H. Peiris (1991) An appraisal of the concept of a traditional Tamil homeland in Sri Lanka, *Ethnic Studies Report*, **IX**, 1, 13–39, January.
29. See Appendix II to chapter 7 of this volume.
30. H.L. de Silva (1987) Indo-Sri Lanka Peace Accord: An appraisal, in S.U. Kodikara (ed), *Indo-Sri Lanka Agreement of July 1987*, Colombo, Lake House, p. 36.
31. See, for example, S.L. Gunasekera, *Indo-Lanka Accord: An Analysis*, Mahajana Publications, Colombo (undated), p. 53.
32. *The Island* (Colombo) (1992) 7 January, p. 1.
33. M.H.M. Ashroff (1987) The Muslim community and the Peace Accord *Logos* (Colombo), **26**, 1, 3 and 4, 48–57, December.
34. *Hindu* (Madras) (1987) 30 August.
35. *Far Eastern Economic Review* (1987) 13 August, p. 8.
36. *India Today* (1987) 15 August, p. 9.
37. *Hindu* (Madras) (1987) 12 August.
38. Source: ICES Data Bank, International Centre for Ethnic Studies, Kandy, Sri Lanka.
39. See, for example, I. William Zartman, Conflict Reduction: Prevention Management and Resolution, in Francis M. Deng and I. William Zartman (eds) (1991) *Conflict Resolution in Africa*, Washington, DC: Brookings Institution, p. 311.
40. See K.M. de Silva's chapter in this book for details of these events.

9 PEACE ACCORDS: SEEKING CONFLICT RESOLUTION IN DEEPLY DIVIDED SOCIETIES

John M. Richardson Jr. and Jianxin Wang[1]

Introduction

The peace accords described in this book did not lead to durable settlements. In this respect they failed. On the other hand, however, they were pioneering attempts at settling one of the most intractable forms of political conflict. In every case a framework for conflict resolution, agreed upon by some, was created and in several cases, the accords temporarily ended violent conflict and provided a breathing space within which further discussions could go forward. Thus, the peace accords can usefully be viewed as experiments, from which there are lessons to be learned. Identifying those lessons is a major purpose of *Peace Accords and Ethnic Conflict* and of this concluding chapter.

Table 9.1 summarizes the outcomes of the accords. The Addis Ababa Agreement was most successful, contributing to nearly ten years of peace between Northern and Southern Sudanese, but now ethnic conflict rages again.[2] About three years of stability followed the independence of Cyprus, mandated by the London-Zurich Accord.[3] In Sri Lanka, violence subsided in the north for about six weeks after the Indo-Lanka Accord was signed, but the accord was a catalyst in a new conflict in the south.[4] The Punjab Agreement and Canada's Meech Lake Accord produced documents, but few tangible results.[5] One could add to this list the several agreements that have attempted to resolve Northern Ireland's ethnic conflict,[6] plus other negotiations and accords, signed and unsigned, that have failed to produce lasting peace. Shortcomings in peace accords point to the two questions addressed in this paper, which reviews both 'scholarly' and 'practical' studies of conflict resolution: (1) Why did the peace accords fail to achieve their objectives? (2) How can those concerned with resolving ethnic conflicts do better?

Apparently, ethnic conflict has not yet captured the interest of most conflict resolution scholars. A computer search of the major book collection in the Washington, DC area devoted to 'conflict resolution'[7]

Table 9.1 Outcomes of Peace Accords

Accord	Outcome
CYPRUS: London-Zurich Agreements (1959)	Greek dominated government proposed constitutional changes in 1963 to modify agreement. Turks withdrew from government. Subsequent unrest resulted in a pro-Greek military coup and occupation of the North by Turkish forces. Turkish Cypriots declared independence in 1983. Subsequent negotiations under UN auspices have failed to produce agreement.
SUDAN: Addis Ababa Agreement (Feb. 1972)	Agreement implemented as the Southern Provinces Regional Self Government Act. Act unilaterally abrogated by President Nimeiri in 1982. Government attempted to implement Sharia nationwide in 1984. Conflict between SPLM/SPLA and Sudan Government forces continues.
INDIA: Punjab Accord (July 1985)	Provisions of the accord have not been implemented. Accord is now 'forgotten' by both sides. Sikh signatory, Sand Longowal assassinated by militants. Conflict between Sikh militant groups and Indian Government forces continues.
CANADA: Meech Lake Accord (June 1987)	Accord initially accepted by provincial premiers, but subsequently failed ratification as a constitutional amendment in two provinces. Status of Quebec unresolved. Accord also raised consciousness about status of aboriginal 'nations'. Aboriginal status issues also unresolved.
SRI LANKA: Indo-Sri Lanka Accord (July 1987)	LTTE failed to honor accord. Indian Peace Keeping Force failed to subdue LTTE. North-eastern Provincial Government officials fled after declaring independence. Conflict between LTTE and Sri Lanka Government forces continues

produced 392 titles of which 121 were devoted to 'international conflict resolution', but only 3 to 'ethnic conflict resolution'. A search of the DWIL periodical index[8] produced 447 titles on 'conflict resolution', 91 on 'international conflict resolution' and seven on 'ethnic conflict resolution'.[9] No doubt the reawakening of ethnic strife in Eastern Europe and the former Soviet Union will evoke new interest in this area and in the practical problem of framing durable peace accords to resolve ethnic conflicts.[10]

Conflict resolution studies relevant to ethnic conflicts: A survey

The literature most relevant to resolving ethnic conflicts can be usefully grouped into three broad categories, (a) surveys of conflict resolution theory, practice and experience; (b) case studies of ethnic conflict resolution and (c) practical guides for negotiators, mediators and facilitators. This section briefly reviews representative works in each category.

Surveys of theory, practice and experience

Most scholars of conflict resolution assume there is commonality between conflicts occurring at the individual, family, group, organizational, national and international levels. Theories of conflict resolution propose that lessons learned from resolving conflicts at one level will be broadly applicable to others. The massive 'St. Martins' series' on conflict resolution recently completed under John Burton's leadership (Burton, 1990a, 1990b; Burton and Dukes 1990a, 1990b) exemplifies this point of view. Burton and Dukes argue that the struggle to satisfy inherent human needs is common to all conflicts, although conflicts may take many different forms. Different forms of conflict may require different conflict resolution strategies, for example negotiation, alternative dispute resolution, mediation or second track diplomacy.

Other works in this genre include Sandole and Sandole-Saroste (1987), Azar and Burton (1987), Shellenberg (1989), Berkovitch (1984) and Kressel and Pruitt (1989). The works of Shellenberg, Berkovitch and Kressel and Pruitt, however, illustrate a more specialized focus. Shellenberg argues that theories of conflict resolution must be based on a broad understanding of theories that address the causes and dynamics of conflict. Berkovitch focuses on the role of third parties in resolving inter-personal, labor management and international conflicts. Kressel and Pruitt report results from applying a single conflict resolution strategy – mediation – across a broad range of conflict levels from individual to international.

Studies by Deutsch (1973), Likert and Likert (1976) and Pruitt and Rubin (1986), illustrate work that draws primarily on social psychological theories and related empirical research dealing with individual, group and organizational behavior. Deutsch, writing in the tradition of George Simmel (1955) and Louis Coser (1956), views conflict positively and argues that the challenge of conflict resolution is to transform destructive conflicts into constructive ones. His work presages the emphasis on 'win–win' solutions associated with contemporary 'problem-solving' approaches to conflict resolution.[11] The Likerts draw upon 'research-based principles and theories of organization and management' to identify more effective systems of organization for constructively managing conflict. Such systems, they argue, are essential for striking a balance between individual freedom and social order in complex industrial societies. Pruitt and Rubin examine causes and consequences of alternative strategies for coping with conflict. Under what conditions, they ask, will individuals engage in the cognitively demanding task of attempting to maximize not only their own outcomes, but those of the other side?

Burton's early classic, *Conflict and Communication* (1969) and a more recent work by Kahn (1988) illustrate a school of thought that emphasizes the importance of communication in conflict resolution. Burton argues that resolving conflicts

> must involve processes by which communication can be made to be effective, [that is]...deliberate conveying and accurate receipt and interpretation of what was intended and should be conveyed, and the full employment of information as received and stored in the allocation and re-allocation of values, interests and goals (p. 49).

Burton's later work emphasizes that effective communication, while important, represents only one facet of conflict resolution. Kahn, however, presents the more simplistic view that enhanced communication alone will be sufficient to resolve most conflicts. She ignores situations – sometimes present in ethnic conflicts – where clearer, more accurate communication may actually widen, rather than lessen differences between protagonists.

Mao Tse Tung's writings are rarely cited in surveys of the conflict resolution literature, but his *On the Correct Handling of Contradictions Among the People* (1957) merits attention from students of ethnic conflict. Mao notes that both 'chauvinism of the majority' and 'parochialism of the minority' are potentially divisive problems in multiethnic societies. His approach to conflict management provides for a multifold strategy emphasizing equal participation, changing attitudes (promoting communication and mutual trust) and economic development. Mao's view that 'contradictions' are rooted in a syndrome of interdependent and divergent attitudes, cultural contexts and economic circumstances offers a sophisticated perspective that is sometimes lacking in proposed and implemented conflict resolution strategies (including the peace accords discussed in this book).[12]

An equally multifaceted perspective is found in the late Edward E. Azar's last book, *The Management of Protracted Social Conflict* (1990). Like his frequent collaborator, John Burton, Azar is properly grouped with scholars who believe that individual, group, organizational, national and international level conflicts (and conflict resolution strategies) have much in common. However Azar argues that an emergent, virulent strain, 'protracted social conflicts' poses unusual problems of intractability for both protagonists and third parties concerned with conflict resolution. Ethnic or communal conflicts typically fall into this category. We will have more to say about protracted social conflict in a subsequent section.

Case studies and comparative case studies
Azar's work also illustrates a second, although rarely encountered genre in the literature: case studies and comparative case studies of ethnic conflict resolution. Azar's first insights about the distinctive character-istics of protracted conflict grew from in-depth study of his native country, Lebanon.[13] This lead provided a basis for further case studies, sponsored by the University of Maryland's Center for International Development and Conflict Management, and to refinement of the 'problem-solving forum' strategy for resolving ethnic conflicts. Forums conducted by the Center produced useful insights, but inconclusive results.[14] Rothchild and Hartzell's study of the Sudan peace process (1990)[15] also focuses on the negotiation process and the potential for successful third party mediation. They identify five preconditions favoring success:

(1) the emergence of identifiable bargaining parties;
(2) evidence of a mutually hurting stalemate;
(3) the existence of leaders determined on a practical solution;
(4) external political actors supporting conflict resolution; and
(5) the presence of a mediator actively on the scene.

Other case studies focus on the need to address deep-rooted cultural, economic and geopolitical issues as prerequisites for resolving ethnic conflicts. For example, de Silva's work on managing ethnic conflict in Sri Lanka (1986)[16] points to the importance of resolving constitutional questions involving language, religion, representation patterns and devolution of power. Garcia's work on the Philippines (1988, 1989) urges that attention be given to protecting human rights, agrarian reform, delivery of basic social services and the resolution of gross economic inequities. Rupesinghe's collection of papers on Uganda (1989) emphasizes the need for political institutions that are more responsive to minority concerns and for more equitable, participatory agricultural development strategies. The authors of these case studies do not agree on what are the essential issues that must be resolved.

Probably these issues differ from case to case and culture to culture. Horowitz's massive comparative study *Ethnic Groups in Conflict* (1985) maintains that while deep-rooted issues must be addressed, some ethnic differences may be inherently unresolvable. He believes that conflict *reduction*, rather than conflict *resolution* is a more practicable goal in ethnically diverse societies. Horowitz identifies five basic mechanisms of conflict reduction (p. 597):

(1) creating proliferating points of power;
(2) raising the saliency of intra-ethnic conflict;[17]
(3) creating incentives for inter-ethnic cooperation;[18]
(4) encouraging alignments based on interests other than ethnicity; and
(5) reducing disparities between groups so that dissatisfaction declines.

He proposes that nations live with ethnic differences, rather than attempting to move beyond them, by 'engineering' institutional structures and procedures that are based upon an understanding of how political incentives intensify or mitigate ethnic tensions. Horowitz believes that 'structural techniques' that 'change the political framework within which ethnic conflict occurs but do not necessarily make promises about outcomes', will be most effective (chapter 15).[19] He is skeptical about 'distributive policies', such as proportional allocation of government positions, that attempt to directly change the ethnic balance of economic opportunities and rewards (chapter 16).[20]

Eric Nordlinger's *Conflict Regulation in Divided Societies* (1972) is an earlier comparative study emphasizing conflict management. The work argues that common characteristics of six cases – Belgium, the Netherlands, Austria, Switzerland, Lebanon and Malaysia – point to a general theory of conflict regulation. Nordlinger claims that these six 'divided societies' were free of conflict for long periods of time because elite leaders of protagonist groups were both dominant and politically skillful. By politically skillful, he means that they successfully implemented one or more of six *conflict regulating practices* (pp. 20, ff):

(1) a stable coalition between governing parties;
(2) the principle of proportionality;
(3) acceptance of a mutual veto;
(4) purposive depoliticization;[21]
(5) mutual adjustment of conflicting values and interests through compromise; and
(6) concessions by the stronger group.

When conflict regulation succeeds, 'at least one of the six practices is invariably present (p. 20).

Horowitz's and Nordlinger's emphasis on conflict regulation (or conflict management), distinguishes their work from most studies of conflict resolution. They are more concerned with stabilizing divided societies over the long run than with ending violent conflicts after they have broken out. Their practices and principles provide useful broad goals for negotiators and mediators, however these goals might be difficult to attain or even unreachable when the positions of protagonist groups have been polarized by extended periods of protracted conflict.

Comparative case studies by Lickleider (1990)[22] and Zartman (1985) point to the problems of negotiating successful ethnic peace accords as well as providing useful insights for negotiators.[23] However neither deals with ethnic conflicts specifically. Lickleider's study *How Civil Wars End* emphasizes the limits of so-called 'general theories' and the need for third party mediators to be deeply immersed in the details of each case.[24] Mediator's roles in his cases vary widely. In Zimbabwe, third party mediation was decisive. In the Sudan, it was helpful but not decisive. In Yemen, third party intervention contributed to peace by creating a common enemy, which helped to bring the warring parties together (this was hardly the third party's goal, however).

Zartman examines four conflicts in Africa[25] that offer promising opportunities for mediation, i.e. they are *Ripe for Resolution* – the title of his work (1985). He introduces the concept of the 'ripe moment' when a mediator with something to offer both sides can sometimes intervene successfully. A 'hurting stalemate' can produce a ripe moment (pp. 266–73), however it appears difficult to define ripe moments and hurting stalemates before the fact (Lickleider, 1990).

If negotiation and mediation can contribute to the resolution of at least some protracted conflicts, what are the essential problem-solving and conflict management skills that will make a difference? A considerable literature exists, based on experiences in negotiation, mediation and collaborative problem solving, that attempts to generalize about such skills and to make them accessible to both practitioner and student. Exemplars of this literature are considered next.

Practical guides to negotiation, mediation and problem solving
Practical guides to negotiation, mediation and problem solving can be divided into those that describe general negotiation skills and those that describe skills specifically applicable to international and/or ethnic

conflicts. A second distinction is between competitive (zero-sum) and problem-solving (positive-sum) approaches.[26] Cohen's *You Can Negotiate Anything* (1980) and Fisher and Ury's widely publicized *Getting to Yes* (1981)[27] provide good examples of works dealing with general negotiation skills.[28] Zartman and Berman's *The Practical Negotiator* (1982), Mitchell's *Peacemaking and the Consultant's Role* (1981) and Touval's *The Peace Brokers* (1982) focus on skills relevant to international and ethnic conflict resolution.[29]

Cohen's guide to 'negotiating anything, at any place' covers transactions from purchasing a refrigerator to reaching agreements with the Soviet Union.[30] Although he gives some attention to problem-solving approaches, his work is most useful as an explication of zero-sum bargaining principles. Cohen sees control over power, time and information as essential to successful negotiations. Threats, exaggeration and lying may be effective tactics. Soviet diplomats are described as good models of effective zero-sum negotiators. Their tactics have included (a) taking extreme initial positions, (b) limiting the authority of negotiators, (c) using emotion as a negotiating tactic, (d) treating adversary concessions as weaknesses, (e) being stingy in their own concessions; and (f) ignoring deadlines.

Advocates of problem-solving approaches maintain that zero-sum strategies are of limited effectiveness except in single, one-shot negotiations over limited resources (Singer, 1990, chapter 2). In complicated negotiations, and especially in resolving conflicts where protagonists will remain in close proximity to one another, a strategy that transforms zero-sum bargaining to mutually supportive problem solving is far more likely to produce stable, long-lasting agreements.

The Harvard Negotiation Project, headed by Roger Fisher and William Ury has been instrumental in both refining and popularizing problem-solving approaches (Fisher and Ury, 1981; Fisher and Brown, 1989). The Project's strategy of 'principled negotiation' advocates looking for mutual gains wherever possible. When interests conflict, outcomes should be based on 'fair standards, independent of the will of either side,' (1981, p. xii). A principled negotiation, then, becomes a collaborative process of agreeing on fair standards and identifying previously unrecognized areas for mutual gain.

The authors propose four basic principles to guide negotiation processes (1981):

1. *Separate the people from the problem* (chapter 2). Adversaries must be recognized as people first and negotiators must attempt to place

themselves in their opponent's shoes. The problems caused by differing perceptions, strong emotions and the need to 'save face' must be taken into account.
2. *Focus on interests, not positions* (chapter 3). Negotiators must recognize that 'behind opposed positions lie shared and compatible interests as well as conflicting ones.... A close examination of the underlying interests will reveal the existence of many more interests that are shared and compatible than ones that are opposed' (p. 43).[31]
3. *Invent options for mutual gain* (chapter 4). Negotiators must separate the creative process of seeking (brainstorming) new options from the more analytical, confronting process of judging and choosing among them.
4. *Insist on objective criteria* (chapter 5). The authors recognize that creativity in inventing options will not entirely obviate the 'harsh reality of interests that conflict' (p. 84). The challenge is to transform the resolution of such conflicts from a test of will to a negotiation on the basis of criteria that are independent of the will of either side. 'Legitimate, practical' criteria can be based on such recognized principles as 'scientific judgement', 'market value', 'professional standards', 'efficiency', and the like.[32]

Although every negotiation is different, Fisher and Ury maintain that the elements of a principled negotiation do not change. 'Principled negotiation is an all purpose strategy' that is as applicable to family disputes as to superpower arms control talks (p. xiii).

Two contending schools of thought are found in works that focus specifically on negotiating national- and international-level political conflicts. The first criticizes traditional diplomacy, argues that international and other forms of conflicts have much in common and advocates an increased role for technically-trained professional mediators. The second school argues that much can be learned from traditional diplomacy, that international conflicts have distinctive characteristics and that mediators must play a political as well as a professional role.

The first school of thought is exemplified by C.R. Mitchell's work on third party mediation (1981). He believes that traditional approaches to negotiation have high risks and, even if successful, fail to produce viable long-term solutions (chapter 1). Traditional negotiators assume that they are in a 'win-lose' situation where compromises, involving concessions by both sides provide the best possible opportunity for a solution (introduction). The shortcomings of traditional approaches could be remedied, the author maintains, by the participation of professionally trained 'consultants' who would be impartial facilitators of the negotiation process. The facilitator's strategy would be similar to Fisher and Ury's principled negotiation. Conflicts would be mediated by altering protagonists' goals, perceptions and range of available alternatives (introduction and chapter 4). Mitchell's model for the consultant's role is the 'workshop' format first proposed by John Burton (1969) and subsequently used by Kelman and Cohen to intervene in the conflict between Greek and Turkish Cypriots (1972).[33]

The works by Zartman and Berman (1982) and especially by Touval (1982) present almost a mirror image of Mitchell's point of view.[34] They argue that much can be learned from diplomats' experiences. In their view, the distinctiveness of national- and international-level political conflicts and negotiations demands, at least in some degree, distinctive conflict resolution strategies.[35]

Zartman and Berman's *The Practical Negotiator* (1982) is the most empirically grounded study of political conflict resolution found in the literature. It draws upon more than ten years of research under the auspices of the Academy for Educational Development's Conflict and Communication program. The resources generated by the project included interviews with numerous practitioners and the results of dialogues between scholars and practitioners in several structured settings.[36] The authors propose a three stage model of the negotiation process. In the *diagnostic phase*, negotiations are initiated and opportunities for a solution to the conflict are identified. In the *formula phase*, specific formulas or rules that could provide a basis for agreement are defined. In the *detail phase* the specific elements of an agreement are negotiated and finalized. For each phase, 'specific behaviors and tactics' that can 'improve the conduct of negotiations and better the chances of success' are proposed. These are summarized in practical 'checklists' which negotiators are advised to 'keep on their desks'.[37]

While Zartman and Berman's work is broadly applicable to both direct negotiations between protagonists and to those in which third parties play a role, Saadia Touval's *The Peace Brokers: Mediators in the Arab Israeli Conflict, 1948–79* (1982) addresses the role of third parties exclusively. It also emphasizes the distinctive characteristics of international/communal conflicts most strongly. The author's 'Peace Brokers' are the individuals or teams that participated in nine distinct attempts to resolve the ongoing strife between Arabs and Israelis.[38] The qualities Touval attributes to successful mediators are similar to those emphasized elsewhere. They should be experienced in conflict resolution and knowledgeable about the specific conflict, the context in which it is waged and the parties involved. Personal qualities should include tact, intelligence, persuasiveness, humility and patience. But in contrast to other analysts, Touval does not believe that successful mediators in international and ethnic conflicts need be or probably will be unbiased. Rather he believes that third parties will bring both recognized biases and external resources to the mediation process. In the cases he examined, mediators' effectiveness in winning concessions from protagonists was due more to the resources at their disposal than impartiality or even negotiating skills. Touval believes that third party mediation in the Middle East must realistically be viewed as another form of power politics, albeit one of the less destructive forms.

Examination of *The Peace Brokers* concludes our brief literature survey. The stage is now set to answer the two questions that introduced this paper; (1) Why did the ethnic peace accords fail? (2) How can those concerned with resolving ethnic conflicts do better?

Why did the ethnic peace accords fail to achieve lasting peace?

We propose two explanations for the failure of the ethnic peace accords to achieve lasting peace. First is the intractability of ethnic conflicts. These conflicts, while they bear some similarity to other disputes, are probably the most complex and difficult to resolve by any conflict resolution method and under any circumstances. Our second explanation concerns shortcomings in negotiating and implementing the accords. Possibly excepting the Addis Ababa Agreement, the negotiation process, content and follow-up of the peace accords fail to exhibit even the most elementary principles that conflict resolution specialists point to as prerequisites for success.

The intractability of ethnic conflicts
A major theme of Donald Horowitz's path-breaking *Ethnic Groups in Conflict* (1985) is, as noted above, that *resolving* ethnic conflicts may be impossible. It may only be possible to *manage* them. He illustrates with the following tale:

> When the Japanese hurriedly evacuated Christmas Island, south of Java, they left some small arms behind. The Malays and Chinese who inhabit the island had enough of fighting, and it is said that they arranged for the Chinese to keep the rifles and the Malays to keep the bolts. The Malays, on the other hand, were to keep the pistols but give the magazines to the Chinese. By these devices, a bloodbath was averted (p. 563).

The Christmas Islanders recognized that their predispositions toward violent ethnic conflict were dangerous, deeply rooted and not susceptible to individual good will. Fortunately, they were able to seize a propitious moment and limit the resources that would support violence. Protagonists and victims of most ethnic conflicts have been less fortunate. Ethnic differences often provoke violence. The resources to sustain violent conflict are readily available. As noted above, violent ethnic conflict often assumes a particularly virulent form, labeled by the late Edward Azar as 'protracted social conflict' (1990).

The focus of protracted conflicts, according to Azar, 'is religious, cultural or ethnic communal identity, which in turn is dependent upon the satisfaction of basic needs such as those for security, communal recognition and distributive justice' (p. 2). Such conflicts 'tend to involve an enduring antagonistic set of perceptions and interactions between communal groups and the state'. Those perceptions and interactions are conditioned by the experiences, fears and belief systems of the contending ethnic groups. Each attributes the worst motivations to the other side. Hostility begets hostility, creating conditions of violent conflict that feed upon themselves (pp. 13–16). Protracted conflict weakens civil society, delegitimizes governmental institutions, destroys the economy and frustrates developmental goals:

> At the onset of conflict, social and economic institutions mediating communal interrelationships may still be functional, and communal boundaries permeable. As conflict protracts, however, communal cleavages become petrified, and the prospects for co-operative interaction and nation building become poor (p. 16). . . . With the continued stress of each conflict, attitudes, cognitive processes and perceptions become set and ossified. War culture and cynicism dominate. Meaningful communication between or among conflicting parties dries up, and ability to satisfy communal acceptance needs is severely diminished (p. 17).

Protracted conflict creates severe obstacles to any peacemaking process. Peacemaking is resisted even though for most of those involved, the economic costs of protracted conflict clearly outweigh any conceivable long-term economic benefit (Azar, 1990, p. 7,ff; Richardson and Samarasinghe, 1992). In part, this is because leaders and members of militant groups, who must be key actors in any peacemaking process, reap both psychic and material benefits from the perpetuation of conflict, while passing the costs to others. They may have little to gain from peace (Richardson and Samarasinghe, 1992). Often militant forces are far from unified; there may be multiple – even rival – key leaders with differing objectives. Sometimes militant leaders and groups comprising one faction seem as hostile to each other as to their adversaries from opposing ethnic groups.[39] For high government officials, the perpetuation of conflict can divert attention from failures in leadership and from intractable social and economic problems (Richardson and Samarasinghe, 1992). For the foot soldiers in protracted conflict, symbolic considerations often weigh more heavily than economic ones (Horowitz, 1985, chapter 4).

Clearly ethnic conflicts *are* protracted. Animosities contributing to a high potential for violent conflict can be traced back over decades and even centuries.[40] When violent conflicts between ethnic groups do break out, they tend to last far longer than wars between nations.[41] Although available data is more anecdotal than comprehensive, the evidence seems overwhelming that genocide, military defeat, exile or enforced separation of contending parties are more likely to mark the end of violent ethnic conflicts than negotiated peace accords.[42]

Shortcomings in the five ethnic peace accords

Formidable challenges clearly await those who would frame ethnic peace accords as negotiator, mediator or external arbiter. For negotiators or mediators the conditions for success would seem to include – at a minimum – bringing authoritative representatives of contending groups together, establishing communication, creating trust, identifying acceptable terms for an accord, ensuring that those terms have adequate support among the adversaries and fully implementing the accord. Possibly, external arbiters can devote less time to building consensus to the degree that they have the capacity to impose and enforce terms of an accord. But imposing terms on militant groups is not easy, as the Indian Peace Keeping Force discovered in Sri Lanka, and an imposed peace, unless supported by some commitment from contending groups, is unlikely to be sustainable.

Table 9.2 summarizes the negotiation process and implementation of each accord discussed in this book. External actors played a role in some: Cyprus, Sri Lanka, and Sudan. In two cases, Cyprus and Sri Lanka, external powers attempted to achieve peace by imposing an accord. Although both accords attempted to deal with some outstanding issues, neither set of negotiations involved all of the protagonists and fundamental points of difference were left unresolved. In Cyprus the proportional representation scheme written into the new nation's constitution never provided a basis for real co-operation. Peace ended when Greek and Turkish Cypriots were able to draw their client

Table 9.2 Negotiation and implementation of ethnic peace accords

Accord	Negotiation and implementation
CYPRUS: London-Zurich Agreements (1959)	Accord was negotiated by 3 external powers – Great Britain, Greece, Turkey – who agreed to serve as guarantors. Cypriots did not participate in the agreements, although they did sign the documents.
SUDAN: Addis Ababa Agreement (Feb. 1972)	Accord was the result of three years of preliminary negotiations and several months of intensive negotiations, following the accession of the Nimeiri Government. Abel Alier, a southerner, headed government delegation and played a key role in maintaining communication between northerners and southerners. Participation of influential outside mediators helped to bring negotiators to Addis Ababa and keep them at work until an accord was reached. As the Sudanese Vice President, Alier subsequently played a key role in implementing the accord, with President Nimeiri's full backing.
INDIA: Punjab Accord (July 1985)	Accord was negotiated by Rajiv Gandhi and more moderate Sikh politicians headed by Akali Dal leader Sand Longowal. Militant Sikh leaders and leaders of states required to make territorial concessions under the agreement did not participate. Neither moderate Sikh leaders nor Gandhi had sufficient mandate to implement the accord. Gandhi is later reputed to have manipulated the 'independent commissions' established under the accord to produce decisions unfavorable to the Sikhs (Gill, pp. 21–2).
CANADA: Meech Lake Accord (June 1987)	Accord was the result of intensive negotiations between Prime Minister Mulroney (Federal Government) and Premier Bourassa (Quebec). Agreement was accepted by other Provincial Premiers, almost without alteration. During three year period allowed for ratification, new governments were elected in two provinces and opposition groups mobilized. Agreement failed ratification.
SRI LANKA: Indo-Lanka Accord (July 1987)	Discussions leading to the accord were precipitated created by Indian military pressure on Sri Lanka. The accord was negotiated by Indian Prime Minister Gandhi and Sri Lankan President Jayewardene with no direct participation of either moderate or militant Sri Lankan Tamils. LTTE leader Prabhakaran acceded to the accord under pressure, but subsequently repudiated it. The Indian government was unable to keep its side of the agreement, to disarm the LTTE and enforce compliance with the accord.

states into a confrontation. In Sri Lanka, the Indian Government was over-optimistic about the ability of its Army to enforce the accord that Rajiv Gandhi had dictated to the LTTE leader, Prabhakaran. When the Liberation Tigers resumed hostilities, within two months after the accord was signed, the Indian Peace Keeping Force was hardly more effective than the Sri Lankan army had been in maintaining order.[43] The one case where external actors played the role of mediator produced the relatively successful Addis Ababa Accord. However distinctive characteristics of the conflict, internally, also contributed to success. The Southern Sudanese rebels negotiated from a strong, if not equal, position with government representatives. Their key role in bringing the Nimeiri regime to power was recognized. President Nimeiri was personally committed to reaching some accord and empowered a skillful negotiator, in the person of Vice President Alier, who could effectively communicate with both sides. Signing of the accord was followed by implementation of its provisions, again under the direction of Vice President Alier.[44]

In contrast to the Sudan, negotiations leading to the Punjab Accord failed to involve key actors with strong interests in the negotiations. The accord provided for major concessions, involving land and water rights, from the leaders of Haryana province. Prime Minister Gandhi first overestimated his ability to persuade recalcitrant provincial leaders and then lost interest in the process when the configuration of forces in Indian provincial politics changed. In failing to ensure the support of militant Sikh leaders, Gandhi committed an error that he was to repeat in the Indo-Sri Lanka Accord, two years later, with equally disastrous consequences.

Among the five accords, Meech Lake is a special case because Canada is a modern nation and because there has been little violent conflict between the English and the *Quebecois*. However there are parallels between the problems encountered in ratifying this accord and those in the Punjab case. Implementation of each accord failed in part because the negotiations excluded parties with strong interests and effective veto power. Prime Minister Mulroney was so focused on resolving outstanding issues between Quebec and the federal government that he neglected the concerns of other provinces and failed to see the impact of the accord on Canada's indigenous peoples.[45]

When one compares recommendations from studies of conflict resolution against what transpired in negotiating and implementing the five peace accords the shortcomings of the accords become apparent. Parties to the accords, especially 'external' third parties made commitments that could not, or would not be kept. The effective veto power of key actors, who were excluded from the negotiations, was either underestimated or ignored. Thus, most of the ethnic peace accords failed to establish communication, build trust, identify mutual interests or resolve fundamental issues among major protagonists. This offers grounds for hope, not pessimism. It suggests that negotiators of ethnic peace accords have something to learn from studies of conflict resolution and that the process of negotiating such accords can be improved.

How can negotiators do better?

Effective mediation and conflict regulation
Studies of ethnic conflict by Horowitz (1985), Azar (1991) and others provide convincing evidence that violent ethnic conflicts will rarely, if ever be 'resolved' by the protagonists alone except through the capitulation, destruction or extermination of one of them. But 'conflict resolution' through military victory is likely to be an uncertain, costly, destructive and time consuming process (Richardson and Samarasinghe, 1992). Even though third party intervention was largely ineffective in negotiating and implementing the accords discussed in this book, we believe that a strong case can be made for effective third party intervention. But what type of third party role is most likely to bring warring parties together and mediate a successful accord. Principles of effective mediation, as described in the literature, may contribute to a successful outcome, but they will not be sufficient. To be effective in resolving ethnic conflicts, third party negotiators must be more than skillful. They must be (or represent) key political actors in their own right who bring influence, strong interests in resolving the conflict and substantial resources to the negotiation process.

Readers will recognize that this conclusion is consistent with Saadia Touval's work on the Middle East peace process (1982) and differs from the view that an effective role can be played by a dispassionate, technically competent mediator who is not politically involved. Although Touval is primarily writing about international conflicts, I believe his findings are relevant to the concerns of this paper. The over thirty years of armed struggle between Israelis and Arabs certainly qualifies as a protracted social conflict.

According to Touval, mediating powers in the Arab-Israeli conflict had strong national security interests in the outcome and were often biased toward one side or the other. However bias did not appear to limit their effectiveness. Serious negotiations were more likely when a mediating power could exert political pressure that would bring the protagonists to the negotiating table. When negotiations commenced, the ability of the mediator to provide benefits for both sides and to reduce risks that adversaries assumed by making concessions were key factors contributing to success. Successful mediators were able to create a 'win-win' situation by providing positive incentives to both sides and serving as credible guarantors against backsliding or cheating.[46]

The Camp David Accords illustrate many of these points.[47] After 13 days of arduous negotiations, Egypt and Israel reached agreement on the terms of a peace treaty and on Israeli withdrawal from the Sinai peninsula. There has been peace between the two nations for more than a decade.[48] The United States used not only political pressure, but the prestige of the US Presidency to bring top-level representatives of two major protagonists to the negotiating table. President Carter provided not only good offices, but substantial financial incentives and military guarantees. In addition to these political, financial and military resources, the President and his aides used many of the techniques of 'problem-solving' negotiation that have been described above.

The story of Camp David Accords illustrates that partial resolution of ethnic conflicts may sometimes be possible without military victory; it also illustrates that the task of framing a sustainable ethnic peace accord should not be undertaken lightly, nor with any certainty about the outcome. Moreover, Camp David may be a model of limited generality. Tensions between Israel and Egypt were high, but a number of circumstances, not easily replicable, contributed to the results achieved.[49] Negotiations were preceded by major political changes in both Israel and Egypt, in which President Sadat's trip to Israel and speech before the Israeli Parliament catalysts. Both Egypt and Israel were already politically beholden to the United States and were major recipients of US Aid. President Carter was perhaps uniquely skilled among US Presidents as a peacemaker and willing to risk the reputation of his Presidency on a favorable outcome.

The circumstances of many ethnic conflicts are less favorable than those faced by the Camp David negotiators. Members of conflicting groups may be intermingled, as in Northern Ireland, Croatia, India and Sri Lanka, making clear territorial demarcations difficult. There may be multiple groups and divided authority on one or both sides, complicating the negotiation process. Leaders of militant groups may have little predisposition toward the give and take of negotiation and see few gains from a peaceful outcome. There may be more than one external power with a stake in the outcome; some external powers may see greater benefits from prolonging conflict than from conflict resolution. Moreover it would be inaccurate to label the Camp David results 'conflict resolution'. Rather, the accords managed to reduce friction between the two protagonists sufficiently so that further negotiation, rather than the use of force, became a mutually acceptable basis for managing potentially violent conflicts and beginning to resolve outstanding disputes.

Mediation has a role to play in resolving violent ethnic conflicts and may sometimes provide a successful basis for long-term conflict management. But given the costs and intractability of such conflicts, implementing conflict reduction or conflict management strategies before violence breaks out would seem to be far more promising and cost effective. Paradoxically, we have far less detailed knowledge about conflict avoidance in ethnically diverse societies than about the minutiae of negotiation, mediation and arbitration. Nordlinger's work on conflict regulating practices identified a promising area of research that, until recently, has received little attention. Horowitz's work on mechanisms of conflict reduction and his comparative analysis of structural versus preferential policies to reduce ethnic conflict represents a significant step forward. Work in this genre can be helpful in preventing the outbreak of violent conflict and in building a durable peace following a successful mediation effort.

Recapitulation

Here is a summary of our major conclusions:

1. If violent conflict has broken out, negotiating a successful ethnic peace accord, without military victory on one side, will require third party intervention.
2. The third party should be substantially more powerful, politically, than any protagonist, should have a strong interest in reaching an accord and be willing to commit substantial resources to implementing its provisions. The United Nations or a regional group such as the European Common Market, ASEAN, SAARC, OAS or OAU might play the third party role if group mediation is backed by major powers.[50]
3. Third party leaders must resist the temptation to try imposing a solution using military force. The use of neutral peace-keeping forces, under conditions agreed to by all key protagonists, may be a temporary expedient.

4. Third party negotiators should be committed to establishing communication, building trust and identifying areas of mutual interest among the protagonists.
5. Use of the 'workshop format' and other conflict resolution techniques can be an important part of the negotiation process, but should be viewed as complementary to the role of a politically powerful, highly committed third party.
6. All key actors with potential veto power over implementation of an accord should be involved in the negotiations.
7. Conflict management is probably a more desirable and attainable goal for ethnic peace accords than conflict resolution. Many ethnic conflicts may be manageable but not resolvable.
8. Successful negotiation of an accord should be viewed as the beginning, not the end of the conflict management process.
9. Potential third party intervenors as well as protagonists should recognize that the most propitious and cost effective time for managing ethnic differences is before violent conflict breaks out.
10. Among conflict management strategies found in the literature, Donald Horowitz's proposals, emphasizing design of political structures to mitigate, diffuse and channel ethnic tensions appear to be the most promising.

As the 1990s begin, a new generation of political leaders is grappling with questions of constitutional and institutional design in ethnically diverse nations. These leaders need to understand more about the causes of ethnic conflict and how alternative institutional structures can either mitigate or exacerbate ethnic tensions. Further, the costs and benefits of attempts to resolve ethnic tensions by force need to be realistically appraised. When tension does lead to conflict, leaders of contending groups and potential third party intervenors need to know which negotiation and mediation strategies are likely to be most effective. Those of us who are scholars need to research these areas more fully. But much is already known and there are lessons to be learned from accords that succeeded only partially, or not at all. While seeking new knowledge, we need to communicate what we know now to political leaders in ways that are clear, powerful and relevant. And we need to apply our current knowledge more widely and effectively.

Notes

1. Dr. Richardson's work on this paper was partially supported by a grant from the US Institute of Peace. Mr. Wang's work was supported by a graduate fellowship from The American University.
2. See chapter 4 in this book; also Rothchild and Hartzell (1988).
3. See chapter 3 in this book.
4. See chapter 7 in this book. Also Kodikara (1989).
5. See chapters 5 and 6 and 2 in this book.
6. See for example Grims and Satriano (1990).
7. The collection is found in George Mason University's Fenwick Library.
8. DWIL provides simultaneous computerized searches of the following indices: *Humanities* Index, from February, 1984; *Social Sciences Index*, from February 1983; *General Science Index*, from May 1984; *Business Periodicals Index*, from July 1982; *Readers' Guide*, from January 1983; *Index to Legal Periodicals* from August, 1981.
9. Donald Horowitz (see esp. 1985) represents the most notable exception to this generalization. Also, the International Centre for Ethnic Studies, under whose auspices this book is written, has conducted a research program focused on ethnic conflict for more than a decade. The keyword search described above certainly did not identify all relevant works dealing with the resolution of ethnic conflict. However we believe it does accurately portray the relatively modest level of attention given to ethnic conflicts by scholars who are more generally concerned with conflict resolution. Whether or not lessons drawn from resolving other types of conflict are relevant to resolving ethnic conflicts will be examined more fully later in this chapter.
10. In the United States, major leadership in initiating studies of ethnic conflict and conflict resolution is being provided by the grants program of the US Institute of Peace (1990).
11. Most notable among these is the work of the Harvard Negotiation Project, directed by Roger Fisher and William Ury. See, for example, Fisher and Ury (1981), and Fisher and Brown (1989). Problem-solving approaches are discussed below.
12. The fact that Mao sometimes used repression to deal with ethnic diversity in China does not detract from the usefulness of his insights.
13. For example, see Azar *et al.*, 1984; Azar and Haddad (1986).
14. Participants in the Center's forums were not in a position to take effective action, although they did have close ties to top decision makers in some instances. This limited their impact on policy making, though most agreed that enhanced communication achieved by the forums was significant personally. For a discussion of antecedents to the 'forum' approach, see Mitchell (1981). This type of third party mediation is discussed more fully below.
15. See also Francis Mading Deng, Negotiating identity: Dishonored agreements in the Sudanese conflict, in this book.
16. As its title *Managing Ethnic Tensions in Multi-Ethnic Societies* suggests, de Silva's work focuses primarily on conflict management rather than

conflict resolution. Thus it is similar in approach to the works of Horowitz (1985) and Nordlinger (1972) discussed below.

17. For example, by creating reserved offices for particular ethnic groups.
18. For example, by establishing electoral procedures that encourage coalition formation involving more than one ethnic group.
19. In his most recent work (1991), Horowitz examines the relevance of these principles for a democratic South Africa.
20. Proportional allocation was the basis of Lebanese political stability for a number of years and was a feature of the London-Zurich agreement. Various proportional allocation schemes have been proposed as conflict regulation mechanisms in Sri Lanka. Nordlinger's earlier work, discussed immediately below, views preferential policies more favorably.
21. Protagonist group leaders agree not to involve the government in public policy areas that impinge upon group members' core values and interests.
22. Lickleider selected his cases from the Singer-Small (1982) data on large scale conflicts that had ended 'at least for some considerable time'. The cases he examined were Sudan – 1972, the American Civil War, Colombia – 1957, Zimbabwe, Yemen, Greece and Nigeria. Only the Sudan, Nigeria and, perhaps, Zimbabwe could properly be termed ethnic conflicts.
23. Deng and Zartman (1991) is a more recent edited volume in the same genre.
24. The ignorance of third party intervenors (Rajiv Gandhi in both cases) seems to have been an important factor in the failure of the Indo-Sri Lanka and Punjab Accords. In the case of the London-Zurich Accord, third party intervenors simply imposed a solution from above.
25. The four cases are the Moroccan-Algerian boundary conflict, the Somali-Ethiopian clash, the territorial struggle between Zaire, Zambia and Angola and the efforts to bring Namibia to independence. Interestingly, the author gives the US relatively high marks as a mediator. Its representatives, he observes, seemed more genuinely interested in resolving the conflicts than in seeing one side win.
26. In competitive negotiations, there are clear winners and losers. The goal is to win. In problem-solving negotiations, the goal is to transform the context of the conflict so that both protagonists can emerge as 'winners'.
27. One reason for the attention given to *Getting to Yes* was news accounts describing the use of Fisher and Ury's 'principled negotiation' method in the process that led to the Camp David Peace Accords. However Touval, in a work discussed below (1982), argues that the principal reasons for the success of President Carter's intervention were the large amounts of aid promised to Egypt and Israel and internal changes in each nation that occurred prior to the negotiations. Our view of the role that principled negotiation played in the accords is discussed below.
28. Linda Singer's *Settling Disputes: Conflict Resolution in Business, Families and the Legal System* (1990) is a more recent work focusing on the growing use of collaborative problem-solving approaches to dispute resolution in the United States.
29. The literature reviewed in this paper does not lend itself to neat categories, and some experts in the field may feel uncomfortable with the categorizations we have made. For example, we have chosen to omit Paul Pillar's thoughtful *Negotiating Peace* (1983) because few of the conflicts it

examines are ethnic conflicts. Kressel and Pruitt (1989) and Berkovitch (1984) have been discussed above, rather than in this section, because their emphasis seems more theoretical than practical.

30. As of 25 December 1991, known officially as the 'former Soviet Union'.

31. The authors offer a useful example from the Camp David Agreements to illustrate this point. Israel wanted to retain control over the Egyptian Sinai Peninsula because they feared a military threat. Egypt insisted on regaining sovereignty over the Peninsula. The interests were reconciled by returning the Sinai to complete Egyptian sovereignty, but demilitarizing large areas.

32. Other principles or criteria listed by the authors include: 'precedent', 'costs', 'what a court would decide', 'moral standards', 'tradition, equal treatment', and 'reciprocity'.

33. As noted above, later use of this approach by Azar and others to mediate conflicts in Lebanon, Falklands-Malvinas and Sri Lanka produced useful, but inconclusive rights (Azar *et al.*, 1984).

34. Touval and Zartman's edited volume, *International Negotiation in Theory and Practice* (1985) might also be included here. However most of the cases discussed in that volume do not seem relevant to violent ethnic conflict.

35. A recent edited volume by de Silva and May (1991) provides examples of ethnic conflicts that are, in fact, becoming more 'international'.

36. As part of the study, a questionnaire was administered to senior negotiators from both the American diplomatic services and to diplomats holding key negotiating positions in other nations. The theme of the questionnaire was 'what do you know now that you wish you had known when you first started?' (p. 7). Fifty United Nations ambassadors and high members of the UN Secretariat participated in a second set of interviews which involved participants in a simulated negotiating experience.

37. For example Zartman and Berman offer the following four guidelines for the 'detail phase' of negotiations (pp. 201, 202): (1) Do not lose the big picture in the little picture. (2) Be clear from the beginning about objectives, and do not confuse means with ends. (3) Steadiness at the brink requires a clear understanding of increments and a sense of both sides' ability to do without an agreement. (4) Concessions are made to convey a message but they are justified by a principle.

38. The mediators discussed in individual chapters of Touval's book are Count Bernadotte, Ralph Bunche, The United Nations Conciliation Commission, The Robert Anderson Mission, The Gunnar Jarring Mission, The William Rogers Initiative and Interim Agreement Talks, the initiative by African presidents, Henry Kissinger's 'shuttle diplomacy', US President Carter's mediation leading to the Camp David Accord.

39. In Sri Lanka, for example, LTTE leader Vellupillai Prabhakaran has systematically exterminated the leaders of other Tamil groups, both moderate and militant.

40. Horowitz points out however that the level at which these animosities are expressed can change, over time and be influenced by changes in constitutional and political arrangements (1985, chapter 3, 15).

41. One factor contributing to the duration of many ethnic conflicts has been

the availability of external support from contending superpowers or regional hegemons (de Silva and May, eds, 1991). With the end of the cold war and breakup of the former Soviet Union, this source of support is diminishing somewhat. On the other hand, international drug dealing seems to be a growing source of funds and armaments for militant groups and perhaps for some governments as well (for an example from Sri Lanka, see de Silva, 1991).

42. Among six ethnic conflicts found among Paul Pillar's terminated wars, for the post World War II period (1983, pp. 21–3), four ended with the capitulation and/or decisive military defeat of one protagonist. One (Cyprus) ended with the enforced separation of the contending groups. In one (Sri Lanka) both class and ethnic conflict rekindled after an initial defeat of one militant group by government forces. As noted above violent conflict is still prevalent in four of the six cases described in this book. In Cyprus stability is enforced by UN peacekeepers and Turkish forces. Other examples of protracted ethnic conflicts not resolved by negotiation include Eritria-Ethiopia, Lebanon, Northern Ireland and Burma. The Ethiopian-Eritrian civil war of more than 20 years ended in 1991 with the military defeat of the Ethiopian army and toppling of the Mengistu regime.

43. 'Civilian casualties' and 'human rights violations' had been one justification for the Indian intervention. However when the Indians decided to force the Tigers from Jaffna, they used a full-scale armored assault, supported by aircraft and artillery. There were many civilian casualties. As the Indian Peace-Keeping Force became transformed from liberator to foreign army of occupation, complaints of human rights violations were just as numerous as those that had been leveled against the – largely Sinhalese – Sri Lankan army.

44. Unfortunately even the peace established by this 'successful' accord proved to be unsustainable. The Addis Accord lacked institutional mechanisms to bridge the differences between North and South and depended too much on the personal support of one man, the President. Those factors proved to be its undoing.

45. Judging whether an accord could have been crafted to meet the multiple, conflicting demands that surfaced in the Meech Lake ratification process is beyond the scope of this paper.

46. This is a summary of major points found in Touval (1982), chapter 11.

47. The accords were negotiated between Egyptian President Sadat and Israeli Prime Minister Begin, with US President Jimmy Carter serving as mediator. The most detailed description of the negotiations is found in *Camp David: Peacemaking and Politics* (1986), by former National Security Staff member William B. Quandt. President Carter provides a more personal account in his autobiography, *Keeping Faith* (1982).

48. The negotiations failed to produce a meaningful agreement for Israeli withdrawal from the West Bank and Gaza Strip, however.

49. Quandt (1986) is pessimistic about the degree to which the lessons of Camp David can be applied to other negotiations.

50. The role of regional groups as mediators is addressed in Wolfers (1985) and Scheman and Ford (1985).

References

Azar, Edward E. *et al.* (1984) *The Emergence of a New Lebanon: Fantasy or Reality*, New York: Praeger.

Azar, Edward E. (1990) *The Management of Protracted Social Conflict*, Hampshire, England: Dartmouth.

Azar, Edward, E., and John W. Burton (1986) *International Conflict Resolution in Theory and Practice*, Sussex: Wheatsheaf.

Azar, Edward E. and R. Haddad (1986) Lebanon: An anomalous conflict, *Third World Quarterly*, 8, pp. 1337–50.

Berkovitch, Jacob (1984) *Social Conflicts and Third Parties: Strategies for Conflict Resolution*, Boulder, Colorado: Westview Press.

Burton, John W. (1969) *Conflict and Communication: The Use of Controlled Communication in International Relations*, New York: Free Press.

Burton, John W. (1990a) *Conflict: Human Needs Theory*, New York: St. Martin's Press.

Burton, John W. (1990b) *Conflict: Resolution and Prevention*, New York: St. Martin's Press.

Burton, John W. and Frank Dukes (1990a) *Conflict: Practices in Management, Settlement and Resolution*, New York: St. Martin's Press.

Burton, John W. and Frank Dukes (1990b) *Conflict: Readings in Management and Resolution*, New York: St. Martin's Press.

Carter, Jimmy (1982) *Keeping Faith: Memoirs of a President*, New York: Bantam Books.

Cohen, Herb (1980) *You Can Negotiate Anything*, Secaucus, New Jersey: L. Stuart.

Coser, Louis (1956) *The Functions of Social Conflict*, Glencoe, Illinois: The Free Press.

Deng, Francis M. and I. William Zartman (eds) (1991) *Conflict Resolution in Africa*, Washington, DC: The Brookings Institution.

Deutsch, Morton (1973) *The Resolution of Conflict*, New Haven: Yale University Press.

De Silva, Kingsley M. (1986) *Managing Ethnic Tensions in Multi-Ethnic Societies: Sri Lanka 1880–1985*, Lanham, Maryland: University Press of America.

De Silva, Kingsley M. (1991) Indo-Sri Lanka relations: A study in the internationalization of ethnic conflict, in de Silva and May (1991), pp. 76–106.

De Silva, Kingsley M. and May, Ronald J. (eds) (1991) *The Internationalization of Ethnic Conflict*, London: Frances Pinter.

Fisher, Roger and Scott Brown (1989) *Getting Together: Building Relationships as We Negotiate*, New York: Penguin.

Fisher, Roger and William Ury (1981) *Getting to Yes*, Boston: Houghton Mifflin.

Garcia, Edmundo (1989) Conflict resolution in the Philippines: The quest for peace in a period of democratic transition, *Bulletin of Peace Proposals*, 20:1, pp. 59–69.

Garcia, Edmundo (1988) *The Transformation of Society*, Quezon City: Cleretian Publications.

Grims, Erika and Mary Kay Satriano (1990) Northern Ireland conflict – agreements, *Ethnic Studies Report*, VII:2, pp. 33–43.

Horowitz, Donald (1985) *Ethnic Groups in Conflict*, Berkeley: University of California Press.

Horowitz, Donald (1991) *A Democratic South Africa*, Berkeley: University of California Press.

Kahn, Lynn S. (1988) *Peace Making: A Systems Approach to Conflict Management*, Lanham, Maryland: University Press of America.

Kelman, Herbert C. and Stephen F. Cohen (1972) The problem solving workshop in conflict resolution, in Richard L. Merritt, (ed) *Communication in International Politics*, Urbana, Illinois: University of Illinois Press.

Kressel, Kenneth and Dean G. Pruitt (1989) *Mediation Research: The Process and Effectiveness of Third Party Intervention*, San Francisco: Jossey-Bass.

Kodikara, Shelton U. (ed.) (1989) *Indo-Sri Lanka Agreement of July 1987*, Dehiwala, Sri Lanka: Sridevi Printers for the International Relations Program, University of Colombo.

Likert, Rensis and Jane G. Likert (1976) *New Ways of Managing Conflict*, New York: McGraw Hill.

Lickleider, Roy (1990) *How Civil Wars End: Preliminary Results from a Comparative Project*, unpublished paper, prepared for delivery at the 1990 Annual Meeting of the American Political Science Association, 30 August–2 September, San Francisco, California.

Mao Tse Tung (1957) *On the Correct Handling of Contradictions Among the People*, Beijing: Foreign Language Press.

Mitchell, C.R. (1981) *Peacemaking and the Consultant's Role*, Farnborough, Hampshire, England: Gower.

Nordlinger, Eric (1972) *Conflict Regulation in Divided Societies*, Cambridge: Harvard University, Center for International Affairs, Occasional Papers in International Affairs, 29.

Pillar, Paul (1983) *Negotiating Peace: War Termination as a Bargaining Process*, Princeton: Princeton University Press.

Pruitt, Dean G. and Jeffrey Z. Rubin (1986) *Social Conflict: Escalation, Stalemate and Settlement*, New York: Random House.

Quandt, William B. (1986) *Camp David: Peacemaking and Politics*, Washington, DC: The Brookings Institution.

Rothchild, Donald and Caroline and Hartzell (1988) *The Peace Process in the Sudan 1972*, paper prepared for delivery at the International Political Science Association meeting, Washington, DC, 30 August.

Richardson, John M. Jr. and S.W. R. de A. Samarasinghe (1992) Costs and benefits of violent political conflict: The case of Sri Lanka, Forthcoming in *World Development*.

Rupesinghe, Kumar (ed.) (1989) *Conflict Resolution in Uganda*, Athens, Ohio: Ohio University Press.

Sandole Dennis J.D. and Ingrid Sandole-Saroste (1987) *Conflict Management and Problem Solving: Interpersonal to International Applications*, New York: New York University Press.

Scheman, L. Ronald and John W. Ford, The organization of American States as mediator, in Touval and Zartman, *International Mediation in Theory and Practice*.

Shellenberg, James A. (1989) *The Science of Conflict*, New York: Oxford University Press.

Simmel, Georg (1955) *Conflict*, New York: Free Press.

Singer, Linda (1990) *Settling Disputes: Conflict Resolution in Business, Families and the Legal System*, Boulder, Colorado: Westview Press.

Touval, Saadia (1982) *The Peace Brokers: Mediators in the Arab-Israeli Conflict 1948-1979*, Princeton: Princeton University Press.

Touval, Saadia and I. William Zartman (1985) *International Mediation in Theory and Practice*, Boulder, Colorado: Westview Press/Foreign Policy Institute, School of Advanced International Studies, Johns Hopkins University.

United States Institute of Peace (1990) *Contributions to the Study of Peacemaking: A Summary of Completed Grant Projects*, Washington, DC: US Institute of Peace, December.

Wolfers, Michael (1985) The Organization of African Unity as Mediator, in Touval and Zartman, *International Mediation in Theory and Practice*.

Zartman, I. William (1985) *Ripe for Resolution: Conflict and Intervention in Africa*, New York: Oxford University Press.

Zartman, I. William and Maureen R. Berman (1982) *The Practical Negotiator*, New Haven: Yale University Press.

INDEX